International Review of Strategic Management

VOLUME 5   1994

MEMBERS OF THE EDITORIAL BOARD

International Review of Strategic Management

VOLUME 5   1994

Edited by

D. E. Hussey

Harbridge Consulting Group Ltd

JOHN WILEY & SONS

CHICHESTER · NEW YORK · BRISBANE · TORONTO · SINGAPORE

Copyright © 1994 by John Wiley & Sons Ltd,
Baffins Lane, Chichester,
West Sussex PO19 1UD, England

National Chichester 01243 779777
International (+44) 1243 779777

International Review of Strategic Management ISSN 1047–7918

Published annually by John Wiley & Sons

Library of Congress Cataloging–in–Publication Data

is available 90–641036

British Library Cataloguing in Publication Data

International review of strategic management—vol 5 (1994)—
658

ISBN 0-471-93958-7

Typeset in 11/12pt Palatino by Mackreth Media Services, Hemel Hempstead
Printed and bound in Great Britain by Bookcraft (Bath) Ltd

CONTENTS

PART THREE: OTHER TOPICS

ABOUT THE CONTRIBUTORS

CHIARA BENTIVOGLI is a director of the Study Department of Banca D'Italia, the Central Bank of Italy in Rome. She has a laurea in economics and a masters degree in business administration. She has published extensively and is currently co-authoring a book on European privatisation programmes.

T. K. DAS is a member of the Management Department of Baruch College, City University of New York. Before joining academia, Dr Das worked in senior corporate level positions in the State Bank of India. He has been a practitioner, lecturer, researcher and writer on strategic change, publishing several books and over 90 articles in professional journals. Among his recent books is *The Subjective Side of Strategy Making: Future Orientations and Perceptions of Executives*.

R. JEFFERY ELLIS is the Ralph Z. Sorenson Term Professor at Babson College in Wellersley, Massachusetts, in the field of strategic management. He is also a fellow at the Warwick Business School Research Bureau in England. The author of about 40 papers and case studies, he recently wrote *Managing Strategy in the Real World*, published by Free Press, New York and Maxwell Macmillan, Oxford. He is a director of the Competitive Intelligence Society. He has undertaken consultancy and research in numerous leading companies on both sides of the Atlantic.

HANS H. HINTERHUBER is a professor of business administration and the Director of the Department of Management at the University of Innsbruck, Austria. He also teaches Strategic Management at the University of Milan, Italy. He holds an MS degree in petroleum engineering from the Mining University of Loeben, Austria, and a PhD in business administration from the University of Venice, Italy. Dr Hinterhuber has worked in management in Italian and German companies. He now serves as a director of a number of companies in Austria, Germany and Italy. His research and consulting work focuses on strategy, strategic management and the management of organizational evolution in different cultures.

SAMUEL K. M. HO has degrees in engineering from the University of Hong Kong, in management from UWIST and a doctorate in information management from Henley. He worked in various management roles in organizations in Hong Kong before joining the City Polytechnic of Hong Kong as a senior lecturer. In 1986 he was awarded the Oshikawa Fellowship by the Asian Productivity Organization (APO). His consequent research among the five industrialized Asian countries was published under the title *Information Technology Development for Small and Medium Enterprises in Asian NICs and Japan.* He was a senior teaching fellow at Warwick University from 1988 to 1993 and is now a principal lecturer at De Montfort University.

GERT HOFSTEDE is a professor of organizational anthropology and international management at the University of Limburg at Maastricht. He founded and is the director of the Institute for Research on Intercultural Cooperation. He is a leading authority on intercultural management and author of many books on the subject, including *Culture and Organizations* (McGraw–Hill, 1991). His work has made a considerable contribution to multinational management.

DAVID HUSSEY has had many years experience in corporate planning, as a practitioner in industry from 1964 to 1975, and as a consultant since 1976. Prior to moving into corporate planning, he was engaged in industrial development work in a developing country. He is managing director of the European operations of a well–known US consultancy, and is the author of several books on the subject of strategic management, including *Corporate Planning: Theory and Practice* (Pergamon, 1974), which won the John Player management author of the year award. He was one of the founders of the Society for Strategic Planning, and has been associated with the official journal of the society, *Long Range Planning*, since its foundation. He is a member of the editorial board of *Strategic Directions*, and a director of the Japanese Society of Strategic Management. He is editor of the *Journal of Strategic Change*, which was launched in 1992.

CAROL FELKER KAUFMAN is an Associate Professor of Marketing at the Business School of Rutgers University, Camden, New Jersey, USA. She received her PhD from Temple University in 1986. Her research interests include the study of time use and perception. She has tested and developed several research methods in the study of time, including the PAI, or Polychronic Attitude Index, an indicator of one's tendencies to combine activities simultaneously. Her publications have appeared in the *Journal of Consumer Research, The Journal of Business and Psychology, The Journal of Advertising Research, The Journal of Consumer Marketing, The Journal of Strategic Change,* and *The Journal of Retailing.* Currently Dr Kaufman is participating in research sponsored by the International Council of Shopping Centers Educational Foundation with Paul Lane. In 1992/1993 she received a research grant in new product development through RITIM, The Research Institute for Telecommunications and Information Marketing, with Paul Lane.

PAUL M. LANE, PhD is an Associate Professor of Marketing and Coordinator of Outreach for the Haworth College of Business with offices on both the Grand Rapids and Kalamazoo campuses. Primary teaching style is experiential and interactive using real companies to develop students' ability to integrate marketing courses. Primary research and practice interests include Time, Strategic Planning, International Business, Entrepreneurship, Qualitative Methods, and Consumer Behaviour. He is an active consultant whose recent clients include private industry, government, economic development organizations, and research foundations. He is a frequent presenter of seminars for both small and large business. In his capacities with Perspective Marketing and the companies that he has worked with in his WMU courses, Dr. Lane has dealt with almost 300 area organizations.

Drs Lane and Kaufman and Jay D. Lindquist and Esther Page-Wood of WMU have authored more than fifty articles on the study of time. The work can be found in the *Journal of Consumer Research, Journal of Business Psychology, The Academy of Management Executive, The Journal of Strategic Change,* and others.

MATHEW GIBSON LYNAS lectures in strategic management, organizational behaviour and human resources management at Aberdeen University. Dr Lynas has a wide-ranging general and specialist management background and is currently on the boards of two large voluntary organizations. His publications are in the areas of organizational development and human resources and small business management.

BRIANCE MASCARENHAS is a professor of International Business and Strategy at Rutgers University, Camden, New Jersey. He holds a

PhD from the University of California, Berkeley. His research interests and consulting are in international competition and market entry strategy. He is the recipient of the 1994 Provost's Award for Teaching Excellence.

GEN–ICHI NAKAMURA is a regular contributor to this book series and a member of its editorial board. He has 20 years business experience and 15 years of academic experience. He has been developing an extensive consultancy practice in Asia, Europe and the United States. He is Chairman and Principal Researcher/ Consultant of SMI 21 Co. Ltd., Principal of Gen–Ichi–Nakamura Associates, Managing Partner of Ansoff, Buchner, Nakamura and Partners in West Germany, and co–founder of the Japan Strategic Management Society. He is also the author of a number of books, primarily on strategic management and related subjects. His recent works are *The Practice of Divestment Strategy* and *Corporate Identity Development within the Context of Strategic Management*. Both are in the Japanese language.

KEITH RITCHIE is an accountant with Halliburton, an international energy services company. He has been involved with charitable organizations since his university days and is presently treasurer of the Multiple Sclerosis Charity of Aberdeen.

PAUL STREBEL is professor of Business Administration at IMD, the International Institute for Management Development in Lausanne, Switzerland. His consulting and executive development activities have been in the areas of value based strategic planning, change management and the anticipation and management of competitive turning points and breakpoints. He has had extensive international experience in Europe, North America, the Far East, South Africa and Australasia. Prior to his present position, Strebel was director of Research of IMEDE, one of the founding institutions of IMD. He was recently a visiting Professor at the Harvard Business School. Dr Strebel received his PhD from Princeton University, his BMA from Columbia University, and his BSc from the University of Cape Town, where he graduated with highest honours. His most recent book is on *Breakpoints: How managers exploit radical business change* (Harvard Business School Press, 1992).

SANDRO TRENTO is the director of the Study Department of Banca D'Italia, the central bank of Italy, in Rome. He has a laurea in economics and a masters degree in business administration. He has published widely, and is currently working on a book with Chiara Bentivogli.

LIISA VÄLIKANGAS is currently a Japan Foundation Fellow and Visiting Scholar at Keio University, Graduate School of Business Administration in Yokohama. Previously, she was associated with IMD in Lausanne, Switzerland, studying the management of corporate change and contributing to the IMD executive programs on the subject. Between 1990 and 1992, she was also the chief analyst for the *World Competitiveness Report*, a publication by IMD and the World Economic Forum, comparing the annual competitiveness of nations. She is finishing her PhD at the University of Tampere, Finland. Her dissertation is about leadership for organizational change, a topic that she is also teaching at the School of International Studies in Tokyo.

WEE CHOW HOU is dean of the faculty of the School of Postgraduate Management Studies at the National University of Singapore. He is also a director of the National Productivity board, the Telecommunication Authority of Singapore and Apollo Enterprises Ltd. Professor Wee has had over 150 articles and papers published, and is the senior author of *Sun Tzu, War and Management* (Addison-Wesley, 1991).

INTRODUCTION

This is the fifth volume of the *International Review of Strategic Management,* and continues to follow the objective of the series, which is to produce an annual critical review of developments and best practice in strategic management. Over the years this will accumulate to a significant reference source. Each book contains its own index. A cumulative index to cover all volumes is included for ease of reference.

Each volume contains a state of the art review article, focused on a particular aspect of strategic management, a number of chapters on a related theme, and a general section. This last part of the content allows inclusion of individual contributions which would be difficult to put in a theme, and provides a way of including other good material which would otherwise have to wait for several editions.

In this volume the theme is global and multinational management, and the state of the art review links to this. It therefore becomes a scene–setting chapter, which attempts to provide an overview to the theme section. As I mention in this chapter, it is a personal view describing what I think is important, and not a full coverage of everything written on the subject.

Most of the chapters in Part Two are, I hope, a little different from what might be expected. Those by Jeffery Ellis and Briance Mascarenhas cover approaches to strategy formulation and, although presenting original view points, are of the type of article that the reader might expect to find.

Wee Chow Hou's comparison of management with Sun Tzu's *The Art of War* is an insightful analysis which has much of value for the multinational strategist, although many of the lessons are equally applicable to the single-country business. It is not the first time that business strategy has been compared to military strategy. Caplan (1965) gives an analysis of the relationships between principles of military strategy and the principles of business planning, using the *US Army Field Manual* as its base. James (1984) makes a detailed comparison of the strategic actions of a number of companies with military tactics, and some of the mistakes and successes of the military. Platts (1993) looks at leadership through the eyes of Confucius, Lao Tzu and Sun Tzu. Chow Hou's scholarly chapter makes a welcome addition to the literature on strategy.

Global strategies have to be implemented, and in the process of implementation people of different nationalities have to work together, either as colleagues or in a customer/supplier relationship. Gert Hofstede has devoted much of his professional life to issues of intercultural management, and his books, and the activities of the institute of which he is a director, offer guidance which is of immeasurable value when considering global and multinational strategy. His contribution to this volume adds a dimension of thought which is often overlooked, and anyone concerned with international operations of any sort will gain much from it.

Strategic management owes much to the Far East, particularly to Japan. Gen-Ichi Nakamura's chapter on the changes in Japan's progression is of great value, and I was very pleased to have it, even more so because he met an impossible deadline so that I could include it in this book. Gen-Ichi will be well known to regular readers of this book series, as he has contributed to most volumes, and provided me with other papers from Japanese authors. It is thanks to his immense personal efforts on behalf of the series that I have been able to include so much from that part of the world. The future of Japan is of interest to all businesses, and particularly those that believe it important to have a firm position in all the main regions of the world.

This part of the book is rounded off by a study of a world industry, watches. There are many lessons for all of us from the history of the watch industry, particularly in the way leadership of the industry has moved from one country to another over the centuries.

Several chapters in Part Three follow an international, if not global, theme, and are thus very appropriate for this book. Samuel Ho provides an A–Z of Japanese management in the context of its transferability to the West. Although now living in the UK, Samuel was from Hong Kong, and his work owes much to some original studies he made in other countries across the region.

I have not previously had a contribution from India, and although T. K. Das is now at an academic institute in the USA, his chapter covers a case study of the implementation of change in the Bank of India, where he was previously employed. Not many people know the scale of this bank. I know that I did not until he told me that it has 13 000 offices worldwide and 300 000 employees. Change in such a vast organization must be on a scale of difficulty that few of us experience, but the lessons that can be drawn are applicable to us all. Another case study of planning covers UK charitable organizations. Although aspects of the business environment are particular to the countries in the UK, the lessons from the study are widely applicable. Charities exist in all countries, and there are particular problems in planning their strategies.

Paul Strebel and Liisa Välikangas provide some useful thinking on organizational change processes, using a force field approach. The implementation of new strategies is an area which was the subject of an earlier volume in this series, which was further developed last year when the theme was vision and leadership. A conceptual article on change is, therefore, very appropriate, and fits well with T. K. Das's practical example.

Finally, we have a contribution which is more difficult to classify, but no less significant because of this. It is about time in strategic thinking, not in the usual sense of reducing the time in processes to gain maximum value but in terms of the different perceptions of time held by different people and cultures. It would have been possible to argue that this chapter is another aspect of intercultural management, and I could have put it in Part Two of the book. However, I felt that the slant of the article was of a more general strategic nature, although I shall not be at all sorry if it is found useful by the formulators of global strategies.

The fifth volume of any book series is something of a landmark, and is not achieved without a lot of help from many people. Editorial boards of books and journals are often passive, which is why I am so grateful for the advice, articles and introductions to authors provided by my very active board. I also have to thank two members of the editorial team of the *Journal of Strategic Change*, Michael Liew of Singapore, and the ever–active Per Jenster of IMD, Lausanne. Both introduced me to authors whose chapters appear in this book.

Thanks are also due to all authors who have appeared in the various volumes, many of whom have written to my broad specifications, while others have amended chapters to make them more suitable for my needs. It is this support that enables an edited book to be successful, and I am thankful for it.

Not everyone knows what goes on when a manuscript reaches the publisher. It takes effort by a number of people to turn it into a quality book, and among the unsung heroes and heroines are the often–maligned copy and style editors. Many small errors, mine and those of contributors, have been picked up by this team, whose efforts have contributed to the readability of the books. They do the jobs that most authors overlook, such as checking that references in the text are actually listed at the end, and spelt the same way in both places.

I hope that the series will continue to add to the body of knowledge about strategic management.

REFERENCES

Caplan, R. H. (1965) Appendix B.   Relationships between principles of military strategy and principles of business planning. In R. N. Anthony (ed.), *Planning and Control Systems: A Framework for Analysis*, Harvard, Boston, MA.

James, B. G. (1984) *Business Wargames*, New York, Abacus Press. My edition by Penguin, London, 1985.

Platts, M. J. (1993) Confucius on leadership. Unpublished paper.

Part One

STATE OF THE
ART REVIEW

GLOBAL AND MULTINATIONAL STRATEGY: DEVELOPMENT OF CONCEPTS

D. E. Hussey

Managing Director, Harbridge Consulting Group Ltd

The history of global and multinational operations as a subset of strategy is a little like the evolution of the history of humankind. Most things have happened in recent years. Humans are reputed to have been on this earth for the best part of 2 million years but `history' only began to happen in the last 2000, and only in the last 100 years have we had such a profusion of documentary evidence that it becomes difficult to sort the wheat from the chaff. Of course, if you are a fan of Sellar and Yeatman, (1930) you may share their tongue-in-cheek view of history:

> History is not what you thought. *It is what you can remember.* This means that the whole of British history can be reduced to 103 Good Things, 5 Bad Kings and 2 Genuine dates, and that it came to an end after the Great War when America became top nation.

Planning must have had a long period when it had no recorded history. It is impossible to believe that business executives never developed a vision for their businesses, or produced plans to support it, until the concepts began to appear in books. In fact, the early books on general management drew much from the real-life

International Review of Strategic Management, Volume 5
Edited by D. E. Hussey © 1994 John Wiley & Sons Ltd

experiences of the great pioneer managers. The recorded history of strategic planning began in the 1960s. A mid-1960s student of the subject who had read Scott, (1962), Steiner, (1963) and Ansoff, (1965) would have only had to add a few *Harvard Business Review* articles, and the publications of the Stanford Research Institute to have covered virtually the entire bibliography. Of course, there were probably a few more publications of note, but not many. By the 1990s the literature had become vast. Mockler, (1993) lists 70 pages of books in print in the USA on strategy and related themes, a list which omits most British books, and all that are in languages other than English. There are more than 25 books per page. The same source lists over 500 dissertations in the field between 1987 and 1993. Within this rich vein, which tends to become richer every year, a number of new themes emerge. Although international strategy and multinational operations did attract writers and theorists from the early days of strategic management's recorded history, the major contributions on global strategy have appeared only since the 1980s.

What can I learn from the Sellar and Yeatman approach to history? The first is that the state of the art as written here is what I remember. We have more than two dates, no bad kings, but a large number of good things. In writing about global and multinational strategy, America is top nation. In originating and applying the ideas, the honours go to the Japanese. Unlike Sellar and Yeatman, I do not think this marks the end of history, but a new beginning. In trying to set down some of the concepts and references which may be helpful to those interested in the topic, I am very conscious that new research and ideas are constantly emerging.

THE CHANGING BACKGROUND

It is not surprising that there has been a change in thinking about global strategy, as the recipes for business success have also undergone fundamental change. In my early career I was involved in trying to bring more industrial development to what was then the Federation of Rhodesia and Nyasaland, since broken up into its three components, Malawi, Zambia and Zimbabwe. The recipe we were exploiting was a simple one. British businesses (in particular) developed an export market in a particular country. Imperial preference offered an incentive for them to concentrate on the countries of the British Commonwealth. Once a market was large enough the next step was to persuade the company to manufacture the product locally. The carrot was that a shield of protective duties would be provided to protect the infant industry. The stick was that approaches were made to non-British companies and to local business executives with the same offer. The British company could choose to invest in a local factory or lose its market completely. Through the post-war years until the early 1960s, this represented the recipe for a good multinational strategy.

Until the mid-1960s it is possible to argue that the whole pattern of multinational growth, whatever the origin of the parent company, was based on the idea that subsidiaries were a little like children. Wherever the market was big enough, the answer was to have a baby company that as far as possible was in the image of the parent. However, the wise parent accepted that, whatever the common genes, the baby would grow up to be different, and would be subject also to different environmental pressures. What would result is a network of manufacturing companies, each responding somewhat differently to local conditions, and somehow trying to gain synergy from more centralised activities such as research and development. Much of the writing on strategy during this period was concerned with how to co-ordinate plans from across the world, rather than how to achieve a common strategy. Indeed, books and articles still stressed this theme until the start of the 1980s, although changes in world competition, and the changed economic emphasis of regional trading blocks, such as the European Community, had brought about the obsolescence of imperial preference. The change in competition was caused by many factors (those interested in the UK position in particular will find much of value in Channon, 1973). Perhaps chief among these was the rise of the Japanese companies who worked on a very different principle of strategic success. Instead of a network of country-by-country factories, their recipe was for one large factory which served the world, gaining great economies of scale and, through lower production costs, overcoming disadvantages of customs tariffs and transportation costs. The final cunning streak was to realise that if real prices were lower, demand would rise, enabling more products to be made at even lower prices.

Both of the descriptions given here oversimplify, but they do serve as a background which helps us to understand why the writing on multinational strategy has changed its tone so much, and why so many of the best contributions are of relatively recent origin. At the same time, we have to recognise that not all businesses fit either of my two polarised models, and that multinational operations will not always be synonymous with global strategies.

STAGES OF ORGANISATIONAL DEVELOPMENT

Before going further it is worth referring to some of the studies in strategy and structure, many of which grew out of an initiative at the Harvard Business School and led to a spate of publications in the early 1970s. The pioneer work was Chandler (1962), who studied the historical development of strategy of DuPont, Standard Oil of New Jersey, Sears Roebuck and General Motors, and the way structure had followed. In fact this catalyst appeared from MIT, that other renowned establishment a little downriver from the Harvard Business School.

Among the studies undertaken were Channon (1973), Stopford (1968) and Rumelt (1974). With the exception of Stopford, the referenced studies did not particularly focus on the international firm. However, there was interest in whether the American patterns were valid for other countries. Channon's work covered the UK, Franco (1974), dealt with companies in continental Europe.

Detailed summaries of this work may be found in Channon (1973) and Galbraith and Nathanson (1978), the latter giving the more detailed account. What is relevant here is where the research has led. Scott (1971) suggested that there were three stages of organisational development. Stage 1 was when the organisation was controlled by the owner, there was little formal structure, and only one product or product line. Stage 2 was still oriented to a single product line, but was more formal with an organisation based on function and all product service transactions were integrated internally. This stage is effectively a grown-up version of the previous stage. Scott's final stage 3 was when the company moved into multiple product lines and multiple channels, and where the structure was based on specialisation of product market relationships.

Smith and Charmoz (1975) suggested stages in the development of a multinational company. This reference appeared in Galbraith and Nathanson (1978):

Phase 1 Overseas expansion. The company establishes businesses in various countries, which report back to the centre.
Phase 2 Development of Subsidiaries. Subsidiaries develop and it is necessary to establish an international division, usually in the parent country, to co-ordinate them. Strategy is probably driven more by the subsidiary than by the parent.
Phase 3 Regionalisation. A regional head office is set up between the international office and the subsidiaries, the world being divided into regions. The region takes on much of the strategic role.

Phase 4 International Consolidation. At this stage the locus of power moves back into the international division, as a new CEO sets about the task of consolidating the disparate activities that have evolved.
Phase 5 Global Development. Regions and the international division disappear, and are replaced by global strategic business units, with the relevant activities in the subsidiaries reporting to the SBU management, usually in the parent company.

Stopford and Wells (1972) suggest stages of a development pattern which may follow alternative paths, but which result in a global matrix. In practice, we can observe a global form which retains a regional role within each SBU. In this form there may be different regional divisions for each SBU.

Galbraith and Nathanson (1978) extended the model developed by Scott (1971) to take account of the additional research. They suggested a five-stage model and identified a number of criteria for each stage. The stages, with their description of the organisational structure were:

Simple: simple functional
Functional: central functional
Holding: decentralised profit centres around product divisions, small headquarters
Multi-divisional: decentralised product or area division profit centres
Global, multi-divisional: decentralised profit centres around worldwide product or area divisions.

The final stage mentioned above was related to observed experience at the time. More recently Bartlett and Goshal (1990) identified a new form which they termed the transnational, which overcame the problems of divided responsibility of the global matrix. The transnational form is an integrated network. The authors describe three historic forms of structure as multinational, global and international. Descriptions of the criteria of each are provided on the dimensions of configuration of assets and capabilities, role of overseas operations, and development and diffusion of knowledge. Only the last criterion is quoted here, and compared with their definition of the transnational:

Multinational: Knowledge developed and retained within each unit
Global: Knowledge developed and retained at the centre
International: Knowledge developed at the centre and transferred to overseas units
Transnational: Knowledge developed jointly and shared worldwide.

The strategic capability, organisational characteristics and management tasks of the transnational form are given below. The three classifications are strategic capability (SC), organisational characteristics (OC) and management tasks (MT). The descriptions are all direct quotations from Bartlett and Goshal (1990).

> Global competitiveness (SC): Dispersed and interdependent assets and resources (OC): Legitimising diverse perspectives and capabilities (MT). Multinational flexibility (SC): Differentiated and specialised subsidiary roles (OC): Developing multiple and flexible coordination processes (MT).
> Worldwide learning (SC): Joint development and worldwide sharing of knowledge (OC): Building shared vision and individual commitment (MT).

EARLY DEVELOPMENT OF STRATEGIC VIEWS

As structure normally changes because of shifts in strategy, it would be very surprising if the writing on strategy did not in some way match the stages of development observed in the evolution of structure. Before looking at the changes in strategic thinking, I should like to stress that in my opinion the evolution of structure discussed above covers two related but different trends. The first is the growth and development of a company within a historical setting. The second is the historical evolution of business as a whole, within which framework the company develops. In the 1960s, few (if any) businesses operated a global strategy as we would now describe it. In theory they could have done so: in practice the economic and political environment of the time put it outside the conventional wisdom of the day. It would have been very surprising to find the concepts of global strategy, as they are now documented, appearing in the literature of an earlier age. Equally, it would have been virtually impossible for the early charter companies, such as the British East India Company, to conceive running a business through a network of international subsidiaries. The way you did things then was to set up your own army and navy, link to the political aims of your government, and set out to conquer and administer territories on the other side of the world.

The pattern of the literature through the 1960s and 1970s was largely about multinational and international strategy, as it was practised in Europe and the USA at the time. Of course, there was original thinking, and useful research, and much of what was written still has validity for those businesses which are not global. It is revealing that the cumulative index of *Long Range Planning* for the first 17 volumes, from its foundation in 1968 to 1984, has headings for international business and multinational companies but not for global. In fact the major books on global strategy did not begin to appear until 1986 and after.

Van Dam (1972) offered an interesting view of multinational strategy which developed from Rostow (1960). This was the only time I had come across Rostow's analysis being used by business, and it interested me because it had formed part of my academic studies earlier. Van Dam developed Rostow's model of the stages of economic growth to 10, into which he classified various countries. He then argued that the planning of a multinational should be geared to the appropriate stage of development of each country. His stages were:

(1)   The dormant society
(2)   Traditional society
(3)   Stage of transition
(4)   Pre-take-off
(5)   Take-off stage
(6)   Age of innovation
(7)   Sustained rapid growth
(8)   Technological superiority
(9)   High mass-consumption
(10)   The affluent society

The model remains useful when applied to a modern approach to global strategy. Classifications of countries into development stages, of course, still continue. Anyone wishing to continue this line of thinking would also find Taylor (1992) useful. He uses the classifications post-industrial, advanced industrial, industrial, transitioning industrial and pre-industrial, and provides information and forecasts under these headings.

The early views of multinational strategic planning were very much that it was the same as planning for a single-country company, with a few complications. Steiner and Schöllhammer (1975) looked at pitfalls of long-range planning in six countries. The questionnaire followed earlier research by Steiner (1972) in the USA. A list of 50 pitfalls had been generated, and respondents were asked to look at these in a number of ways. One table shows the ten most important pitfalls to be avoided. In order of priority, and much summarised, these were:

Delegation of planning by top management to a planner
Top management engrossed in current problems
Failure to develop suitable long-range goals
Failure to develop a planning climate in the company
Failure of top management to review plans with departmental and
divisional heads
Failure to involve line management
Treating planning as something separate from the planning process
Failure of top management to understand long-range planning
Failure to appoint a senior person as corporate planner
Failure to use plans as standards for measuring personal
performance.

Questions were asked about organisational structure, but not
whether the respondents were head offices or subsidiaries of
multinational companies. At this time the question did not seem to
be important. The pitfalls were all defined on the basis of the earlier
US survey, and did not consider the special problems of
multinational firms. For example, I would hypothesise from
experience that the biggest pitfall today is the company that operates
in a global business, but believes that it does not.

Brandt, Hulbert and Richers (1980) studied the planning problems
and practices of multinational firms, particularly the relationship
between head office and subsidiary. What they saw was the tension
caused by the trend for head offices to take a stronger strategic
control over foreign subsidiaries, at a time when there was more host
government pressure for subsidiaries to be responsible to local
needs, increased economic and political turbulence, keener local
competition, and increasing customer sophistication. Among their
conclusions was the need for multinational head offices to cease
running subsidiaries just by the financial figures, for greater
flexibility in planning systems and for ways of bringing more
subsidiary managers into the process. The thinking in this article
was very much about the planning process rather than the strategy
itself.

Another stream of articles through the 1960s and 1970s dealt with
the specific problems of being international: country risk and
currency fluctuations being two examples. I have not referenced
these. However Ringbakk (1976) is worth special mention, as he
draws attention to the growing turbulence of the environment in
which multinationals operate, and suggest that this will affect the
strategies that can be followed. Much of this thinking was further
developed by Channon with Jalland (1979). This book began to

develop thinking about different approaches to planning according to the structure of the company, broadly following the concepts identified earlier in this chapter. Subsequent chapters dealt with specific issues and problem areas, such as international treasury management, tax and political risk. In my own view it was a watershed between the earlier writings (many of which tended to assume that head offices would determine how much could be invested in a country, but apart from that, the strategy was a local or regional concern) and the emergence of a body of knowledge about the formulation of global strategy.

MODERN THINKING ABOUT GLOBAL STRATEGY

Transnational and multinational companies polarise into two strategic types: multi-domestic and global. A multi-domestic strategy works through a co-ordinated series of country operations, possibly grouped into regions, where strategies are designed as a response to local market conditions. The global company looks at the world as one market, and in many but not necessarily all of its operations will act on a global basis.

Strategic management for the multi-domestic companies presents only a few additional problems over those faced by a national business. These arise mainly from the complications of distance, language, national cultural differences, the management of additional profit centres and the need to take account of more than one national business environment. Most are well covered in the earlier references, except for one fundamental question: should they be multi-domestic businesses?

To answer this question we have to know what it is that drives a company to change from a strategy of having subsidiaries which respond individually to their own markets to an organisation which, in the extreme case, clones an identical response to every market. What options lie between these extremes?

Yip (1989, 1992) argues that there are four groups of factors which are the drivers for an industry to become global: market, cost, government and competitive.

Market

The factors here include a convergence of market requirements in different parts of the world, as life styles and tastes draw closer together. Customer organisations (buyers), who are themselves global, increasingly expect their suppliers to offer a global service. There are now more areas of the world which enjoy a relatively affluent lifestyle. However, this last point should not be overstressed, as the population in the less developed world is expected to continue to increase as a percentage of total world population (see Taylor, 1992).

World travel creates a requirement for the same services to be available on a global basis. Visa or American Express are good examples of markets where a worldwide service is needed, and which give the companies concerned an advantage over a credit card that can be used only in the country of issue.

Demand is related to price, which in turn has connections with cost. The nature of many markets is that the volume of the market only exists because world requirements are compressed into a few factories, thus enabling costs to tumble through economies of scale and the experience curve effect. The vast increase in instant information, through the explosion of information technology, has meant that facts about the markets and business environment are known quickly, enabling a fast response.

Costs

In addition to the volume effect on costs that can be achieved by a global approach, global operations are forced by technological change and the trend to shorter product life cycles. World volumes may be needed in order to afford the required level of research and development, and the capital costs of new production requirements. Because of issues like this, many industries have seen a concentration that would have been unnecessary 40 years ago. The number of players in the world's aerospace industry has fallen as development and production costs have risen, and it is now inconceivable that anyone could contemplate entering this industry on a small scale, based only on the demand from domestic airlines.

Information technology has also helped the cost factor. Computer-aided design (CAD) and computer-aided manufacture (CAM) enable products to be designed in any country, and instantaneously be made available in any other location. This makes it easier for manufacture to be located in areas of lowest cost, and design and development in areas of highest talent.

Government

Recent years have seen the amalgamation of separate countries into vast trading blocs, of which the best example is the European Union. In addition to creating a larger accessible market, EU regulations have removed many non-tariff barriers by setting common standards for many products. Many difficulties in reaching a standardised product, essential for true global operations have thus fallen away. Overall, barriers to trade have been steadily reduced despite occasional setbacks as in the 1992 GATT negotiations. There has also been a world trend to privatise industries previously in the public sector. Thus the opportunity for global expansion in telecommunications now exists, when it was impossible in the 1970s.

Competitive

Although certain niche strategies may sometimes be successful in an industry where most players are global, increasingly it is being realised that the rules of the game are changing, and that it is next to impossible to defeat a global player through a country-by-country strategy. One reason behind the demise of the British and American motorcycle industries was that the companies concerned had been driven out of their markets before they realised that the new competitors were thinking in world terms. The reason behind the success of the global strategies is partly the lower costs that can be achieved through a mixture of high volumes and standardised products and partly because the decision base is different. In one grocery products assignment I handled in the late 1980s my client operated on a country-by-country basis in most European countries. The leading competitor operated on the basis that Europe was one market. Whereas my client demanded that each country made its target profits, the competitor took a global view and would willingly reduce profit in a particular country to combat any attempt by the other players to increase their market share. This was always possible, as my client, in common with the other competitors, took marketing decisions piecemeal at the country level, and never mounted a co-ordinated attack in all countries at the same time.

While many companies have evolved into global players, there is an increasing tendency for at least some organisations to be global from start-up. Jolly *et al.* (1992) studied four companies from different countries which had a global vision from start-up, and implemented that vision immediately. The companies were Logitech, a Swiss-based manufacturer of desktop aids for computers;

Technophone, a British firm providing hand-portable telephones: Connor Peripherals, started in the USA to commercialise high-performance Winchester disk drives: and Lasa, which established itself simultaneously in the USA and Europe. Lasa is also in the high-technology computer-related field. While a few years ago it might have been sufficient to watch the strategies of those companies that already had a presence in many countries, the signs are that we may see more global start-ups in the future. The pressure to go global is therefore based not only on what can be seen today but also on the way it might develop in the future.

Ohmae (1985) argues that for long-term success, global businesses have to have a sound position in all of the three geographic centres of the world: the USA, Japan/South-east Asia and Europe. Those that stay in only one or two of these areas are unlikely to succeed in the long run, because the volumes of production which will fall to those competitors that do penetrate the total triad will give an immense cost advantage. The argument is based on the fact that these areas contain some 600 million people in the largest and most sophisticated markets of the world.

One effect of this thinking has been to position alliances as a popular strategic option from about 1980 to the present. This is partly because the scale of investment is now so huge in many industries that it is difficult for even large companies to bear the risk, and because structural change in certain industries such as defence has led to shrinking markets and overcapacity, Western firms find it hard to operate in Japan on a greenfield basis. In many industries the number of companies available for acquisition at reasonable cost has fallen, leaving alliances as the favoured strategy. Ohmae (1990) provides a useful analysis of the logic for alliances and advice on how to make them work. He particularly discusses the Western desire for control:

> When Americans and Europeans come to Japan, they all want 51 percent. That's the magic number because it ensures majority position and control over personnel, brand decisions and investment choices. But good partnerships, like good marriages, don't work on the basis of ownership or control. It takes effort and commitment and enthusiasm from both sides if either is to realise the hoped-for benefits. You cannot own a successful partner any more than you can own a husband or wife.

Figure 1.1 illustrates the fact that for the individual company, globalisation is a strategic decision. The diagram is derived from

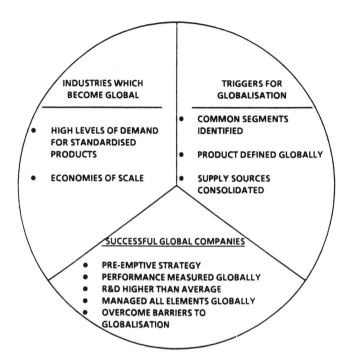

INDUSTRIES WHICH
BECOME GLOBAL

- HIGH LEVELS OF DEMAND
  FOR STANDARDISED
  PRODUCTS

- ECONOMIES OF SCALE

TRIGGERS FOR
GLOBALISATION

- COMMON SEGMENTS
  IDENTIFIED

- PRODUCT DEFINED GLOBALLY

- SUPPLY SOURCES
  CONSOLIDATED

SUCCESSFUL GLOBAL COMPANIES

- PRE-EMPTIVE STRATEGY
- PERFORMANCE MEASURED GLOBALLY
- R&D HIGHER THAN AVERAGE
- MANAGED ALL ELEMENTS GLOBALLY
- OVERCOME BARRIERS TO
  GLOBALISATION

Figure 1.1   Global competition (from Cvar, 1986)

points made by Cvar in a 1986 study of patterns of success and failure in global competition. The analysis suggests that there are certain characteristics in industries that become global in that there has to be the opportunity for high levels of demand for standardised products which also give rise to economies of scale. Globalisation is not a naturally occurring state but is made by people and the triggers are the identification of common segments in different countries that enable a product to be defined globally. In turn, this enables supply sources to be consolidated, so that the competitive cost advantages can be gained.

The study also showed that the successful global companies had five factors in common. They had all developed a pre-emptive strategy, effectively becoming the agency that created the global market. All managed their companies on a global concept and measured their performance on this basis. It was also observed that all had higher than average R&D compared with their industry. All had demonstrated a measure of singlemindedness in overcoming obstacles to globalisation.

The implication of the global dimension is that for many companies strategic thinking has to stretch beyond the country dimensions that may have been traditional in the industry. Whether the company seeks to create a global business, on the lines suggested by Cvar, or whether it chooses to let a competitor initiate this process, is a matter for the individual company. Once the industry goes global the opportunities for the company with only a local market view will certainly change, and may diminish.

Prahalad and Doz (1987) produced one of the landmark books in global strategy, particularly important because little really new was available until this time. They suggest that the key factors in deciding how to operate are the need for integration on a global basis, contrasted with the need for local responsiveness. If these two concerns are seen as two sides of a matrix, it follows that different businesses can be positioned on the matrix and an appropriate strategy decided. However, the authors point to a factor which most strategists will have already observed, that the number of industries where global integration is the dominant factor increases every year. The pressures are created by customers and competitors, and it is dangerous to assume that an industry which has local responsiveness as the key factor today will remain like this in the future.

Figure 1.2 is a diagram which was inspired by the Prahalad and Doz matrix. Tables 1.1 and 1.2 provide a set of questions to enable organisations to plot the industry situation, and the way their company is operating. In Figure 1.2 the need for a globally integrated approach is seen as one end of a spectrum, the other end of which is a need for a totally local response to the market. The vertical arm of the quadrant measures whether the company is operating in a global or multi-local way. Quadrants B and C are, on the face of it, potentially appropriate company responses. Quadrant A could be appropriate if the company has been able to identify niches in each market which are defensible. However, my experience is that the statement 'we are niche players' is often a rationalisation to avoid thinking about the strategy and often has no basis of fact behind it. It is hard to think that an answer which fell in quadrant D could be appropriate, and behaving globally in markets that cannot become global seems like a quick route for disaster.

I have not yet refined and tested Figure 1.2 in real situations, as I have with most other methods and models which have been described in my various publications. So far, its use has been restricted to teaching the concepts of global strategy through the medium of case studies. More work is required on the questions and

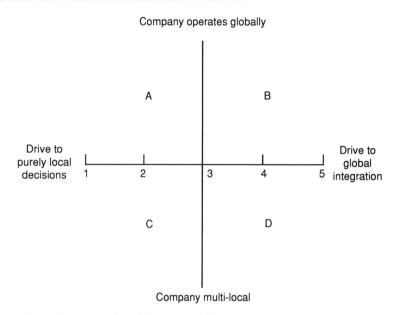

Figure 1.2   Company fit with competitive need

the scoring, but I have included it here because the line of thinking it follows is valid.

The point should be made that different degrees of globalness may be appropriate for different functions in the organisation. Thus design might be integrated globally, manufacture to a significant extent, while certain aspects of marketing, such as advertising, might be different for each country. Once again, the answer is not a formula that can be applied to give one right answer, but management's strategic response to the circumstances as it sees them.

OTHER ISSUES

We might have grouped the other issues under the heading managing the global/multinational company. *Business International* (1972) summarised the views of Perlmutter. He argued the advantages of a super-giant company and put forward the view that 200–400 companies would be super-giants. It may be possible on the basis of current understanding to quarrel with the idea of the massive diversified organisation, but his classification of companies into ethnocentric and polycentric is still of value. The ethnocentric firm has most of top management and staff in the home country,

Table 1.1   Global/local responsiveness questionnaire

Please circle one number on each scale according to the position of the industry

Marketing and sales

1.	Market requirements diverse	1	2	3	4	5	Market requirements homogenous
2.	Few opportunities for cross–country standardisation	1	2	3	4	5	Many opportunities for cross–country standardisation
3.	Numerous market segments	1	2	3	4	5	Few market segments
4.	Distribution channels differ by country	1	2	3	4	5	Distribution channels the same in all countries
5.	Customers all local operations	1	2	3	4	5	Customers all global operations
6.	Low customer pressure for worldwide service	1	2	3	4	5	High customer pressure for worldwide service
7.	Competitors all local buying	1	2	3	4	5	Competitors all global buying
8.	Numerous competitors in world	1	2	3	4	5	Few competitors in world
9.	High fiscal barriers to trade	1	2	3	4	5	Low fiscal barriers to trade
10.	Many non–fiscal barriers	1	2	3	4	5	No non–fiscal barriers

Research and development

11.	Low rate of technological change	1	2	3	4	5	High rate of technological change
12.	Low level of R&D effort	1	2	3	4	5	High level of R&D effort
13.	Short development time for new products	1	2	3	4	5	Long development time for new products
14.	Long product life cycle	1	2	3	4	5	Short product life cycle

Operations

15.	Low scale efficiencies	1	2	3	4	5	High scale efficiencies
16.	Low procurement scale economy	1	2	3	4	5	High procurement scale economy
17.	Flat experience curve	1	2	3	4	5	Steep experience curve
18.	High transport costs as % total costs	1	2	3	4	5	Low transport costs as % total costs

Table 1.2 Questionnaire: how does your company operate?

Tick the statement which most accurately describes how your company operates

	A	B	C
Executives' focus of vision	Local view ☐	Co–ordinate but define locally ☐	One view of the world ☐
Manufacturing	Each subsidiary has its own plant ☐	Plants at country level but co–ordinate ☐	Few plants serving the world ☐ Few centres, global orientation ☐
R&D	At country level ☐	Co–ordinated centres ☐	Same everywhere ☐
Quality concepts	Set at country level ☐	Common principles ☐ Some common features in all companies ☐	
Culture	Each company differs ☐	Through synergy ☐	Same everywhere ☐
Decisions try to maximize profit	At local level ☐	☐	On world view ☐
Control systems	Local ☐	Local but internationally co–ordinated ☐	Global ☐
New product development	Local ☐	Co–ordinated local ☐	Centralized globally ☐
Marketing management	Independent, local ☐	Co–ordinated ☐	Global ☐
Area of markets	One or few countries ☐	Strong in at least one Triad region ☐	Strong in whole Triad ☐

Score 1 for each tick in column A
Score 3 for each tick in column B
Score 5 for each tick in column C
Total score =
Average score =

takes decisions centrally and applies home standards to evaluate people and performance. The polycentric firm is the opposite, and accepts and uses the differences in markets and people, with a minimum of involvement of head office. We have covered the evolution of structure, and the changing views of strategy, and these demonstrated that this simple classification which is coupled with the belief that it is the polycentric companies that will survive, is far too simplistic. Yet in its rationale it identifies one area which is important, and which will repay more careful attention. This is the cultural differences between countries, which must be considered to achieve effective management.

Geert Hofstede is the leading writer here. Hofstede (1991) is not his first book on the subject, but includes refinements of his earlier concepts. He offers a five dimensional model which allows those aspects of culture which are important for management to be measured between countries on a consistent basis. The dimensions are:

• Degree of integration of individuals within groups
• Differences in the social roles of women versus men
• Ways of dealing with inequality
• The degree of tolerance of the unknown
• The trade-off between the long-term and short-term gratification of needs

Using Hofstede's measures it is possible to understand why different countries take such widely different views to many of the actions and edicts of the European Union. The UK has a very high tolerance of the unknown, and therefore many EU rules are seen as bureaucratic nonsense. Other countries with a much lower tolerance see the rules as a way of creating some certainty in an uncertain world, and therefore essential. Hofstede's work continues through a research institute (IRIC) which is based in Holland. The database from which the conclusions are drawn now contains about 200 000 managers. The value of this work in the context of global strategy is that it aids implementation, and careful attention to it may modify strategy, and will certainly cause additional factors to be considered in how businesses are managed.

Trompenaars (1993) offers an alternative approach. His database included 15 000 employees around the world. It is mentioned in order to provide a perspective for anyone wishing to gain a wider knowledge of the concepts.

Porter (1986) contains many contributions by various authors which deal with issues of management, such as co-ordinating international manufacturing and technology, different roles of international market and government relations in the global firm. As mentioned previously, Channon with Jalland (1979) also covered a number of management matters.

The first comprehensive book on human resource management in the multinational which I have discovered was Desatnick and Bennett (1977). This contains much that is still useful, although it does not cover the truly global organisation. It is perhaps worth observing that the collection of articles from *Long Range Planning* under the theme of strategic human resource management (Rothwell, 1991), although it has some excellent material, contains nothing on the issues of human resource management in global and multinational companies. Moreau and Vitrant (1980) covered expatriate employees, useful in very particular circumstances, but not claiming to be about the global company. The book is available only in French.

Coulson-Thomas (1992) provides the most up-to-date and comprehensive guide to management, particularly the human resource issues, in the multinational. It is based on a number of interviews and research studies directed by the author, and relates the ...management processes for formulating, sharing and implementing vision and strategy to advice on motivating, empowering and equipping people across international boarders. It deals with the dynamics of a changing situation.

CONCLUSION

There is much that is useful in the pages of all the works mentioned in this chapter, and I know that my Sellar and Yeatman view of history means that there are other contributions that I have omitted because I have either not seen them or have forgotten them. This makes this chapter a very personal view on the subject. Yet whatever has been omitted, I am left with the view that the really important books have still to be written. There is still much to be explored in the area of strategy formulation, and the literature on strategic human resource management in a global context is very slight (not surprising because there is not very much on strategic human resource management in a single-country operation context). There is wide scope for the development of new ideas across the whole arena of multinational and global management.

My history as promised has given more than two dates, but only as references so that you can find the works mentioned (and also to keep the publisher's copy editor from having a nervous breakdown).

I must have come close to referring you to 103 good things. I have no bad kings to offer, as I edited them out, but I should like to propose five good kings who, I think, have taken our thinking forward: C. K. Prahalad, George Yip, Yves Doz, Geert Hofstede and Kenichi Omhae. Unlike British history, I think we are at the beginning and not yet even close to the end.

REFERENCES

Ansoff, H.I. (1965) *Corporate Strategy*, New York, McGraw-Hill.

Bartlett, C.A. and Ghoshal S. (1990) *Managing Across Borders*, paperback edition 1991 with some additions, Boston, MA, Harvard Business School Press.

Brandt, W. K., Hulbert, J. M., Richers, R. (1980) Pitfalls in Planning for Multinational Operations, *Long Range Planning*, **13.6**, December.

Business International (1972) *Managing the Multinationals: Preparing for Tomorrow*, London, Allen & Unwin. (This book was based on a study and conference organised by *Business International* and was compiled by T. Aitken; however, his name is buried in the text and does not appear on the title page).

Chandler, A. D. (1962) *Strategy and Structure: Chapters in the History of the American Enterprise*, Cambridge, MA, The MIT Press.

Channon, D. F. (1973) *The Structure and Strategy of British Enterprise*, London, Macmillan.

Channon, D. F. with Jalland, M. (1979) *Multinational Strategic Planning*, London, Macmillan.

Coulson-Thomas, C. (1992) *Creating the Global Company*, Maidenhead, McGraw-Hill.

Cvar, M. R. (1986) Case studies in global competition: patterns of success and failure, In Porter, M. E. (ed.), *Competition in Global Industries*, Boston, MA, Harvard Business School.

Desatnick, R. L. and Bennett, M. L. (1977) *Human Resource Management in the Multinational Company*, Farnborough, Gower.

Franco, L. (1974) The move toward a multi-divisional structure in European organisations, *Administration Science Quarterly*, June.

Galbraith, J. R. and Nathansan, D. A (1978) *Strategy Implementation: The Role of Structure and Process*, St Paul, MN, West Publishing.

Hofstede, G. (1991) *Cultures and Organizations: Software of the Mind*, Maidenhead, McGraw-Hill.

Jolly, V. K., Alahuhta, M. and Jeannet, J.-P. (1992) Challenging the incumbents: how high technology start ups compete globally, *Journal of Strategic Change*.

Mockler, R. J. (ed) (1993) *Strategic Management: A Research Guide with Bibliographies*, Planning Forum and Strategic Management Research Group, Oxford, Ohio.

Moreau, M. and Vitrant, D. (1980) *Guide de L'Expatriation*, Paris, Enterprise Moderne d'Edition.
Ohmae, K. (1985) *Triad Power*, New York, Free Press.
Ohmae, K. (1990) *The Borderless World*, New York, Harper Business.
Porter, M. E. (ed.) (1986) *Competition in Global Industries*, Harvard Business School, Boston, MA.
Prahalad, C. K. and Doz, Y. (1987) *The Multinational Mission*, New York, Free Press.
Ringbakk, K.-A. (1976) Strategic planning in a turbulant International Environment, *Long Range Planning*, **9.3**, June.
Rostow, W. W. (1960) *The Stages of Economic Growth: A Non-Communist Manifesto*, New York, Cambridge University Press.
Rothwell, S. (1991) *Strategic Planning for Human Resources*, Oxford, Pergamon Press.
Rumelt, R. (1974) *Strategy, Structure and Economic Performance*, Division of Research, Harvard Business School, Cambridge, MA.
Scott, B. (1962) *Long Range Planning in American Industry*, New York, American Management Association.
Scott, B. R. (1971) *Stages of Corporate Development*, Harvard Business School, Cambridge, MA.
Sellar, W. C. and Yeatman, R. J. (1930) *1066 and All That*, London, Methuen, (reprinted 1990), London, Folio Society.
Smith, W. and Charmoz, R. (1975) Coordinate line management. Working paper, Searle International, Chicago, Illinois, February.
Steiner, G. A. (ed.) (1963) *Managerial Long Range Planning*, McGraw-Hill, New York.
Steiner, G. A. (1972) *Pitfalls in Comprehensive Long Range Planning*, Oxford, OH, The Planning Executives Institute.
Steiner, G. A. and Schöllhammer, H. (1975) Pitfalls in multinational long range planning, *Long Range Planning*, **8.2**, April.
Stopford, J. (1968) *Growth and Change in the Multi-National Field*, Unpublished doctoral dissertation, Harvard Business School, Cambridge, MA.
Stopford, J. and Wells, L. T. (1972) *Managing the Multinational Enterprise*, New York, Basic Books.
Steiner, G. A. (1972) *Managerial Long Range Planning*, New York, McGraw-Hill.
Taylor, C. W. (1992) *A World 2010: A New Order of Nations*, Strategic Studies Institute, US Army War College, Carlisle Barracks, Pennsylvania, PA.
Trompenaars, F. (1993) *Riding the Waves of Culture*, London, Economist Books.
Van Dam, A. (1972) Corporate planning for Asia, Latin America and Africa, *Long Range Planning*, **5.4**, December.
Yip, G. (1989) Global Strategy in a world of nations, *Sloan Management Review*, Fall.
Yip, G. (1992) *Total Global Strategy*, Englewood Cliffs, NJ, Prentice Hall.

Part Two

GLOBAL AND MULTINATIONAL
STRATEGY

2

CULTURAL CONSTRAINTS IN MANAGEMENT THEORIES

Geert Hofstede

Institute for Research on Intercultural Cooperation—Maastricht, the Netherlands

MANAGEMENT THEORISTS ARE HUMAN

Lewis Carroll's *Alice in Wonderland* contains the famous story of Alice's croquet game with the Queen of Hearts. Let me quote from it:

> Alice thought she had never seen such a curious croquet-ground in all her life; it was all ridges and furrows; the balls were live hedgehogs, the mallets live flamingoes, and the soldiers had to double themselves up and to stand on their hands and feet, to make the arches (Carroll, 1955 [1865], p.110).

You probably know how the story goes. Alice's flamingo mallet turns its head whenever she wants to strike with it; her hedgehog ball runs away; and the doubled-up soldier-arches walk around all the time. The only rule seems to be that the Queen of Hearts always wins.

Alice's croquet-playing problems are a suitable parable for any attempts to build culture-free theories of management: any concepts available for this purpose are themselves alive with culture, having been developed within a particular cultural context, and they have a will of their own in guiding our thinking towards the conclusion we wanted to arrive at in the first place. As the same reasoning may also be applied to the arguments I am about to present, I had better tell you my conclusions before I continue, so that you know the rules of my game in advance. I plan to take you on a trip around the world and demonstrate that there are no such things as universal management theories.

Diversity in management *practices* as we go around the world has been recognized in US management literature for more than 30 years (Harbison and Myers, 1959), and the term 'comparative management' has been in use since the 1960s (Farmer and Richman, 1965). However, it has taken much longer for the US academic community to accept that not only practices but also the validity of *theories* may stop at national borders, and I wonder whether even today everybody would agree with this statement. An article I published in *Organizational Dynamics* in 1980 and which carries the subtitle 'Do American Theories Apply Abroad?' raised an upheaval way beyond what I had expected. The article argued, with empirical support, that generally accepted US theories like those of Maslow, Herzberg, McClelland, Vroom, McGregor, Likert, Blake and Mouton may not or only very partly apply outside the borders of their country of origin—assuming they do apply within those borders. Among the requests for reprints, by the way, a larger number were from Canada than from the USA itself.

My argument is that not only are employees human—a discovery from the 1930s, with the Human Relations school (Mayo, 1933)—but managers are also human, an idea introduced in the late 1940s by Herbert Simon's 'bounded rationality' (Simon, 1947) and elaborated in Richard Cyert and James March's *Behavioral Theory of the Firm* (1963). Management scientists, theorists and writers are human too: they grew up in a particular society in a particular period, and their ideas cannot but reflect the constraints of the environment they know.

The idea that the validity of a theory is constrained by national borders is more obvious in Europe, with all its borders, than in a huge borderless country like the USA. In the sixteenth century Michel de Montaigne from France wrote a statement which was made famous by Blaise Pascal about a century later: 'Vérité en-deça des Pyrenées, erreur au-delà': 'There are truths on this side of the Pyrenées which are falsehoods on the other', the Pyrenées being the border mountains between France and Spain. In present-day France this sense of relativity has been applied to the borders between disciplines in the work of Pierre Bourdieu, who in his book *Homo Academicus* has dealt with the sociology of social scientists (Bourdieu, 1984, 1988). Surprisingly, he has not (yet?) referred explicitly to national differences.

MANAGEMENT AS AN AMERICAN INVENTION

The word 'management', as far as I can trace it, was first used in the English language in its present meaning in the nineteenth century. The British economist John Stuart Mill (1806–1873) referred to 'managers' and 'management' for describing the persons and the process of running joint stock companies; he did not like them. Since the 1880s the word 'management' appeared occasionally in writings by American engineers, until it was canonized by Frederick W. Taylor in *Shop Management* in 1903 and in *The Principles of Scientific Management* in 1911. In its present meaning, it is an American invention.

The linguistic origin of the word is from Latin *manus* (hand) via the Italian *maneggiare*, which is the training of horses in the *manege*. However, it has also been associated with the French *menage*, as the art of running a household (Mant, 1977, p. 20). The theatre of present-day management contains elements of both *manege* and *menage* and different managers and cultures may put different accents.

In the American meaning of the word, 'management' is used not only to describe an activity but also a class of people. Managers are people who (1) do not own a business but act on behalf of the owner and (2) do not produce themselves but are indispensable for making others (workers) produce through a process called 'motivation'. They carry a high status, and many American boys (as well as quite a few girls) aspire to joining the managerial class. In the USA, the manager is a culture hero.

You are not invited to follow me on our trip around the world. We will look at management in its context in other successful modern economies: subsequently in Germany, Japan, France, Holland, and among the Overseas Chinese. Then we will also pay some attention to management in the much larger part of the world that is still poor, especially in South-east Asian and Africa, and in the new political configurations of Eastern Europe, in particular in Russia, returning to the USA via mainland China.

GERMANY

One could hardly say that the manager is a culture hero in Germany. If anyone, it is the engineer rather than the manager who plays the hero role there. Frederick Taylor invented his Scientific Management in a society of immigrants: one in which large numbers of workers with quite diverse backgrounds and skills had to be put to work together. In Germany this heterogeneity never existed. Elements of the medieval guild system have survived in historical continuity until the present day: in particular, a very effective apprenticeship system both on the shopfloor and in the office, in which practical work and classroom courses alternate. At the end of the apprenticeship the worker receives a certificate, the *Facharbeiterbrief*, which is recognized throughout the country. About two-thirds of the German worker population holds such a certificate and the corresponding occupational pride. For comparison, in Britain two-thirds of the worker population have no occupational qualification at all. Quite a few German company presidents have worked their way up from the ranks through an apprenticeship.

These highly skilled and responsible German workers do not necessarily need a manager, American style, to 'motivate' them. They expect their boss or *Meister* to assign their task and to be a superior expert in order to resolve their technical problems. Comparisons of matched German, British and French organizations have shown the Germans to have the highest rate of personnel in productive roles and the lowest both in leading and in staff roles (Maurice *et al.*, 1980). Business schools are virtually unknown in Germany. Native German management theories concentrate on formal systems (Kieser and Kubicek, 1983). The inapplicability of American concepts of management in this situation became quite apparent when in 1973 the US consulting firm of Booz, Allen and Hamilton, commissioned by the German Ministry of Economic Affairs, wrote a study of German management from an American point of view. The report is highly critical and writes, among other things, that 'Germans simply do not have a very strong concept of management' (Lawrence, 1980, pp. 88–93). Since 1973, according to my personal experience, the situation has not changed much. However, during this period, in comparison with the USA the German economy has performed in a superior fashion in virtually all respects, so a strong concept of management might have been a liability rather than an asset.

JAPAN

The manager, US style, is equally missing in Japan. In the USA the core of the enterprise can be said to be its managerial class. The core of the Japanese enterprise consists of its permanent worker group; workers who, for all practical purposes, are tenured and who aspire at life-long employment. They are distinct from the non-permanent employees, that is, most women as well as subcontracted teams led by gang bosses, to be laid off in slack periods. University graduates in Japan first join the permanent worker group and subsequently fill various positions, moving from line to staff as the need occurs while paid according to seniority rather than position. They take part in Japanese-style group consultation sessions for important decisions, which extend the decision-making period but guarantee fast implementation afterwards. Japanese are, to a large extent, controlled by their peer group rather than by their manager.

Three researchers from the East–West Center of the University of Hawaii, Joseph Tobin, David Wu and Dana Danielson, did an observation study of typical preschools in three countries: China, Japan and the USA. Their results have been published both as a book and as a video (Tobin *et al.*, 1989). In the Japanese preschool, one teacher handled 28 4-year olds. The video shows one particularly obnoxious boy, Hiroki, who fights with other children and throws teaching materials down from the balcony. When a little girl tries to alarm the teacher, the latter answers: 'What are you calling me for? Do something about it!' In the US preschool, there is one adult for every nine children. This class has its problem child too, Kerry, who refuses to clear away his toys. One of the teachers has a long talk with him and isolates him in a corner, until he changes his mind. It does not take much imagination to realize that managing Hiroki 30 years later will be a different process from managing Kerry.

American theories of leadership are ill-suited for the Japanese group-controlled situation. The Japanese have over two decades developed their own 'PM' theory of leadership, in which P stands for Performance and M for Maintenance. The latter is less a concern for individual employees than for maintaining social stability (Misumi and Peterson, 1987). In view of the amazing success of the Japanese economy in the past 30 years, many Americans have sought for the secrets of Japanese management (e.g. Pascale and Athos, 1981; Ouchi, 1981), hoping to be able to copy them. There are no secrets of Japanese management, however; it is even doubtful whether there is such a thing as management, in the American sense, in Japan at all. The secret is in Japanese society; and if any group in society should be singled out as carriers of the secret, it is the workers, not the managers.

FRANCE

The manager, US style, does not exist in France either. In a very enlightening book, unfortunately not yet translated into English, the

French researcher Philippe d'Iribarne (1989) describes the results of in-depth observation and interview studies of management methods in three subsidiary plants of the same French multinational: in France, in the USA, and in Holland; and he relates what he finds to information about the three societies in general, going back to history where necessary to trace the roots of the completely different behaviors in the completion of the same tasks. He identifies three kinds of basic principles (*logiques*) of management. In the USA, the principle is the *contract* between employer and employee, which gives the manager considerable prerogatives, but within its limits. This is really a labor *market* in which the worker sells his or her labor for a price. In France, the principle is the *honor* of each class in a society which has always been and remains extremely stratified, in which superiors behave as superior beings and subordinates accept and expect this, conscious of their own lower level in the national hierarchy but also of the honor of their own class. The French do not think in terms of managers versus non-managers but in terms of *cadres* versus *non-cadres*; one becomes cadre by attending the proper schools and one remains it forever. Regardless of their actual task, cadres have the privileges of a higher social class, and it is very rare for a non-cadre to cross the ranks.

The conflict between French and American theories of management became already apparent in the beginning of the twentieth century, in a criticism by the great French management pioneer Henri Fayol (1841–1925) on his US colleague and contemporary Frederick W. Taylor (1856–1915). The difference in career paths of the two men is striking. Fayol was a French engineer whose career as a *cadre supérieur* culminated in the position of Président-Directeur-Général of a mining company. After his retirement he formulated his experiences in a pathbreaking text on organization: *Administration industrielle et générale*, in which he focused on the sources of authority. Taylor was an American engineer who had started his career in industry as a worker and attained his academic qualifications through evening studies. From Chief Engineer in a steel company he became one of the first management consultants. Taylor was not really concerned with the issue of authority at all; his focus was on efficiency. He proposed to split the task of the first-line boss into eight specialisms, each exercised by a different person; an idea which eventually led to the matrix organization.

Taylor's work appeared in a French translation in 1913, and Fayol read it and showed himself generally impressed but shocked by Taylor's 'denial of the principle of the Unity of Command' in the case of the eight-boss-system (Fayol, 1970 [1916], p. 85). However, this principle was and is much holier in France than in the USA.

Seventy years later André Laurent, another of Fayol's compatriots, found that French managers in a survey reacted very strongly against a suggestion that one employee could report to two different bosses, while US managers in the same survey showed fewer misgivings in this respect (Laurent, 1981). Matrix organization has never become popular in France as it has in the USA.

HOLLAND

In my own country, Holland, or as it is officially called, the Netherlands, the study by Philippe d'Iribarne found the management principle to be a need for *consensus* between all parties, predetermined neither by a contractual relationship nor by class distinctions, but based on an open-ended exchange of views and a balancing of interests. In terms of the different origins of the word 'manager', the organization in Holland is more *menage* (household) while in the USA it is more *manege* (horse drill).

At my university, the University of Limburg at Maastricht, every semester we receive a class of American business junior students who take a Program in European Studies. We asked both the Americans and a matched group of Dutch students to describe their ideal job after graduation, using a list of 22 job characteristics (Hofstede and Vunderink, 1994). The Americans attached significantly more importance than the Dutch to earnings, advancement, benefits, a good working relationship with their boss, and security of employment. The Dutch attached significantly more importance than the Americans to freedom to adopt their own approach to the job, being consulted by their boss in his or her decisions, training opportunities, contributing to the success of their organization, fully using their skills and abilities, and helping others. This list confirms d'Iribarne's findings of a contractual employment relationship in the USA, based on earnings and career opportunities, against a consensual relationship in Holland. The latter has centuries-old roots. It should be remembered that the Netherlands were the first republic in western Europe (1609–1810), and a model for the American republic. The country has been and still is governed by a careful balancing of interests in a multi-party system.

In terms of management theories, both motivation and leadership in Holland are different from what they are in the USA. In Abraham Maslow's Hierarchy of Needs, for example, he puts self-actualization above esteem above belongingness and love. In Holland self-actualization presupposes consensus which carries elements of both esteem and belongingness; but this is a concept which simply does not figure in Maslow's categorization (Maslow, 1970). Leadership in Holland presupposes modesty, as opposed to assertiveness in the USA. No USA leadership theory known to me has room for that. I hope you do not interpret me in such a way that working in Holland is a constant feast; there is a built-in premium on mediocrity and jealousy, as well as ritual consultations in order to maintain the appearance of consensus and the pretense of modesty. There is unfortunately another side to every coin. The perceptive observer will have recognized an expression of Dutch modesty in this statement.

THE OVERSEAS CHINESE

Among the champions of economic development in the past 30 years we find three countries mainly populated by Chinese living outside the Chinese mainland: Taiwan, Hong Kong and Singapore. Moreover, Overseas Chinese play a very important role in the economies of Indonesia, Malaysia, the Philippines and Thailand, where they form an ethnic minority. If anything, the 'little dragons', Taiwan, Hong Kong and Singapore, have even been more economically successful than Japan, moving from rags to riches and now counted among the world's wealthy industrial countries. Yet very little attention has been paid to the way in which their enterprises have been managed. I can highly recommend a recent book, *The Spirit of Chinese Capitalism*, by Gordon Redding (1990), the British dean of the Hong Kong Business School, who bases his insights on personal acquaintance and in-depth discussions with a large number of Overseas Chinese business people. The title of his book is obviously a paraphrase on Max Weber's *The Protestant Ethic and the Spirit of Capitalism* (1930). Few of Redding's interviewees are Protestants, but they are possessed by a strong ethic.

The Overseas Chinese enterprises lack almost all characteristics of modern management, American style. They tend to be small, co-operating for essential functions with other small organizations through networks based on personal relations. They are family-owned, without the separation between ownership and management typical in the West, or even in Japan and South Korea. They normally focus on one product or market, with growth by opportunistic diversification; in this, they are extremely flexible. Decision making is centralized in the hands of one dominant family member, but other family members may be given new ventures to try their skills. They are low-profile and extremely cost-conscious, applying the Confucian virtues of thrift and persistence. Their size is kept small by the assumed lack of loyalty of non-family employees, who, if they are any good, will just wait and save until they can start their own family business. Overseas Chinese prefer economic activities in which great gains can be made with few staff, like commodity trading and real estate. They employ few professional managers, except their sons and sometimes daughters who have been sent to prestigious business schools abroad, but who upon return continue to run the family business the Chinese way.

The origin of this system, or—in Western eyes—this lack of system is found in the history of Chinese society, in which there were no formal laws, only formal networks of powerful people guided by general principles of Confucian virtue; in which the favors of the authorities could change from one day to another, so that no-one could be trusted except one's kinsfolk—of whom, fortunately, there used to be many, in an extended family structure. The Overseas Chinese way of doing business is also very well adapted to their position in the countries in which they form ethnic minorities, often envied and threatened by ethnic violence.

Overseas Chinese businesses following this unprofessional approach command a collective Gross National Product of some US $200 billion, equal to the GNP of Australia. There is no denying that it works.

MANAGEMENT TRANSFER TO POOR COUNTRIES

So far we have visited five countries or areas in the industrially developed, i.e. rich, part of the world: Germany, Japan, France, Holland, and the little dragons of East Asia. In none of these countries are organizations and businesses run according to the American management theory books, although elements of the theories can be fruitfully used here and there; but different elements in different places.

Four-fifths of the world population live in countries that are not rich but poor. After the Second World War and decolonization, the stated purpose of the United Nations and the World Bank has been to promote the development of all the world's countries in a War on Poverty. After 40 years it looks very much like we are losing this war. If one thing has become clear, it is that the export of Western—

mostly American—management practices *and* theories to poor
countries has contributed little or nothing to their development.
There has been no lack of effort and money spent for this purpose:
students from poor countries have been trained in the USA, and
teachers and Peace Corps workers have been sent to the poor
countries. If nothing else, the general lack of success in economic
development of other countries should be a sufficient argument to
doubt the validity of Western management theories in non-Western
environments.

If we take a closer look at different parts of the world, the
development picture is not equally bleak all over, and history is
often a better predictor than economic factors for what happens
today. There is a broad regional pecking-order, with East Asian
leading: the little dragons having passed into the camp of the
wealthy; then follow South-east Asia (with its Overseas Chinese
minorities), Latin America (in spite of the debt crisis), South Asia,
and Africa always trails behind. Several African countries have only
become poorer since decolonization. Regions of the world with a
history of large-scale political integration and civilization generally
have done better than regions in which no large-scale political and
cultural infrastructure existed, even if the old civilizations had
decayed or have been suppressed by colonizers. It has become
painfully clear that development cannot be pressure-cooked; it
presumes a cultural infrastructure that takes time to grow. Local
management is part of this infrastructure; it cannot be imported in
package form. Assuming that with so-called modern management
techniques and theories outsiders can develop a country has proved
a deplorable arrogance. At best, one can hope for a dialogue between
equals with the locals, in which the Western partner acts as the
expert in Western technology and the local partner as the expert in
culture, habits and feelings.

RUSSIA AND CHINA

The crumbling of the former Eastern block has left us with a
scattering of states and would-be states the political and economic
future of which is extremely uncertain. The best predictions are those
based on a knowledge of history, because historical trends have
taken revenge on the arrogance of the Soviet rulers who believed
they could turn them around by brute power. One obvious fact is
that the former bloc is internally extremely heterogeneous, including
countries traditionally closely linked with the West by trade and

travel, like the Czech Republic, Hungary, Slovenia and the Baltic states, as well as others with a Byzantine or Turkish past; some having been prosperous, others always extremely poor.

The industrialized Western world and the World Bank, from what I read in the newspapers, seem committed to helping the former Eastern bloc countries develop, but with the same technocratic neglect for local cultural factors that proved so unsuccessful in the development assistance to other poor countries. Free market capitalism, introduced by Western-style management, is supposed to be the answer from Albania to Russia. Is it? What are the chances of success of this philosophy?

Let me limit myself to the Russian republic, a huge territory with some 140 million inhabitants, mainly Russians. We know quite a bit about the Russians as their country was a world power for several hundreds of years before Communism, and in the nineteenth century it produced some of the greatest writers in the world's literature. If I want to understand the Russians—including how they could so long support the Soviet regime—I tend to reread Lev Nikolayevich Tolstoy (1828–1910). In his famous novel, *Anna Karenina* (1876), one of the main characters is a landowner, Levin, whom Tolstoy uses to express his own views and convictions about his people. Russian peasants used to be serfs; serfdom had been abolished in 1861, but the peasants, now tenants, remained as passive as before. Levin wanted to break this passivity by dividing the land among his peasants in exchange for a share of the crops, but the peasants only let the land deteriorate further. Here follows a quote:

> [Levin] read political economy and socialistic works . . . but, as he had expected, found nothing in them related to his undertaking. In the political economy books—in [John Stuart] Mill, for instance, whom he studied first and with great ardour, hoping every minute to find an answer to the questions that were engrossing him—he found only certain laws deduced from the state of agriculture in Europe; but he could not for the life of him see why these laws, which did not apply to Russia, should be considered universal . . . Political economy told him that the laws by which Europe had developed and was developing her wealth were universal and absolute. Socialist teaching told him that development along those lines leads to ruin. And neither of them offered the smallest enlightenment as to what he, Levin, and all the Russian peasants and landowners were to do with their millions of hands and millions of acres, to make them as productive as possible for the common good (Tolstoy, 1978 [1876], pp. 366–7).

In the summer of 1991, the Russian lands yielded a record harvest, but a large share of it rotted in the fields because no people were to be found for harvesting. The passivity is still there, and not only among the peasants. And the heirs of John Stuart Mill (who, as you will remember, may have coined the word 'management') again present their universal recipes which simply do not apply.

In the summer of 1990 my wife and I travelled by train through Russia and China. The contrast between the two countries could not have been sharper. In Russia there was political freedom—our first time in that country that people spontaneously told us what they thought—but dramatic economic stagnation and passivity. In China there was no freedom of expression, but a booming internal economy and activity. The Russian railways are wide-gauge, in contrast to those in Europe and in China, and we twice had the bogies under the carriages changed, at the Polish–White Russian and the Mongolian–Chinese borders. When this happens the carriages are pulled into a shed, disconnected, lifted, and the old wheels are rolled away and replaced by a new set; all of this with the passengers inside the carriages. The contrast between the two borders could not have been bigger. At Brest-Litowsk, on the Polish–White Russian border, dirty Russian men in an even dirtier shed worked slowly at their routine. At Erlian, on the Chinese–Mongolian border, our Chinese female carriage attendants got out, put on aprons, and with some help from local operators performed the job in a clean shed and in record time.

Citing Tolstoy, I implicitly suggest that management theorists cannot neglect the great literature of the countries to which they want their ideas to apply. The greatest novel in Chinese literature is considered to be Cao Xueqin's *The Story of the Stone*, also known as *The Dream of the Red Chamber*, which appeared around 1760. It describes the rise and fall of two branches of an aristocratic family in Beijing, who live on adjacent plots in the capital. Their plots are joined by a magnificent garden with several pavilions in it, and the young, mostly female, members of both families are allowed to live in them. One day the management of the garden is taken over by a young woman, Tan-Chun, who states:

> I think we ought to pick out a few experienced trustworthy old women from among the ones who work in the Garden—women who know something about gardening already—and put the upkeep of the Garden into their hands. We needn't ask them to pay us rent; all we need ask them for is an annual share of the produce. There would be four advantages in this arrangement. In the first place, if we have people whose sole occupation is to look after trees and flowers and so on, the condition of the Garden will improve gradually year after year

and there will be no more of those long periods of neglect followed by bursts of feverish activity when things have been allowed to get out of hand. Secondly there won't be the spoiling and wastage we get at present. Thirdly the women themselves will gain a little extra to add to their incomes which will compensate them for the hard work they put in throughout the year. And fourthly, there's no reason why we shouldn't use the money we should otherwise have spent on nurserymen, rockery specialists, horticultural cleaners and so on for other purposes (Cao, 1980 [1760], Vol. 3: p.69).

As the story goes on, the privatization—because that is what it is—of the Garden is carried through, and it works. When in the 1980s Deng Xiaoping allowed privatization in the Chinese villages, it also worked. It worked so well that its effects started to be felt in politics and threatened the existing political order; hence the knockdown at Tienanmen Square of June 1989. But it seems that the forces of privatization are getting the upper hand again in China. If we remember what Chinese entrepreneurs are able to do once they have become Overseas Chinese, we should not be too surprised. But what works in China—and worked two centuries ago—does not have to work in Russia, not in Tolstoy's days and not today. I am not offering a solution; I only protest against a naive universalism that knows only one recipe for development, the one supposed to have worked in the USA.

A THEORY OF CULTURE IN MANAGEMENT

Our trip around the world is over and we are back in the USA. What have we learned? There is something in all the countries we visited that can be called 'management', but its meaning differs to a larger or smaller extent from one country to the other, and it takes considerable historical and cultural insight into local conditions to understand its processes, philosophies and problems. If already the word may mean so many different things, how can we expect theories of management to apply abroad? One should be extremely careful in making this assumption, and test it before taking it as proven. 'Management' is not a phenomenon that can be isolated from other processes taking place in a society. We have seen during our trip around the world that it interacts with what happens in the family, at school, in politics and government. It is obviously also related to religion and to beliefs about science. Theories of management always had to be interdisciplinary, but if we cross national borders they should become more interdisciplinary than ever.

Earlier I published an empirically derived theory of culture applicable to management (Hofstede, 1980b, 1991). The theory states, briefly, that cultural differences between nations can to some extent be described using first four, and now five, bipolar *dimensions*. The position of a country on these dimensions allows to make some predictions on the way the national societies operate, including their processes of management and the kind of theories applicable to their management.

My definition of 'culture' differs from some other very respectable definitions. Culture is *the collective programming of the mind which distinguishes one group or category of people from another*. In the part of my work I am referring to now, the category of people is the nation.

Culture is a *construct*, that means it is 'not directly accessible to observation but inferable from verbal statements and other behaviors and useful in predicting still other observable and measurable verbal and nonverbal behavior' (Levitin, 1972, p. 492). It should not be reified; it is an auxiliary concept that should be used as long as it proves useful but bypassed where we can predict behaviors without it.

The same applies to the *dimensions* I introduced. They are also constructs that should not be reified. They do not 'exist'; they are tools for analysis which may or may not clarify a situation. In my statistical analysis of empirical data the first four dimensions together explain 49% of the variance in the data. The other 51% remain specific to individual countries. But at least I have a tool that allowed me to reduce the complexity by half.

The first four dimensions were initially detected through a comparison of the values of similar people (employees and managers) in 64 different national subsidiaries of the IBM Corporation. People working for the same multinational, but in different countries, represent very well-matched samples from the populations of their countries, similar in all respects except nationality. The same dimensions have later been found in multi-country studies of other matched populations (Hofstede and Bond, 1984; Hoppe, 1990). What gave me confidence initially that I was on the right track is that very similar dimensions had been predicted in a review article of the anthropological literature (Inkeles and Levinson, as far back as 1954), as common basic problems worldwide, with consequences for the functioning of societies, of groups within those societies and of individuals within those groups. If one really finds something fundamental in the social sciences, there must be others who found it before.

The first dimension has been labelled *Power Distance*, and it can be defined as the degree of inequality among people which the population of a country considers as normal: from relatively equal (that is, small power distance) to extremely unequal (large power distance). All societies are unequal, but some are more unequal than others.

The second dimension is labelled *Individualism*, and it is the degree to which people in a country prefer to act as individuals rather than as members of groups. The opposite of individualism can be called *Collectivism*, so collectivism is low individualism. The way I use the word, it has no political connotations. In collectivist societies a child learns to respect the group to which it belongs, usually the family, and to differentiate between in-group members and out-group members (that is, all other people). When children grow up they remain members of their group, and they expect the group to protect them when they are in trouble. In return, they have to remain loyal to their group throughout life. In individualist societies, a child learns very early to think of itself as 'I' instead of as part of 'we'. It expects one day to have to stand on its own feet and not to get protection from its group any more; and therefore it also does not feel a need for strong loyalty.

The third dimension has been called *Masculinity* and its opposite pole *Femininity*. It is the degree to which 'tough' values like assertiveness, performance, success and competition, which in nearly all societies are associated with the role of men, prevail over 'tender' values like the quality of life, maintaining warm personal relationships, service, care for the weak, and solidarity, which in nearly all societies are more associated with the role of women. Women's roles differ from men's roles in all countries; but in tough societies, the differences are larger than in tender ones.

The fourth dimension has been labelled *Uncertainty Avoidance*, and it can be defined as the degree to which people in a country prefer structured over unstructured situations. Structured situations are those in which there are clear rules as to how one should behave. These rules can be written down, but they can also be unwritten and imposed by tradition. In countries which score high on uncertainty avoidance, people tend to show more nervous energy, while in countries which score low, people are more easy-going. A (national) society with strong uncertainty avoidance can be called rigid; one with weak uncertainty avoidance, flexible. One way of describing countries where uncertainty avoidance is strong is to say that in these countries a feeling prevails of 'what is different, is dangerous'. In weak uncertainty avoidance societies, the feeling would rather be 'what is different, is curious'.

The fifth dimension was added on the basis of a study of the values of students in 23 countries carried out by Michael Harris Bond, a Canadian working in Hong Kong. He and I had co-operated in another study of students' values which had yielded the same four dimensions as the IBM data. However, we wondered to what extent our common findings in two studies could be the effect of a Western bias introduced by the common Western background of the researchers: remember Alice's croquet game. Michael Bond resolved this dilemma by deliberately introducing an Eastern bias. He used a questionnaire prepared at his request by his Chinese colleagues, the *Chinese Value Survey* (CVS), which was translated from Chinese into different languages and answered by 50 male and 50 female students in each of 23 countries in all five continents. Analysis of the CVS data produced three dimensions significantly correlated with the three IBM dimensions of power distance, individualism and masculinity (*The Chinese Culture Connection*, 1987; Hofstede and Bond, 1988). There was also a fourth dimension, but it did not resemble uncertainty avoidance. It was composed, both on the positive and on the negative side, from items that had not been included in the IBM studies but were present in the Chinese Value Survey because they were rooted in the teachings of Confucius, the great Chinese philosopher of 500 BC. I labelled this dimension *Long-term* versus *Short-term Orientation* (Hofstede, 1991). On the long-term side one finds values oriented towards the future, like thrift (saving) and persistence. On the short-term side one finds values rather oriented towards the past and present, like respect for tradition and fulfilling social obligations.

Table 2.1 lists the scores on all five dimensions for the USA and for the other countries we have just visited on our world trip. The table shows that each country has its own configuration on the four dimensions. Some of the values in the table have been estimated based on imperfect replications or personal impressions. The different dimension scores do not 'explain' all the differences in management I described earlier; in order to understand management in a country, one should have both knowledge of and empathy with the entire local scene. However, the scores should suffice to make us aware that people in other countries may think, feel and act very differently from us when confronted with basic problems of society.

Table 2.1 Culture dimension scores for ten countries

	PD	ID	MA	UA	LT
USA	40 l	91 h	62 h	46 l	29 l
Germany	35 l	67 h	66 h	65 m	31 m
Japan	54 m	46 m	95 h	92 h	80 h
France	68 h	71 h	43 m	86 h	30[a] l
Netherlands	38 l	80 h	14 l	53 m	44 m
Hong Kong	68 h	25 l	57 h	29 l	96 h
Indonesia	78 h	14 l	46 m	48 l	25[a] l
West Africa	77 h	20 l	46 m	54 m	16 l
Russia	95[a] h	50[a] m	40[a] m	90[a] h	10[a] l
China	80[a] h	20[a] l	66[a] h	60[a] m	118 h

[a] Estimated.
PD = Power Distance; ID = Individualism; MA = Masculinity; UA = Uncertainty Avoidance; LT = Long-term Orientation.
h = top third, m = medium third, l = bottom third (among 53 countries and regions for the first four dimensions; among 23 countries for the fifth).

IDIOSYNCRACIES OF AMERICAN MANAGEMENT THEORIES

In comparison to other countries, the US culture profile as I found it presents itself as below average on Power Distance and Uncertainty Avoidance, highly individualistic, fairly masculine and short-term oriented. The Germans show a stronger Uncertainty Avoidance and less extreme Individualism; the Japanese are different on all dimensions, least on Power Distance; the French show larger Power Distance and Uncertainty Avoidance, but are less individualistic and somewhat feminine; the Dutch resemble the Americans on the first three dimensions, but score extremely feminine and relatively long-term oriented; Hong Kong Chinese combine large Power Distance and weak Uncertainty Avoidance, Collectivism, and are very long-term oriented; and so on.

The American culture profile is reflected in American management theories. I will just mention three elements not necessarily present in other countries: the stress on market processes, the stress on the individual and the stress on managers rather than on workers:

(1) *The stress on market processes*: In the U.S.A. in the 1970s and 1980s it became fashionable to look at organizations from a point of

view of 'transaction costs'. Economist Oliver Williamson has
opposed 'hierarchies' to 'markets' (Williamson, 1975). The
reasoning is that human social life consists of economic
transactions between individuals. We found the same in
d'Iribarne's description of the US principle of the contract
between employer and employee, the labor market in which the
worker sells his or her labor for a price. These individuals will
form hierarchical organizations when the cost of the economic
transactions (such as getting information, finding out whom to
trust, etc.) is lower in a hierarchy than when all transactions
would take place on a free market. From a cultural perspective
the important point is that *the 'market' is the point of departure or
base model*, and the organization is explained from market
failure. A culture that produces such a theory is likely to prefer
organizations that internally resemble markets to those that
internally resemble more structured models, like those in
Germany of France. The ideal principle of control in
organizations in the market philosophy is *competition* between
individuals. This philosophy fits a society that combines a not-
too-large Power Distance with a not-too-strong Uncertainty
Avoidance and Individualism; besides the USA, it will fit all
other Anglo countries.

(2) *The stress on the individual*: I find this again and again in the
design of research projects and hypotheses; also in the fact that
in the USA psychology is clearly a more respectable discipline
in management circles than sociology. Culture, however, is a
collective phenomenon. Although we may get our information
about culture from individuals, we have to interpret it at the
level of collectivities. There are snags here known as the
'ecological fallacy' and the 'reverse ecological fallacy' (Hofstede
et al., 1993); none of the US college textbooks on methodology I
know deals sufficiently with the problem of multi-level analysis.
Culture can be compared to a forest, while individuals are trees.
A forest is not just a bunch of trees: it is a symbiosis of different
trees, bushes, plants, insects, animals and micro-organisms, and
we miss the essence of the forest if we describe only its most
typical trees. In the same way, a culture cannot be satisfactorily
described in terms of the characteristics of a typical individual.
There is a tendency in the US management literature to
overlook the forest for the trees and to ascribe cultural
differences to interactions among individuals. A striking
example is the book *Organizational Culture and Leadership* by
Edgar H. Schein (1985). On the basis of his consulting

experience he compares two large companies, nicknamed 'Action' and 'Multi'. He explains the differences in culture between these companies by the group dynamics in their respective boardrooms. Nowhere in his book does he draw any conclusions from the fact that the first company is an American-based computer firm and the second a Swiss-based pharmaceutics firm; this information is not even found in the book. This stress on interactions among individuals obviously fits a culture identified as the most individualistic in the world, but it will not at all be understood by the four-fifths of the world population for whom the group prevails over the individual.

One of the conclusions of my own multi-level research has been that 'culture' at the national level and 'culture' at the organizational level—corporate culture—are two very different phenomena, and that the use of a common term for both is confusing (Hofstede et al., 1990; Hofstede, 1991). If we do use it, we should also pay attention to the occupational and the gender level of culture. National cultures differ primarily in the fundamental, invisible values held by a majority of their members, acquired in early childhood, whereas organizational cultures are a much more superficial phenomenon residing mainly in the visible practices of the organization, acquired by socialization of the new members who join as young adults. National cultures change only very slowly if at all; organizational cultures may be consciously changed, although it is not necessarily easy. This difference between the two types of culture is the secret of the existence of multinational corporations that employ, as I showed in the IBM case, employees with extremely different national cultural values. What keeps them together is a corporate culture based on common practices.

(3) *The stress on managers rather than workers*: The core element of a work organization worldwide is the people who do the work. All the rest is superstructure, and I hope to have demonstrated to you in our trip around the world that it may take many different shapes. In the US literature on work organization, however, the core element, if not explicitly then implicitly, is considered the manager. This may well be the result of the combination of extreme individualism with fairly strong masculinity, which has turned the manager into a culture hero of almost mythical proportions. For example, he—not really she—is supposed to make decisions all the time. Those of you who are or have been managers must know that this is a fable. Very few management decisions are just 'made' as the myth suggests it.

Managers are much more involved in maintaining networks; if anything, it is the rank-and-file worker who can really make decisions on his or her own, albeit on a relatively simple level.

An amusing effect of the US focus on managers is that in at least ten American books and articles on management I have been misquoted as having studied IBM *managers* (or even *'executives'*) in my research, whereas my book clearly describes that the answers were from IBM *employees*. My observation may be biased, but I get the impression that compared to 20 or 30 years ago less research in the USA is done among employees and more on managers. But managers derive their *raison d'être* from the people managed: culturally, they are the followers of the people they lead, and their effectiveness depends on the latter. In other parts of the world, this exclusive focus on the manager is less strong, with Japan as the supreme example.

CONCLUSION

I started with Alice in Wonderland. In fact, the management theorist who ventures outside his or her own country into other parts of the world is like Alice in Wonderland. He or she will meet strange beings, customs, ways of organizing or disorganizing and theories that are clearly stupid, old-fashioned or even immoral—yet they may work, or at least they may not fail more frequently than corresponding theories do at home. Then, after the first culture shock, the traveller to Wonderland will feel enlightened, and may be able to take his or her experiences home and use them advantageously. All great ideas in science, politics and management have travelled from one country to another, and been enriched by foreign influences. The roots of American management theories are mainly in Europe: with John Stuart Mill, Lev Tolstoy, Max Weber, Henri Fayol, Sigmund Freud, Kurt Lewin and many others. These theories were replanted in the USA and they developed and bore fruit. The same will happen again. The last thing we need is a Monroe Doctrine for management ideas.

AUTHOR'S NOTE

Another version of this chapter appeared in the *Academy of Management Executive*, **VII**, No. 1, February 1993, 81–94, and is reprinted with permission.

REFERENCES

Bourdieu, P. (1988a) *Homo academicus*, Paris, Éditions de Minuit. English translation Cambridge Polity Press and Stanford University Press, 1988.
Bourdieu, P. (1988b) Vive la crise! For heterodoxy in social science. *Theory and Society*, **17**.
Cao, Xueqin (1980 [1760]) *The Story of the Stone*, translated by David Hawkes, Volume 3. Harmondworth, Penguin.
Carroll, L. (1946 [1865]) *Alice in Wonderland*, Harmondsworth, Penguin.
Cyert, R. M. and March, J. G. (1963) *A Behavioral Theory of the Firm*, Englewood Cliffs NJ, Prentice Hall.
d'Iribarne, P. (1988) *La logique de l'honneur: Gestion des entreprises et traditions nationales*, Paris, Éditions du Seuil.
Farmer, R. N. and Richman, B. M. (1965) *Comparative Management and Economic Progress*, Homewood, IL, Irwin.
Fayol, H. (1970 [1916]) *Administration industrielle et générale*, Paris, Dunod.
Harbison, F. and Myers, C. A. (1959) *Management in the Industrial World: An International Analysis*, New York, McGraw-Hill.
Hofstede, G. (1980a) Motivation, leadership and organization: Do American theories apply abroad? *Organizational Dynamics* **9**, No. 1, 42–63.
Hofstede, G. (1980b) *Culture's Consequences: International Differences in Work-Related Values*, Beverly Hills, CA, Sage Publications.
Hofstede, G. (1991) *Cultures and Organizations: Software of the Mind*, Maidenhead, McGraw-Hill.
Hofstede, G. and Bond, M. H. (1984) Hofstede's culture dimensions: an independent validation using Rokeach's Value Survey. *Journal of Cross-Cultural Psychology*, **15**, No. 4, 417–33.
Hofstede, G. and Bond, M. H. (1988) The Confucius connection: from cultural roots to economic growth. *Organizational Dynamics*, Spring, **16**, No. 4, 4–21.
Hofstede, G. and Vunderink, M. (1994) *A case study on masculinity/femininity differences: American students in the Netherlands vs. local students*. In Bouvy, A. M., Van de Vijer, F. J. R., Boski, P. and Schmitz, P. (eds), *Journeys into Cross-cultural Psychology*, Lisse Neth., Swets and Zeitlinger, 329–342.
Hofstede, G., Neuijen, B., Ohayv, D. D. and Sanders, G. (1990) Measuring organizational cultures. *Administrative Science Quarterly*, **35**, 286–316.
Hofstede, G., Bond, M. and Luk, C. L. (1993) Individual perceptions of organizational cultures: a methodological treatise on levels of analysis. *Organization Studies*. 14, No. 4, 483–503.
Hoppe, M. H. (1990) *A Comparative Study of Country Elites: International Differences in Work-related Values and Learning and their Implications for Management Training and Development*, Unpublished PhD dissertation, University of North Carolina at Chapel Hill.
Inkeles, A. and Levinson, D. J. (1969 [1954]) National character: the study of modal personality and sociocultural systems. In Lindsey, G. and Aronson, E. (eds), *The Handbook of Social Psychology*, 2nd edn, Vol. 4, Reading, MA, Addison-Wesley, 418–506.

Kieser, A. and Kubicek, H. (1983) *Organisation*, Berlin, Walter de Gruyter.

Laurent, A. (1981) Matrix organizations and Latin cultures. *International Studies of Management and Organization*, Winter, **10**, No. 4, 101–14.

Lawrence, P. (1980) *Managers and Management in West Germany*, London, Croom Helm.

Levitin, T. (1973) Values. In Robinson, J. P. and Shaver, P. R. (eds), *Measures of Social Psychological Attitudes*, Ann Arbor, MI, Institute for Social Research, University of Michigan, pp. 489–502.

Mant, A. (1979) *The Rise and Fall of the British Manager*, London, Pan Books.

Manslow, A. H. (1970) *Motivation and Personality*, 2nd edn, New York, Harper & Row.

Maurice, M., Sorge, A. M. and Warner, M. (1980) Societal differences in organizing manufacturing units: a comparison of France, West Germany, and Great Britain. *Organization Studies*, **1**, No. 1, 59–86.

Mayo, G. E. (1933) *The Human Problems of an Industrial Civilization*, Boston, MA, Division of Research, Harvard Business School.

Misumi, J. and Peterson, M. F. (1987) Supervision and leadership. In Bass, B. M. and Drenth, P. J. D. (eds), *Advances in Organizational Psychology: An International Review*, Newbury Park, CA, Sage.

Ouchi, W. G. (1981) *Theory Z*, New York, Addison-Wesley.

Pascale, R. and Athos, A. G. (1981) *The Art of Japanese Management*, New York, Simon & Schuster.

Redding, S. G. (1990) *The Spirit of Chinese Capitalism*, Berlin, Walter de Gruyter.

Schein, E. H. (1985) *Organizational Culture and Leadership*, San Francisco, CA, Jossey-Bass.

Simon, H. A. (1976) *Administrative Behavior: A Study of Decision-Making Processes in Administrative Organization*, 3rd edn, New York, Free Press.

Taylor, F. W. (1903) *Shop Management*, New York, Harper & Bros.

Taylor, F. W. (1911) *The Principles of Scientific Management*, New York, Harper & Bros.

The Chinese Culture Connection (a team of 24 researchers) (1987) Chinese values and the search for culture-free dimensions of culture. *Journal of Cross-Cultural Psychology*, **18**, No. 2, 143–64.

Tobin, J. J., Wu, D. Y. H. and Danielson, D. H. (1989) *Preschool in Three Cultures: Japan, China and the United States*, New Haven, CT, Yale University Press.

Tolstoy, L. N. (1978 [1876]) *Anna Karenin*, translated by Rosemary Edmonds, Harmondsworth, Penguin.

Weber, M. (1970 [1948]) *Essays in Sociology* (H. H. Gerth and C. W. Mills, eds), London, Routledge & Kegan Paul.

Weber, M. (1976 [1930]) *The Protestant Ethic and the Spirit of Capitalism*, London, George Allen & Unwin.

Williamson, O. E. (1975) *Markets and Hierarchies: Analysis and Antitrust Implications*, New York, Free Press.

3

STRATEGIC FINESSE: INCREMENTALLY DECISIVE GLOBAL STRATEGIES

R. Jeffery Ellis

Babson College and Warwick University Business School Research Bureau

Conventionally, strategic management has been regarded as driven primarily by an intellectual process that recognizes and develops competitive advantages. In this article we present an alternative view of successful strategic management as the result of constant action that seeks advantage by pursuing one or more of five different kinds of strategic finesse. Systematic fieldwork demonstrates that success is more essentially a constant and incremental pursuit of finesse in the capturing of proximate opportunities. When one or more of five patterns are fulfilled, proponents can 'finesse' their competitors by step improvements in their competitive position. This article is of importance to managements facing global competition, both those aspiring to an improved competitive position and those defending a strong position against competitors.

More than at any time, most of the economic regions of the world are entering a period of global competitiveness. Each region promises different bases of competition, increasing challenges exponentially and threatening to dislodge many present competitive positions. More Far Eastern nations are becoming globally competitive and competing vigorously against each other, which is stimulating additional competitive capabilities. European companies

International Review of Strategic Management, Volume 5
Edited by D. E. Hussey © 1994 John Wiley & Sons Ltd

are benefiting further from an integrating European Union and gaining advantages both of scale and of the cross-fertilization of cultures and technologies. North American companies are increasing productivity, quality and rates of innovation, and are adopting more effective models for global business. Former Communist nations are learning to deploy their high levels of education into making and selling competitive products. Emergent nations in South America and in other continents are resolving their debt problems, building more stable political systems and are often entering expanding free-trade areas.

Increases in both the quantity and diversity of global competitors redoubles the challenge of competition as the different cost structures and business philosophies of other nations find opportunities that established world players are less able to exploit. This article argues for outmaneuvering competitors through a cumulation of individually minor improvements which, in combination, ultimately lead to a gain that finesses competitors into a less attractive position. Indeed, most successful Japanese and South Korean companies have already embraced the ideas of finesse. Most successful future global competition is likely to follow these patterns of strategic finesse.

STRATEGIC FINESSE

A Strategic Finesse is a long-run step improvement in strength and position relative to competitors attained after persistent attention to individually small gains in performance or position. This is achieved by the constant pursuit of useful opportunities often at the peripheries or cutting edges of the business. Alternatively, finesse can be attained by a continuous striving for design improvements and better systems and operations within the core of the business. These activities incrementally build and integrate one with another until a capability and position is obtained that allows the company to finesse competitors into an inferior position. The path to a finesse may not be clear at the outset, but constant incremental moves can gradually build the means and eventually reveal the route to a quantum improvement in position relative to competitors.

A step gain in competitive position can be achieved in three different general ways depending on the situation and the chosen emphasis of management:

(1) As a Grand Finesse, where long-run technological and skill

development leads to a major advance that allows the company to restructure its industry in its favor.

(2) As a Flank Finesse, in which a company breaks through to a stronger market position after patient product and market development. This occurs in three distinct forms: (i) a Fifth Column Flank Finesse, (ii) a Back Door Flank Finesse or (iii) a Design Edge Flank Finesse.

(3) As a Detail Finesse, where repeated operating improvements lead the company eventually to a significant advantage over competitors.

Hence, strategic finesse can take one or more of five different approaches. The managerial implications for enabling each of these different routes to strategic development are distinct and are explained in this article.

Grand Finesse

A grand finesse offers customers wholly new and superior cost and quality such as when the South Korean shipbuilding industry secured the majority of the world market after some years of gaining experience and scale with low value-added shipbuilding. Many new technologies harbor this same potential to restructure a market or industry such as the capacity of recombinant DNA technology to replace or, alternatively, to manufacture some drugs by human extraction and purification. A company vision may be built around a hoped-for grand finesse such as Sony's recently espoused intention of marrying their consumer electronics hardware with CBS and Columbia pictures software to redefine and potentially dominate the entertainment industries.

Flank Finesse

A flank finesse implies a smaller scale by exploiting less attractive market segments which are poorly served by existing suppliers until sufficient scale, networks and learning have been achieved to become a significantly more dominant competitor. Recently, Nippon Life, a huge Japanese Mutual Life Insurance Company, purchased a shell company in Delaware, joint ventured with small American companies for processing and similar services, and began to sell Japanese insurance products to Japanese corporations in the United States. Eventually, however, sufficient scale together with experience of the American market may make it possible for Nippon Life to sell insurance products designed for the American market to American corporations. Early sales may be unattractive but the Japanese company has found an undefended flank that provides them with a foothold in the United States perhaps to ultimately finesse themselves into a profitable position involving major channels, markets and future dominance.

Detail Finesse

A detail finesse involves close attention to manufacturing and service operations until superiority is achieved in some critical way. To continue the example of selected small air-conditioning units, Japanese manufacturers progressively built toward a detail finesse through careful attention to the details of products and operations so that uniquely compact and efficient air conditioners could eventually be made by them. It is the availability of these unique products offering valued consumer advantages that has allowed these competitors to gain entry into United States markets through 'back-door' channels.

Some Advantages of Strategic Finesse

Focusing an organization's efforts on winning against competitors by the incremental improvement of technology, products, markets and operations carries many benefits. For example, the target of ultimately finessing competitors into an inferior position as described here:

(1) Provides a simple and clear statement of purpose and action that can be understood by all levels of an organization.
(2) Allows managers and operatives to first recognize tasks critical to competitive success and then to work on them in ways that are most likely to be effective against rivals.
(3) Directs attention to broader and more subtle aspects of competition such as flanking and operating superiority which are likely to matter much more in the long run than head-to-head competitive practices such as price or promotion wars.

For these reasons, most general managers and their staffs serve their organizations best by focusing on the adaptation and strengthening of existing strategy pursuing Strategic Finesse rather than deliberating on various grand designs for strategy.

It is argued here therefore that managers who face increasing global competition can obtain the most leverage for their corporations by pursuing a series of opportunities and improvements that:

(1) Enhance and enable the existing capabilities of their organizations,
(2) Capture market and other opportunities at the margins of their business so long as these exploit or develop the organization's central capabilities, and
(3) Promise the potential eventually to finesse their corporations into superior competitive positions.

These concepts and conclusions follow from recent thinking and observation of strategy, diverse consulting experiences and some results of a systematic study of 24 strategy formations in fourteen corporations described in (Ellis, 1988). The sample on which these concepts and conclusions are based contain many of the world's best-known and apparently best-managed corporations.

THE GRAND FINESSE

The grand finesse addresses large-scale opportunities that cannot be captured adequately by competitors. In their most aggressive guise, these take the form of plays that recast the competitive structure of whole or part of an industry. Some grand finesses literally exceed the resources of others to compete, financially or technologically. They are most often the result, however, of the diligent pursuit of individually small advances step by step until the combination of technology and skills is suddenly sufficient to permit the grand finesse of restructuring an industry in favor of the company.

A classical and apt example is provided by Hattori-Seiko. The ability and willingness of Hattori-Seiko to sustain development of quartz time-keeping technology over many years enabled their remarkable success in winning leadership in the world watch industry from the Swiss cartel. From the truck-mounted quartz timepiece at the 1960 Tokyo Olympiad, the company persisted doggedly with incremental improvements on this intrinsically superior technology until a quartz-driven watch was made and sold competitively against traditional technology. This grand finesse was achieved through a series of smaller actions which together built a decisive technical capability that ultimately enabled access to the world's markets for Seiko.

The world watch industry provides other useful examples of grand finesses that radically revise the relative importance of the different players in an industry. On a smaller scale, Hattori-Seiko's persistence with liquid-crystal displays was a decisive factor in initially winning the digital segment of the watch industry. Companies such as Texas Instruments confined development to the less costly, but ultimately inferior, light-emitting diode technology. Another well-known example of a grand finesse in this industry was when Timex used improvements in process technology and the availability of mass advertising and channels of distribution to produce and market robust, inexpensive and disposable pin-lever watches that captured a major share of the US and some European markets in the 1950s.

The financial and other returns from a successful grand finesse can, of course, be enormous. The opportunity to create a grand finesse or to be the victim of one has increased greatly with the potentials of newer technologies. Biotechnologies promise whole new ways of producing present foods and drugs and of creating new foods and medicines. High-technology ceramics eventually promise automobile engines weighing only a few pounds. Electronic imaging technologies presage, for example, paperless offices, newly structured distribution channels and radical developments in service delivery. Syntheses of technologies can provide enormous potential for grand finesse. For example, the computing and communication industries have been much heralded as progressively converging as time goes by. This is the promise pursued by NEC, AT&T and many other communication and computer companies.

Recognizing the opportunity or threat of a grand finesse is not difficult. Gauging the timing is, however, troublesome because unpredictable leaps in technology are often necessary, such as finding ways to avoid catastrophic breakage in ceramic engines. It is also challenging or impossible to know the implications of a breakthrough for the structure and profitability of an industry. A new technology may often be licensed or otherwise spread through an industry's pattern of suppliers and customers as well as manufacturers. For example, the invention at Pilkington Glass of float-glass technology carried the threat of severely damaging the position of other large glass manufacturers. The potential impact was blunted, however, by Pilkington's decision to license the process for royalties across the industry, largely preserving the relative positions of competitors and building the industry as a whole.

These dynamics make the management of intelligence and action surrounding potential grand finesses extremely challenging. There is a premium on a constant flow of information and action within so that insights can be more deeply grounded and enhanced by the opportunity to infer a pattern over time. It is often necessary to increase sensitivity to unfamiliar technologies or to neighboring industries that may affect the home base.

To pursue a grand finesse usually requires:

(1)   Some superior access to the substitute technology, and
(2)   Tenacious experimentation, not just in the laboratory but also in the factory and in the marketplace.

A grand finesse often makes most sense, therefore, when applying some existing technological position in largely unexploited markets, especially when the organizational and cultural conditions are similar to those already practised in the organization.

However, many grand finesses are less benign internally, mandating two additional requirements:

(3)   Different decision and operating processes respecting novel cost structures or ways of operation, and
(4)   Adaptation of the culture and purpose of an organization.

A separate or only partially integrated organization devoted to the grand finesse may be a way of managing these internal requirements. The ideal is, therefore, maximum relatedness in technology and organizational character but minimum relatedness between the new and established sources of revenue.

When an established participant in a stable industry is facing a grand finesse in its existing markets the situation is grave. If the management decides on a response, it is probably facing not only the need for new operations and new culture but also cannibalization of existing sales positions. These stiff requirements explain why grand finesse is often accomplished by outsiders to an established industry, by formerly disadvantaged competitors, by entrepreneurial ventures, or by emergent competitors from other nations. Many established competitors are served best by slowing rather than accelerating a grand finesse in their core markets.

A prudent strategy for a grand finesse stresses alert intelligence that facilitates bold action. Information is gathered sensitively and interpreted intensively to provide an early warning system with maximum intelligence in place. Action stresses experimentation in the laboratory and exploratory marketing. The emphasis is on trials and learning at every turn. This inventory of intelligence allows decisive action, when the time is right.

Some keys to effective intelligence and action for grand finesse in this predominantly readiness state include:

- A focus on information that strongly displays the potentially superior qualities of substitute technologies. A vigorous testing of technologies in the laboratory, even to the extent of prototype development, may be advisable.
- Careful scrutiny and explanation of the unusual approaches to management adopted by firms pursuing a grand finesse. These might include different cost structures, special government legislative situations, new supplier relationships or any other aspect of the business. It is often important to incorporate intelligence from poorly understood economies and cultures since these often have a special capacity to build toward a grand finesse.
- Tracking of the visions of companies with the potential for grand finesse as these are communicated in corporate speeches, institutional advertising and in other ways. The most revealing information might well exist only in local languages.

A management group following these precepts is well prepared to defend the challenge of a grand finesse, or to decide to pursue a grand finesse aggressively when an appropriate one is shown.

The essential challenge in a grand finesse is mobilizing a whole organization to comprehend and then execute the challenging assignments necessary to achieving a grand finesse. The need here is to influence management thinking and practice around the potentials of a grand finesse. This is best regarded as managing a process of thinking and action itself as it occurs among management. This involves the joint activities of: (1) monitoring and perhaps influencing management's attention to new technologies, new competencies and reinterpreted visions as these are prompted and emerge in the thinking of management, and (2) proactively preparing or organizing information and insights that can be used to move along this kind of thinking as and when its need is felt by management. In this way, managers can: stimulate thinking around the potential of a grand finesse; service the gradually forming realization of the grand finesses within the management team; and provide concrete insight into constructive initiatives that can be taken to move the organization forward to a greater understanding of these potentials.

A grand finesse often revolves around the peripheries of a market or a technology. This respects the necessarily emerging quality of a grand finesse as the uncertainties and patterns of investment are revealed over time and as higher-value applications are first garnered. This observation suggests that sensitive intelligence and exploratory action at the periphery can show the intentions and abilities of others as well as the major lessons that competitors are learning.

THE THREE FLANK FINESSES

A flank finesse exploits small opportunities overlooked or undersupported by the established competitors. An accumulation of such footholds in markets, technologies or supply arrangements eventually provides a significant improvement in the company's competitive position in the industry. The flank finesse looks for opportunities that build experience, quality, and position in ways that do not engender competitor retaliation. Action takes place around the flanks of established competitors. The idea of flanks is important because this is where competitors are weakest, where they are less likely to respond and where they are less likely to realize possible long-run implications of seemingly fragmented and unconnected actions. Additionally, avoiding competitor retaliation suggests that opportunities can prove both less expensive and more likely to succeed.

There are three forms of flank finesse which are dubbed: (1) the fifth column; (2) the back door; and (3) the design edge:

(1) *The fifth-column flank finesse*: This finesse forms a network of several joint ventures and contract relationships with other firms until a complete new capability is developed by the firm. Many of these relationships involve invited participation within the activities of competitors, implying a fifth column as an organized body sympathizing with and working for a competing company. While even the spirit of individual contracts may be honored, in combination with other relationships, an aggressive company may well achieve new competencies not intended by any one of the collaborating parties individually. NEC is reported to have secured exceptional competence in the integration of computer and communications technologies, partly through an ingenious

collection of joint ventures and contract arrangements with various partners (Prahalad and Hamel, 1990).

(2) *The back-door flank finesse*: This finds ways of providing customer advantages by distributing through specialized or unusual channels or serving minority customer groups which are underrecognized by competitors. The term 'back door' indicates the sense that the competitor has slipped quietly into the market without attracting the attention or retaliation of existing occupants. A back-door flank finesse becomes possible when sufficient learning and large enough scale has been obtained to become eventually one of the leaders in the industry. Dell Computers provides an example of a back-door flank finesse, where a 19-year-old college drop-out offered desktop computers to specialized vertical markets through mail order and direct sales channels until the company became an established player in the computer industry.

(3) *The design-edge flank finesse*: This flank finesse follows from exploiting the speed and value of response to customer needs and the advantages that improving technology provide for customers and operations. Through time, a succession of fast responses can gain a small share or additional competence and lead to increasingly higher value and bellwether needs in a customer industry. A design-edge flank finesse becomes possible when some new level of service or design is evident that can provide a permanent edge over competitors. An example is provided by one of the specialized semiconductor design and manufacturing companies. Global data transmission between design teams moves designs from the United States to Japan to Europe and back to the United States so that semiconductor designs are pursued 24 hours each day. These arrangements provide the company with competitively superior customer response as well as the capacity to integrate technological advances more rapidly than traditional competitors. Eventually, a design-edge flank finesse may be possible for this semiconductor design and manufacturing company as its cumulative experience and reputation reveal an opportunity to provide decisively different customer value that cannot be copied by competition.

Flank finesses are probably most potent when they are directed towards unfilled and emerging needs or corners of markets because more valuable experience is gained and possibly even less competitive resistance is encountered.

The Fifth-column Flank Finesse

The fifth-column finesse can take many forms wherever collaborative arrangements are made between two corporations. The enormous number and forms of strategic alliances between companies is reported widely. Their logic is powerful as the strengths of one company are parlayed into those of another, linking perhaps the product superiority of one company with unusual access to the markets of another, or integrating a supplemental technology into a product which may then appeal to a broader or higher-value market. A fifth-column finesse has the apparent quality of a purely symbiotic relationship between the two partners while, perhaps in combination with linkages to other companies, the junior partner has the ultimate goal of becoming a fully competent player in the same or some related industry.

The fifth-column finesse can take a particularly elegant form in the supply of components or subassemblies to the final sellers of the product or 'original equipment manufacturers (OEMs)'. Supplying OEMs provides the opportunity to improve manufacturing skills and to gain more knowledge of the total system. A network of OEM supply arrangements can, over time, build full competences enabling the junior partner to become an independent participant as an OEM itself.

The increasing participation of newly industrializing nations in the world automobile company provides an example. It has benefited the most established automobile companies based in the most industrialized countries to sponsor manufacture of components in less technologically developed ones. As these efforts continue, an increasingly comprehensive network of component manufacturers becomes available to a company that aspires to the design and assembly of an automobile of its own. Indeed, contractual and collaborative help is also available from design houses and machinery suppliers (for example, for the design of the overall vehicle and for the setting up of factories for fully assembled automobiles).

The Back-door Flank Finesse

The back-door finesse finds a series of neglected corners in which a company can strengthen its position without much risk, and eventually gain significantly over competitors. An example is participation in even relatively unattractive national markets underserved by established competitors. The entry of US insurance companies into small markets in the Far East such as Taiwan, Singapore, Indonesia and others represents individually minor and unexciting initiatives. These insurance markets are small, comprising only the most basic of life and property risks while mature insurance markets in Europe, North America and Japan substantially include health, savings, pensions, and major property and personal liabilities. However, participation in numerous, presently unglamorous national markets may prove pivotal in the formation of a small group of global insurance companies of superior size and profitability, finessing companies which have chosen not to pursue such opportunities into potentially inferior national status. Several back-door participations can help aid world recognition, cumulate experience and build scale.

This same back-door principle of exploiting small opportunities that others do not choose to pursue applies similarly to small corners within national markets. Corners can be found in almost any aspect of supplying and serving markets for a back-door flank finesse, for example:

- In non-traditional distribution channels such as in mail order for personal computers.
- In direct wholesale supply for cash as in store milk delivery.
- In direct retail supply as in television shopping networks for jewellers.
- In specialized end uses such as dangerous applications for chemicals.
- In especially complex uses such as intensively interactive applications for computer software.
- In relatively overlooked supply possibilities such as from newly industrializing nations or from manufacturers that typically supply other industries.

It is partly points of difference between competitors that make nooks and crannies within a market relatively more attractive to one competitor than another. This distinction is easiest to grasp in terms of cost advantage where a lower cost position obviously affords profitable ventures in less attractive markets. Similarly, unique technology may enable certain applications or market segments to be attractive opportunities that would not be viable for others. But other distinctions can afford profitability that eludes other competitors in less attractive corners of the market. A unique position in a given customer industry or geographic region may make it possible to attack a corner more profitably than competitors.

To pursue a back-door flank finesse requires focusing on a future pattern of market positions rather than the individual profitability of any one early market initiative. Eventual profitability grows from the interlocking pattern of market initiatives over time. Properly managed, the pattern builds into a back-door flank finesse that permanently places the company in an advantaged position compared to its competitors by, for example, a stronger presence in a certain region, or a stronger position within a particular type of application or customer group.

The Design-edge Flank Finesse

The third form of flank finesse, design edge, exploits the inability of competitors to respond quickly and flexibly to incremental change in the design of products and services. The aspiring competitor anticipates customer or other changes at the edges or flanks of the product or service and, because of prior preparation or systems that can produce designs faster, responds more quickly to design opportunities in the market, to changes in taste or to minor improvements in utility. The US market for part-time four-wheel drive vehicles with high ground clearance has slipped from the Jeep Cherokee, once the most popular private vehicle in the country, toward several Japanese makers. While some Japanese products may have been inferior adaptations of delivery trucks initially, they have gradually won important shares of this segment by continuously innovating often rather superficial aspects of the design of these specialized vehicles.

In particular, the Japanese suppliers of Jeep-like vehicles were quick to exploit the inability or unwillingness of Jeep to supply the market promptly with four-door versions of the Cherokee that was critical to families with young children for whom this kind of vehicle otherwise promised special value. Gradually, however, these new entrants were the first to provide a number of other features valuable to customers. These included relatively trivial improvements from an engineering perspective but which added great value for consumers such as back-seat headrests and seats that folded into beds.

It was through similar approaches that many Japanese companies finessed American manufacturers. For example, Xerox's fall from dominance in the photocopier industry was abetted by the feature-upon-feature improvement of products by their competitors. Gains from proficiency in response may be expected to yield more design-edge flank finesses in the future as computer-integrated manufacturing systems are gradually extended to permit 'on-line' changes in manufacturing operations, thereby allowing small design improvements to be implemented with great speed. The individual market share or other gains may be small, but a succession of such gains builds expertise and experience ahead of competitors potentially offering a design-edge flank finesse, permanently subjugating competitors to lesser positions.

The potential for a design-edge flank finesse increases when a reputation as a problem solver results in customers inviting a supplier to get closer to their business and the leading-edge challenges they face. These benefits form part of the rationale for IBM's present pursuit of customer-driven quality. While starting from a position of supreme strength, this commitment to innovation close to the customer enables the organization to be more responsive to customers needs and how they change. IBM's customer-driven quality also defends their flanks against the entry and strengthening of competitors.

Creating Flank Finesse

The three forms of flank finesse (fifth column, back door and design edge) individually provide gains over competitors but flank finesses are most powerful when a combination of all three forms builds a complete and exceptional core of expertise and experience. The benefit is greatest when a pattern of flank finesses surround a competitor and begin to weaken the competitor's core. The suppliers to OEMs today are the possible OEMs of tomorrow. Participants in back-door channels and those serving relatively less attractive customer groups today can build the strength to enter more attractive channels and more attractive customer groups tomorrow. Design gains can, over a period of time, yield exceptional competence which, when parlayed into broader market initiatives, can build leading competitive positions.

Managers face several challenges in finding and defining flank finesses, and in recognizing early the use of flank finesses by competitors. Creating flank finesse requires;

(1) Resourcefulness and sensible imagination in finding and pursuing opportunities that are unapparent yet combine to a competitive advantage.
(2) A capacity to draw reliable insights on the likely reaction of competitors to collections of actions.

(3)   An ability to synthesize the potential importance of peripheral, secondary and tactical opportunities pursued by competitors.

Finding flank opportunities

To find opportunities that are unapparent, it is necessary to closely survey markets, competitors, suppliers, technologies and other aspects of a business within the industry but often outside of the areas of most intense activity. Ferreting out opportunities in cracks and crevices demands attention to media and enterprises that are not of direct relevance to day-to-day competitive behavior. Suitable intelligence often exists in more specialized media, and in trade shows and the like that are at the edges of the normal areas of investigation. Attention to a competitor's local media may be particularly revealing because issues may be reported there that are important competitively but are not of sufficient general importance to be covered nationally.

Assessing competitors' reactions

Many of the most attractive opportunities are those to which competitors are unwilling or unable to retaliate. This makes them less expensive, more likely to succeed, and possibly helps lead to a distinctive market position for the ultimate finesse. Competitive intelligence professionals can help line managers considerably by developing an assessment of the likely response and retaliation of competitors. The limitations of competitors can become apparent by examining their recent history and current structure and resources. Many corporations are blind-sided concerning some opportunities because of prior misfortunes with similar experiences or simply because they are pursuing different goals, have other priorities or have financial demands that prevent them from availing themselves of the opportunity. In other cases, competitors may possess intractable faults that can prevent them from responding to some challenges. In any case, well-reasoned judgements can be made by role-playing the likely thinking of a competitor.

Detecting competitors' flank finesses

To synthesize the overall finesse or intention hidden in a competitor's quiet accumulation of competences and strengthening of position requires, first, a sensitive tracking of some of the further ranging activities of competitors and, second, a perceptive interpretation of what has been observed. The larger the number of small and seemingly fragmented initiatives identified over a longer time frame, the more reliably can the true direction or intention of a competitor be assessed. More important than the rather straightforward need to track the moves of competitors is the thoughtful synthesis of the patterns that they portend. For this process, it helps to deduce the long-run motivations and intentions of the competitor in question. Role-playing techniques can be very useful to uncover a competitor's purpose behind a series of moves as well as to assess likely competitor responses.

THE DETAIL FINESSE

In a detail finesse, a series of individually minor improvements or innovations cumulate to a significant difference in service and operations that competitors cannot, then, match. Many of our finest competitors embody this frame of mind; Federal Express, DHL, American Hospital Supply, Porsche, United Parcels Services, L.L. Bean, Honda, Toyota, and Matsushita, for example. Among other things, these competitors stand out for eliciting criticism and ideas and responding to them from customers, suppliers and also from their own employees. Corporate value systems inculcate this philosophy. Such organizations have the capacity to identify and meet needs faster and better.

A detail finesse occurs when incremental improvements bring about a critically new level of service or operations for which customers pay a premium or switch their allegiance from others. It often provides exceptional and enduring returns. Guaranteed delivery of packages by the next morning, just-in-time delivery of components with zero defects and immediate execution of stock buy and sell orders for small investors are some examples of a quantum improvement of service or of operations that brings about a detail finesse putting competitors into a long-run inferior position. Nearly always implying an improvement in time or of quality, a detail finesse that puts the company a major step forward results from a whole series of details that eventually build to a critical mass enabling the finesse.

Naturally, detail improvements in cycle times, quality, time to market and operating processes should be pursued independently of any intention eventually to finesse competitors. The opportunity for a detail finesse may only become revealed after many small improvements are implemented one at a time. It is only shown by experience how they can be consolidated into a step improvement in performance that puts competitors into an inferior position.

To pursue detail finesse it is necessary to make organization members clearly aware of expectations. This requires more than telling. Benchmarks of competitors, deliberately challenging relationships with the most demanding customers and internal disciplines for imaginative thinking are useful perspectives to this end.

Some dimensions relevant to instilling perspectives enabling detail finesse include:

- Giving managers and operators concrete examples which both prove the realism of expectations and provide some guidelines to follow.
- Selecting the most demanding customers and suppliers and working intensively with them, especially those at the leading edge of needs and innovation. This puts constant pressure on managers and operators to rise to the highest standards and most demanding applications, and keep up with the most progressive ideas.
- Encouraging managers and operators to find more original ideas than competitors. A thinking discipline is necessary that always challenges current ways of doing things and also explores all possible methods of exploiting new techniques (such as when a new technology becomes available.)
- Putting constant pressure on issues as an incentive to redefine situations. For example, the management of a manufacturing plant eager to expand was limited by capacity. Instead of accepting the operation as it had been defined for a decade, the team stripped down all the production steps and reassembled them into a different production sequence. A 30% increase in capacity was achieved with a negligible investment.

There is a constant need to lift managers and operators to find new ways to do things. Incentives for new efforts and rewards for achievements are major factors in making this happen.

Managers and their staffs can greatly influence an organization in a drive towards a detail finesse. Benchmarks, the selection of demanding customers and the provoking of original thinking either depend on or are driven by timely flows of the most useful information to that end. Working towards a detail finesse can help build competitive positions of great strength over time, especially when incorporated into the philosophy of a company, reinforced by systems and a suitably challenging environment, and when employees feel urgency and pressure to originate and implement improvements.

FINESSE IN COMPETITIVE INTELLIGENCE

A finesse, therefore, is an unalterable gain over a competitor achieved by pursuing many incremental opportunities and actions that issue from and build toward a bold result. Sometimes a grand finesse is pursued that seeks to alter the way an industry performs or the way it is structured in favor of the protagonist. At other times, one or more of three types of flank finesse (fifth column, back door or design edge) are pursued to profit from marginal opportunities that eventually build experience and position until competitors at the core of the industry are weakened. Alternatively, a detail finesse results from a gradual improvement in the day-to-day activities of a business until a quantum improvement in service time or quality becomes possible.

In addition to the individual implications for each type of finesse described in the appropriate sections above, three overriding implications are indicated for managers wishing to implement a finesse-based strategy in their organization:

(1) The need to distinguish separately each of the three different perspectives presented by each of grand, flank and detail finesse within management activities because of their different natures.
(2) The need to broaden the horizon and vision of managers to embrace broader issues of competitiveness captured in finesse.
(3) The need to incorporate specialized competitive intelligence activities symbiotically into line-management action because of the impossibility of line managers finding the time and temperament necessary to systematically track, assimilate and interpret information relating to issues of finesse.

Each of these implications is addressed below.

Three Distinct Managerial Perspectives

Superior management action is the progenitor and facilitator of strategy through finesse. However, most managerial systems and organizations do not distinguish adequately between the three different competitive environments implied by each main type of finesse. Because of the important differences between the three types of finesse, it is indicated here that clear distinctions should be drawn concerning each of grand finesse, flank finesse and detail finesse.

Indeed, the three types of finesse suggest a corresponding specialization within the organization. To capture the perspective of grand finesse requires longer time frames, conceptual thinking, broad-gauge data collection and inspired interpretation of the meaning of information. Flank fitnesses embrace moderate time frames, analytical thinking, persistent and resourceful collection of fine-grain data, and careful but synthetic understanding of information. Detail fitnesses involve urgent time frames, concrete thinking, energetic but straightforward data collection and an instrumental appreciation of the meaning of information.

These differences make it constructive to view managerial activities as three parallel endeavors or functions in favor of, for example, strategic (grand finesse), market (flank finesse) and tactical (detail finesse). For larger organizations, this implies three suborganizations, each addressing the three types of finesse. More usually, however, this suggests a constant recognition within smaller managerial units that the three types are recognized and managed collaterally. Temporary discriminations can be made according to needs by using personnel, systems and approaches in combinations that respect the type of finesse under investigation at a particular time.

Broaden the Vision of Management

Managements have historically stressed the more obvious manifestations of competitiveness such as price and product changes and have been less cognizant of the special abilities and privileged positions on which corporate and business competitiveness depends. The understanding of finesse powerfully indicates that the frame of reference of managers should be broader to embrace all the competences and positions of competitors. The importance of technological competencies has long been recognized but little attention has been paid to special abilities in manufacturing or distribution or procurement, for example. There is an increasing need to gather information on and understand the meaning of special competencies held by a competitor in all the spheres of its endeavors.

Similarly, there is an increasing need to understand benefits that accrue to a competitor from both special geographic positions and from special business positions. Geographically, for example, it is necessary to understand the advantages that accrue from different configurations of national subsidiaries and other associated businesses networks across the world. These may blend technological strengths of certain countries or special advantages surrounding costs or tariffs, for example.

Special business positions that can convey advantages are unbounded in nature but include, for example, forms of ownership, technologies, special strength within segments, networks of suppliers, customer contracts, joint ventures, and so forth. As well as recognizing such advantages, the manager or their competitive intelligence professional must interpret these advantages in terms of their integration and the transfer of special attributes between several positions. The need is now compelling for managers and their staffs to understand their organizations in their full strategic, market and operating complexity and to deduce the actions that lead the organization to its optimum position. Competitors should also be understood as complex wholes that uniquely integrate all business activities, competitive positions and external relationships.

Finesse in Action

Distinguishing managerial efforts according to the three kinds of finesse, and arguing for intelligence to include all the activities associated with a competitor, are useful reminders that the three finesses are most effective in combination. Indeed, detail finesses build competence that facilitate fifth-column, back-door and design-edge finesses. Equivalently, all the three flank finesses can, especially in combination, provide the basis of a grand finesse as expertise and experience builds.

A passion for finesse presents a new and more powerful way of thinking about strategy. When successful, a grand finesse upstages a competitor, a flank finesse surrounds and then dislodges a competitor and a detail finesse takes a company ahead of its competitors. The importance of finesse as strategy is, however, much greater. Finesse implies an incremental, step-by-step approach to achieving a competitive intention. This gradualist notion provides opportunities for learning so that greater strength can be achieved with the flexibility to alter emphasis in the light of experience. Finesse also imparts the capacity for surprise, a discipline on pursuing opportunities early and a motivating level of energy for an organization. Finesse transcends most approaches to strategy by forcing a process of incremental refinement and finding ways of inexpensively overwhelming competitors.

ACKNOWLEDGEMENTS

The author acknowledges the support of the Board of Research of Babson College, the assistance of Susan Hamilton, and the professional consideration of Farshad Rafii.

FURTHER READING

Ellis, R. J. (1988) *Managing Strategy in the Real World: Conclusions and framework from field studies of business practice*, New York, Lexington Books, Free Press, Macmillan; and Oxford, Maxwell/Macmillan.

Ghoshal, S. and Westney, D. E. (1991) Organizing competitor analysis systems. *Strategic Management Journal*, January, 17–33.

Hamel, G. and Prahalad, C. K. (1989) Strategic intent. *Harvard Business Review*, May–June.

Hamel, G. and Prahalad, C. K. (1991) Corporate imagination and exploratory marketing. *Harvard Business Review*, November–December.

Mintzberg, H. (1987) Crafting strategy. *Harvard Business Review*, July–August.

Mintzberg, H. and James Brian Quinn, J. B. (1992) *Strategy Process*, Englewood Cliffs, NJ, Prentice Hall.

Porter, M. E. (1990) *The Competitive Advantage of Nations*, New York, Free Press.

Prahalad, C. K. and Hamel, G. (1990) Core competence of the corporation. *Harvard Business Review*, May–June.

4

NEW TECHNOLOGY ADOPTION AND MULTINATIONAL MARKET EXPANSION

Briance Mascarenhas

Rutgers University

A central debate concerns the nature of the multinational company, with two views espousing opposite directions of causality between innovation and multinationality. The 'proactive' view posits that multinational companies seize technical innovations in anticipation of their international market potential. In contrast, the 'reactive' view holds that multinational expansion is a consequence of once-adopted technical innovations since know-how is less efficiently communicated internationally between independent organizations than through a firm's internal hierarchy.

To resolve this debate and help to develop a theory of innovation that incorporates international expansion, this study examines two sets of hypotheses concerning (1) the adoption of a new-technology innovation, the semi-submersible rig, among oil-drilling firms, and (2) the multinational expansion of firms. Taken together, these two sets of hypotheses provide insights about innovation over a firm's life cycle. The next section develops these two hypotheses.

HYPOTHESES

Technical Innovation Adoption

Empirical research on technical innovation adoption has consistently observed the explanatory power of firm size and age. Larger firms

International Review of Strategic Management, Volume 5
Edited by D. E. Hussey © 1994 John Wiley & Sons Ltd

are likely to adopt innovations because of economies of scale in introducing innovations (Ettlie, 1983; Kimberly and Evanisko, 1981; Mohr, 1969), greater resources to experiment with innovation and more internal differentiation resulting in interest groups receptive to and eager to champion innovations (Pierce and Delbecq, 1977).

Older firms are unlikely to adopt innovations because they have established niches (Kimberly and Evanisko, 1981) and operating routines which may not be compatible with change. Industry newcomers often obtain entry by product innovation while established firms respond by emphasizing process innovations associated with existing products (Abernathy and Utterback, 1988).

Arguments exist both for and against a firm's prior multinationality encouraging the adoption of technical innovation, possibly neutralizing one other. On the one hand, a firm's presence in multiple countries increases a technical innovation's market and profit potential (Caves, 1982). Mansfield *et al.* (1979) argue that firms may cut innovation activities if the results cannot be exploited internationally. Operating in multiple markets also increases the likelihood of a firm's presence in a market that fits an innovation's characteristics (Utterback, 1974). On the other hand, multinationality may distinguish a firm's desire and ability to change. Diversification through operations in multiple countries shields managers from unfavorable environments, and thus from survival pressures to innovate. Multinational firms with established operations in multiple countries may not want to adopt new technologies that will potentially cannibalize their existing products.

Innovations do not diffuse rapidly or widely through organizations (Kimberly, 1981) because of resistance, particularly in multinational companies which span wide geographical, cultural and regulatory differences. Consequently, innovations are not adopted for their international leveraging potential:

H1:   After controlling for industry market conditions, the adoption of the technical innovation is:
       Positively related to an organization's prior size
       Negatively related to its age
       Unrelated to its prior multinationality.

International Expansion

New technical know-how provides firms with a motivation and needed edge to compete in a foreign market with local firms more familiar with their local environment (Johnson, 1970). International transfers of new technical know-how, however, are subject to substantial communication difficulties and uncertainties and are more easily performed internally (Teece, 1977, 1981). As a result of this internalization of transactions, multinational companies emerge with foreign investments in multiple countries. Consequently, firms which adopt and continue to use the new technology are expected to embark on multinational expansion.

Size has been found positively related to international expansion. Using static analyses and industry averages, Horst (1972), Vernon (1966) and Wolf (1977) observed a positive relationship between multinationality and firm size. Larger firms' resources enable them to overcome size-related overseas entry barriers and to readily amortize the fixed foreign investment start-up costs by staking a large investment (Caves, 1982):

H2:   After controlling for industry market conditions, multinational
      expansion:
      Is positively related to the technical innovation adoption
      period
      Is positively related to firm size.

Collectively, the two hypotheses posit the following pattern of innovation over a firm's life. Industry newcomers and resource-rich firms are prone to adopt the technical innovation. Firms that continue to use the technical innovation gradually extend the innovation to new international markets. This market-expansion process corresponds to the rapid growth stage of the product life cycle (Porter, 1980). As firms become established multinationally, however, their prior propensity to adopt technical innovations diminishes.

METHODOLOGY

The two sets of hypotheses are examined with longitudinal data from the offshore oil-drilling business. Offshore drilling is conducted by firms with drilling rigs contracted out for underwater oil exploration to oil companies and governments. In general, these drilling companies explore for oil but do not engage in production once it is discovered. Customers of drilling companies are composed of independent oil companies, oil majors and national oil companies owned by the state. Contracts between drilling companies and their customers specify the length of time drilling is to be conducted in a country and a day- or foot-rate of payment. Drilling companies assume the operational risks of drilling, such as cost-overruns and accidents associated with high-pressure, high-temperature drilling.

Several industry characteristics make the industry suitable for examining the hypotheses. First, the industry is composed of local and international firms, based in different countries. Second, though firms and their activities are dispersed internationally, detailed and comparable information exists on all firms in the worldwide industry population for an extended period. Third, the technical innovation can be defined, and the incidence and length of adoption clearly observed in the population.

The study covered the period from 1962, when the semi-submersible was developed, to 1984. In 1984 the industry was composed of over 100 firms based in more than 30 countries with over 800 offshore rigs operating worldwide. Offshore drilling had its beginnings in the 1930s. Three types of offshore rigs existed prior to development of the semi-submersible rig: submersible, jack-up and drillship (Hammett, 1984).

A submersible rig is built on a platform which rests on the seabed. The platform's height limits the water depth at which drilling can be undertaken and the platform's large surface area in contact with water makes it unstable in agitated water conditions. Consequently, the submersible rig is typically used for shallow drilling in calm waters.

The jack-up is a drilling rig on a platform elevated over the water and supported by three or four girder-legs resting on the seabed which reduces the surface area exposed to the water. The jack-up is thus often used to drill in agitated water conditions but in shallow water depths (less than 250 feet) because it is bottom-supported.

The drillship is a rig mounted on a ship which drills through the hull. Since the ship floats and is not bottom-supported it can drill in deep waters (up to 6000 feet). The large area of the ship in contact with waves on the water's surface, however, reduces the drillship's stability, and thus drillships are used typically for drilling in deep but calm waters.

Operating constraints provided an opportunity for a rig which could drill under conditions not ideal for the three types of rigs: in deep, agitated water conditions. The Shell Oil Company developed the technology for such a rig, the semi-submersible, in 1962. This is a rig resting on a platform above the water surface connected to pontoons which float but have most of their surface area below the agitable water's surface. Thus, the rig can drill in deep water because it floats and its limited exposure to the water's surface increases its stability.

Thus the semi-submersible rig represents the largest departure from the submersible rig, which is suitable for shallow and stable water conditions. The semi-submersible rig offers a higher water-depth drilling capability than the jack-up rig, which can drill in shallow but agitated waters. Also, relative to the drillship, which can drill in deep, stable waters, the semi-submersible rig provides an edge in drilling in unstable water conditions.

A semi-submersible rig requires an investment of about $60 million, compared with about $30 million for a drillship, $20 million for a jack-up rig and $10 million for a submersible rig. Operation of the semi-submersible rig also requires managing a longer supply line when drilling farther away from the shore and special know-how to adjust engine thrusters to neutralize water currents and waves.

Data Collection

Personal interviews were held with over 20 industry participants and observers, including top executives of domestic and foreign drilling companies, the trade association and financial analysts following the industry. These exploratory interviews helped to identify major industry trends, understand the business and probe firm activities.

Information on a firm's characteristics, including the possible adoption and discontinuation of the new rig, was then obtained from an industry data service firm, Offshore Data Services. This firm closely tracks the characteristics of each industry rig worldwide, including rig type, location and company ownership. The data service covers all the firms in the industry and its information service is extensively used by the industry. Annual data about each rig were obtained for the period 1962–1984. A cross-check of the information from the data service firm with rig disclosures in annual reports and 10-K statements of publicly traded US drilling companies for which data were available (about 22% of all firm-years of data) did not reveal discrepancies. Similar data cross-checks were not possible with the remaining firms because of more limited disclosure requirements, because they were based overseas or were not publicly traded.

During the study period, 1962–1984, 187 firms existed for the entire or a part of the period. During the 23-year period, about 37% (70/187) of these firms adopted the technical innovation.

Variable Measures

To examine the two hypotheses, the following variables were defined and measured:

- *Technical innovation adoption*: whether or not a firm used the semi-submersible rig in its field operations. This variable was measured by a dummy variable equal to 1 if a firm used the semi-submersible rig, 0 otherwise.
- *Drilling age*: the length of time a firm had experience in drilling, measured by the number of years of drilling operations before adoption if adopter, or before the last year of operation if non-adopter.
- *Prior multinationality*: the extent to which a firm was a multinational company before adopting the semi-submersible rig. This variable was measured by the number of countries in which a firm had rigs operating in the year prior to semi-submersible rig adoption if adopter, or the last year of operation if non-adopter.
- *Prior drilling size*: the size of an organization's drilling operations, measured by the number of rigs in a firm's fleet in the year prior to semi-submersible rig adoption if adopter, or the last year of operation if non-adopter. A log transformation was performed to adjust for curvilinearity (Kimberly, 1976).
- *Future multinationality*: a firm's multinational change after possible adoption of the new technology. This variable is measured by the change number of countries of operation per year beginning in the year after technical innovation adoption for adopters, and from the first year of drilling operations for non-adopters.
- *Drilling size*: firm size in drilling, measured by the number of rigs in firm's fleet in the year of innovation adoption if adopter or the last year of operation if non-adopter. A log transformation was performed to adjust for curvilinearity (Kimberly, 1976), which often produces a closer fit.
- *Technical innovation adoption period*: length of time a firm used the semi-submersible rig, measured in number of years. Adoption period includes information on both the incidence and the duration of the technical innovation adoption, while an adoption dummy variable includes only information on the incidence. Adoption period was used rather than a dummy variable denoting whether or not adoption occurred because over 33% (24 of 70) of adopters subsequently discontinued the innovation.
- *Industry boom*: whether or not adoption occurred during a period when world oil prices were relatively high, measured by a dummy variable equal to 1 if adoption of the semi-submersible rig occurred between 1973 and 1981, 0 otherwise.

• *Industry boom period*: the length of time in years that a firm had drilling activities between 1973 and 1981, when oil prices were relatively high.

DATA ANALYSIS

Technical Innovation Adoption

Hypothesis 1 suggests that after controlling for industry market conditions, technical innovation adoption is (1) positively related to a firm's prior size, (2) negatively related to its age and (3) unrelated to its prior multinationality.

The binary nature of the dependent variable, *Technical innovation adoption*, whether or not a firm adopted the innovation, led to the use of logistic regression with maximum likelihood estimation in LIMDEP (Greene, 1989).

The independent variables were *Prior drilling size, Drilling age, Prior multinationality* and *Industry boom*. When an event precedes another, the subsequent event is unlikely to be a cause for the preceding one (Hellevik, 1984). Accordingly, variables expected to be causes in Hypothesis 1, *Prior drilling size* and *Prior multinationality*, were lagged 1 year.

Table 4.1 details the technical innovation adoption model. The results are consistent with Hypothesis 1. Strong market conditions (*Industry boom*) driven by higher oil prices encouraged oil exploration and the adoption of the semi-submersible rig. Industry newcomers (*Drilling age*) and larger (*Prior drilling size*) organizations are prone to adopt the technical innovation. However, *Prior multinationality* is unrelated to the technical innovation.

The *Prior multinationality* variable is not significant (at the 0.05 level) even when the analysis is repeated excluding the *Size* variable. No material changes in results are observed when the *Prior drilling size* and *Prior multinationality* variables are lagged by two years instead of one.

Multinational Expansion

Hypothesis 2 suggests that after controlling for industry market conditions, multinational expansion is positively related to (1) the technical innovation adoption period and (2) firm size. A multiple regression model, employing OLS estimation, was run using *Future*

Table 4.1 Logistic regression model of technical innovation adoption ($n = 187$)

Independent variables	Mean	S.D.	Coeff. estimate (t-statistic)
Intercept			−0.44[a] (−3.04)
Drilling Age	7.20	6.04	−0.02[a] (−4.46)
Prior Drilling Size	2.34	1.19	1.01[a] (5.81)
Prior Multinationality	1.24	0.77	−0.01 (−0.13)
Industry Boom	0.35	0.48	0.34[a] (5.51)
Maximized log			−91.0
Baseline log			−123.7
p-value			0.00

[a] Coefficient significant at the 0.01 level.

multinationality as the dependent variable. The independent variables were *Drilling size, Technical innovation adoption period* and *Industry boom period*.

The multinational expansion model results are shown in Table 4.2. The sample size is smaller, because the *Future multinationality change* variable cannot be defined for firms founded or adopting the technology in the last year of the study period. Also, without a lag, the *Drilling size* mean and standard deviations are larger during this period when firms were generally growing.

The evidence is consistent with Hypothesis 2. *Technical innovation adoption period* is positively related to subsequent multinational expansion, significant at the 0.01 level. Interviews and closer analysis of the data suggested that many firms used the new technology to penetrate markets where they had no prior presence. Multinational expansion is also significantly associated with larger firm size (*Drilling size*), significant at the 0.01 level. Further, these relationships hold when controlling for industry market conditions, which suggests that the industry boom was associated with multinational expansion.

The analysis was repeated using a dummy variable denoting whether or not a firm adopted the technical innovation instead of *Technical innovation adoption period*. This dummy variable turned out

Table 4.2 Regression model of multinational expansion (n = 181)

Independent variable	Mean	S.D.	Coef. estimate (t-statistic)
Intercept			−1.70[a] (−5.12)
Drilling Size	3.19	1.79	1.68[a] (6.19)
Technical Innovation Adoption Period	3.47	4.83	0.19[a] (5.79)
Industry Boom Period	3.45	2.62	0.04 (0.64)
p-statistic			39.86
d.f.			177
p-value			0.00
Adjusted R^2			0.39

[a] Coefficient significant at the 0.01 level.

to be insignificant, suggesting that it is firms that persist with the technical innovation that expand internationally.

CONCLUSION

A central debate concerns the origin and nature of the multinational company. Are multinational companies proactive organizations that seize innovations in anticipation of their international market potential? Or do multinational companies reactively emerge as a result of extending once-acquired technology into new foreign markets?

To shed light on this debate about the intertemporal relationship between technical innovation and multinational expansion, this study examined (1) the factors associated with the adoption of a technical innovation, the semi-submersible rig in oil drilling and (2) the factors encouraging a firm's multinational expansion.

The findings of this study suggest that technical innovation is adopted under favorable industry market conditions by larger firms, which have more resources and internal differentiation, and industry newcomers, which are less restrained by established ways of doing business. A firm's prior multinationality, however, is unrelated to adoption of the new technology.

Multinational expansion is found positively associated with favorable industry market conditions, firm size and the continued but not mere adoption of the technical innovation. Continued use of the new technology increases a firm's experience and credibility with the rig for obtaining foreign market orders. Of course, new foreign-market orders also enable continued use of the semi-submersible rig. An alternative explanation is that firms able to sustain the commitment to a new technology could also sustain a commitment to overcoming foreign-market entry barriers.

Juxtaposing the findings about the adoption of the technical innovation and multinational expansion helps to develop a theory of innovation over a firm's life cycle. Technical innovations are adopted by industry newcomers and large organizations. While a substantial proportion (about a third) of new-technology adopters discontinue the innovation, firms which continue to use the technical innovation expand multinationally. Eventually, as firms become established internationally their prior proclivity to adopt later technologies diminishes. Later technologies may cannibalize sales of their existing products or their performance may be buffered by international diversification from operations in multiple countries.

The findings help to clarify the central debate between the two diametrically opposed views of the relationship between technical innovation and multinationality. No evidence is found that multinationality increases technical innovation. Neither is evidence found that mere technical innovation adoption directly and unequivocally results in multinational expansion. Evidence was found, however, that continued use of the technical innovation is associated with multinational expansion.

The interrelationship between technical and multinational expansion highlights a problem of sustaining firm innovation. The strategic problem that emerges from this study concerns how top executives can sustain technical innovativeness after a firm has become established multinationally.

The findings also have implications for international transfer of know-how and worldwide economic development. National governments wanting to encourage the inflow of innovations into their economies should not rely on multinational firms already operating within their markets. Public policy should make it easier for local firms and new multinational firms to enter, and in so doing introduce more technical innovations.

Finally, this study has focused on one technical innovation which could be observed in an international context. Additional research and evidence are needed on other technical innovations in a similar wide and longitudinal context.

REFERENCES

Abernathy, W. J. and Utterback, J. M. (1988) Patterns of industrial innovation. In Tushman, M. L. and Moore, W. L. (eds), *Readings in the Management of Innovation*, 2nd edn, Cambridge, MA, Ballinger.

Baranson, J. (1970) Technology transfer through the international firm. *American Economic Review*, **60**, May, 435–40.

Caves, R. E. (1982) *Multinational Enterprise and Economic Analysis*, Cambridge, MA, Cambridge University Press.

Daft, R. L. (1978) A dual-core model of organizational innovation. *Academy of Management Journal*, **21**, 193–210.

Downs, G. W. and Mohr, L. B. (1976) Conceptual issues in the study of innovation. *Administrative Science Quarterly*, **21**, 700–14.

Ettlie, J. E. and Vallenga, D. B. (1979) The adoption time period for some transportation innovations. *Management Science*, **25**, 429–43.

Ettlie, J. E. (1983) Organizational policy and innovation among suppliers to the food processing industry. *Academy of Management Journal*, **26**, 27–44.

Evan, W. M. and Black, G. (1967) Innovation in business organizations: some factors associated with success or failure. *Journal of Business*, **40**, 519–30.

Greene, W. (1989) LIMDEP. Econometric software: New York.

Gruber, W., Mehta, D. and Vernon, R. (1967) The R&D factor in international trade and international investment of U.S. industries. *Journal of Political Economy*, **75**, February, 20–37.

Hammett, D. (1984) Deepwater drilling—foresight, risk, and reward. In Moss, J. (ed.), *Exploration and Economics of the Petroleum Industry*, Vol. 22, New York, Matthew Bender, 1984, pp. 227–48.

Hellevik, O. (1984) *Introduction to Causal Analysis*, Boston, MA, Allen & Unwin.

Horst, T. (1972) Firm and industry determinants of the decision to invest abroad: an empirical study. *Review of Economics and Statistics*, **54**, 258–66.

Johnson, H. G. (1970) The efficiency and welfare implications of the international corporation. In Kindleberger, C. P. (ed.), *The International Corporation*, Cambridge, MA, MIT Press.

Kimberly, J. R. (1976) Organization size and the structuralist perspective: a review, critique, and proposal. *Administrative Science Quarterly*, **21**, 571–97.

Kimberly, J. R. (1981) Managerial innovation. In Nystrom, P. and Starbuck, W. (eds), *Handbook of Organizational Design*, 1, Oxford, Oxford University Press.

Kimberly, J. R. and Evanisko, M. J. (1981) Organizational innovation: the influence of individual, organizational, and contextual factors on hospital adoption of technological and administrative innovations. *Academy of Management Journal*, **24**, 4, 689–713.

Mansfield, E., Romeo, A. and Wagner, S. (1979) Foreign trade and U.S. research and development. *Review of Economics and Statistics*, **16**, February, 49–57.

Mohr, L. (1969) Determinants of innovation in organizations. *American Political Science Review*, **63**, 111–26.

Pierce, J. L. and Delbecq, A. L. (1977) Organization structure, individual attitudes, and innovation. *Academy of Management Review*, January.

Porter, M. E. (1980) *Competitive Strategy*, New York, Free Press.

Teece, D. J. (1977) Technology transfer by multinational firms: the resource cost of transferring technical knowhow. *Economic Journal*, **87**, June, 242–61.

Teece, D. J. (1981) The multinational enterprise: market failure and market power considerations. *Sloan Management Review*, **22**, 3–17.

Tushman, M., Newman, W. and Romanelli, E. (1986) Convergence and upheaval: managing the unsteady pace of organizational evolution. *California Management Review*, **29**, No. 1.

Utterback, J. (1974) Innovation in industry and the diffusion of technology. *Science*, **183**, 620.

Van de Ven, A. H. (1986) Central problems in the management of innovation. *Management Science*, **32**, No. 5.

Vernon, R. (1966) International investment and international trade in the product cycle. *Quarterly Journal of Economics*, **80**, May, 190–207.

Vernon, R. (1979) The product cycle hypothesis in a new international environment. *Oxford Bulletin of Economics and Statistics*, **41**, November, 255–67.

Wolf, B. M. (1977) Industrial diversification and internationalization: some empirical evidence. *Journal of Industrial Economics*, December.

5

SUN TZU'S *ART OF WAR*: SELECTED APPLICATIONS TO STRATEGIC THINKING AND BUSINESS PRACTICES

Chow Hou Wee

National University of Singapore

INTRODUCTION

Sun Tzu's *Art of War*, written around 400–320 BC, is the oldest military classic known in Chinese literature. It is also probably the most revered and well-known military text outside China. The significance and importance of Sun Tzu's work in influencing military thought has seldom been questioned. For example, this book is known to influence Japanese military thinking as Sun Tzu's writings were already introduced to Japan around AD 716–735 (Griffith, 1982). Even in the 1990/91 Gulf War, Sun Tzu was cited repeatedly by reporters and analysts. The wide acceptance of Sun Tzu's thinking can be noted by the fact that his works have been translated into many languages, and the book can be found among the 'must read' list in major military schools around the world.

What is perhaps less known is the applicability of Sun Tzu's *Art of War* to business practices. Yet it is interesting to note that the idea of an analogy between the world of business and that of the battlefield is not a novel one. The metaphor is accepted, consciously or not, in

International Review of Strategic Management, Volume 5
Edited by D. E. Hussey © 1994 John Wiley & Sons Ltd

such familiar phrases as the US–Japan trade war and a militaristic turn of phrase in the boardroom now borders on being a cliché. It was in July 1985 that the *New York Times Magazine* carried Theodore White's argument that while America may have won the military war, Japan was busy winning the economic war. Several years later, *International Business Week* (9 April 1990) and *Asia Magazine* (8–10 May 1992) both carried the headline 'Car Wars' on their covers. Both issues featured prominently the continuous US–Japan–Europe rivalries in their conquest for market shares in the world automobile industry. In an earlier issue of *International Business Week* (22 January 1990), Carla Hills was also featured prominently on its cover and in its cover story as the US 'Trade Warrior'. In her role as the new US trade negotiator, it was reported that she would have to battle with the Japanese and European policy makers, while keeping the US protectionists at bay.

Military jargons, clichés, and analogies have also found their way into the writings of renowned journalists, executives and scholars. For example, Enricho and Kornbluth (1987) described how Pepsi won the 'Cola Wars' against Coke. Saporito (1992) documented that price wars would never end for companies in the airline, automobile, computer, food, retailing and steel industries because of over-investments in the past. This had forced many companies in these industries to chase market share at all costs. Labich (1992a,b) used the term 'Sky Wars' to describe the battle for market share among the three leading aircraft manufacturers Airbus, Boeing and McDonnell-Douglas. This was followed by Zellner (1992), who reported how the American airlines are killing each other through price wars, and Labich (1992b), who documented how deregulation in the airline industry had led many of Europe's airlines to war. More recently, Schlender (1993b) commented on how the American manufacturers of personal computers had begun to attack the Japanese market with new spiffy machines, innovative software and sharply lower prices.

Various studies relating the application of military strategies to business practices had been undertaken (e.g. Kotler and Singh, 1981; Stripp, 1985). In a publication by Ries and Trout (1986), they chose to rely on the works of German general Karl von Clausewitz to illustrate the parallels between military concepts and marketing practices. In addition, Kotler *et al.* (1985), Lazer *et al.* (1985) and Ohmae (1982) and many others had often described the Japanese economic conquest of the world very much like a well-orchestrated military campaign. In a more recent article, Sullivan (1992) cited the works of Abegglen and Stalk (1985) in describing Theory F (for fear) as one of the factors for the success of Japan. According to Theory F, large Japanese corporations were obsessed with analyzing their competitors so as to exploit competitive advantages. In addition, they had a growth bias in their strategic orientation.

Few writers, however, had given recognition and acknowledgement to the oldest known military treatise in the world, Sun Tzu's *Art of War*. Yet this manual, written in China centuries before the birth of Christ, can be said to contain the foundations on which all modern military strategies are based. It is proposed that the achievement of Sun Tzu's *Art of War* transcends the military context and offers the basis for an insight into the nature of modern business practices. In particular, and this is an underlying thesis, a study and understanding of Sun Tzu provides a valuable platform for exploring the exact nature of the analogy between business and war and in doing so, it offers a pregnant framework for interpreting one of the most startling economic trends in the late twentieth century: the relative rise of the Japanese economy at the expense of the US economy.

There are other reasons for focusing on Sun Tzu's works. With the opening of China, there is an increased desire to know their thoughts, especially in the area of strategic management and practices. This is necessary if one wishes to do business with them. Here, it is significant to note that while the Chinese have turned to the Western world for much help in the area of training and consulting, they have also begun actively to research their own classics to relate their applications to management. Sun Tzu's *Art of War* has emerged as a favourite, and today, there are many publications in China that attempt to relate this classic to strategic thinking and practice (e.g. Li *et al.*, 1984; National Economic Commission, 1985). These are in addition to many similar publications that exist today in Hong Kong, Taiwan, Japan and South Korea. In fact, Sun Tzu is a highly regarded guru in these countries.

If one subscribes to the belief that the twenty-first century may belong to the Asia–Pacific region, it is important to note that its key players—Japan, Taiwan, South Korea, Hong Kong and Singapore— have many cultural similarities that could be traced to their roots in China. Together with China, they can form a significant economic force that few countries can ignore. Without doubt, there is a need for practitioners and researchers in the Western world to begin understanding the philosophy and thinking of the oriental mindset. Sun Tzu's *Art of War* may provide an useful start in this learning process.

A detailed exposition on how Sun Tzu's works can be applied to business practices can be found in Wee (1989, 1990) and Wee *et al.* (1991). The purpose of this article is to highlight some of the salient concepts that are embedded in the works of Sun Tzu, which could be applied to strategic thinking and business practices. Without doubt, there are many other concepts in the works of Sun Tzu that could be used for business practices. What will be highlighted here represent only the 'tip of the iceberg' on the application possibilities of Sun Tzu's *Art of War* to modern business operations and management.

STRATEGY, STRUCTURE AND BEHAVIOUR

One of the most important aspects in the conduct of war is the relationship between strategy, structure and behaviour. In the words of Sun Tzu: 'To control a large force in combat is similar to that of a small force. It is a matter of formations and signals.' He went on to say: 'Order and disorder depend on organization.'

Implicit in these sayings is that structure actually breeds behaviour, regardless of the size of the army. As such, the way a general organizes an army would affect the behaviour of the troops in battle. In the same way, the way a company is organized and structured will also determine the behaviour of the employees. For example, if a company wants to become international, it must be structured in such a way so as to reward those employees with international experience. Otherwise, no one would want to work abroad.

What, then, determines structure? In war, it is always *strategy*. In other words, the strategy must be the genesis of any organizational design and structure. Undeniably, with proper feedback, one's strategy could be modified. However, the starting point for any planning exercise in war has to be strategy. For example, in the 1991 war against Iraq, the US-led forces decided on the strategy before embarking on how to organize for combat. In fact, General Norman Schwarzkopf was himself a product of the strategy.

There is a definitive requirement as to why structure and organization must follow the crystallization of the strategy in war. First, there is a need for *flexibility*. This is because battle conditions are quite fluid, and the general on the ground must be given the maximum flexibility to organize and restructure his troops and formations depending on the battle situations. Second, as battle conditions change, the general must change his strategy accordingly. In other words, he has to constantly reorganize according to his strategy. Although he begins with a battle plan, that plan can never be cast in stone. He must constantly reorganize his troops for battles as he changes his plan (strategy) to meet the dynamic conditions of war. In sum, he has to be very proactive and seize on any available opportunity to win. This was true of ancient wars, and is still applicable today. Figure 5.1 shows the relationships between strategy, structure, and behaviour.

Interestingly, there is no lack of support in the business literature for the relationship between strategy and structure. For example, Chandler (1962) concluded that once a corporate strategy is in place, its structure will follow. More recently Bartlett and Ghoshal (1989, p. 20) argued that organizational structure should fit the strategic requirement of the business and the firm's dominant strategic capability. Similar views were expressed by Lorange and Vancil (1976), Henderson (1979), Lorange (1980, 1982), and Ohmae (1989). Unfortunately, there are other scholars who counter argue that it is often the other way around—that is, it is often the structure that drives the strategy (e.g. Pascale, 1990, p. 100). This lack of consensus on how strategy affects structure or vice versa has influenced to some extent, the way many companies manage themselves for competition.

It is important to point out that there are fundamental differences in the likely outcome/behaviour between a strategy-led versus a structure-led approach. These differences are shown in Table 5.1. In the current highly competitive and technology-driven environment, it would be more logical to subscribe to a strategy-led approach as it would result in behaviour/outcome as illustrated in the left column of Table 5.1. In fact, even Japanese companies are discovering that

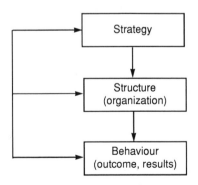

Figure 5.1   Strategy, structure and behaviour

Table 5.1   Strategy-led versus structure-led behaviour

Strategy → Structure	Structure → Strategy
(1) Believes in flexibility (fluidity)	(1) Creates rigidity ('Cast in stone')
(2) Able to cope in an uncertain and dynamic environment	(2) Prefers to operate in a static or stable environment
(3) Change is a necessity	(3) Change is to be avoided
(4) Adopts a proactive approach	(4) Develops a reactive posture
(5) Tends to promote creativity	(5) Tends to build bureaucracy
(6) Stimulates learning in the organisation	(6) Retards progress in the organisation
(7) Able to tackle risks head-on	(7) Avoids risks if possible

their bureaucratic structures are now affecting their competitiveness (Schlender, 1993a). Companies should dismantle fixed organizational charts, and instead organize their companies around their strategies and the changing environment (Dumaine, 1991; Katzenbach and Smith, 1993; Kirkpatrick, 1993).

THE NEED TO BE COMBAT-READY ALL THE TIME

It is very important to emphasize that in the realm of the military, the army must always maintain a highly vigilant state of combat-readiness. Thus, even though there may be no war, troops are trained to the highest level of combat-fitness in *peacetime*. In fact, it is during peacetime that the army can seize on the opportunity to build up its resources so as to act as a deterrent to any hostile move by the enemy. This principle is well illustrated by Sun Tzu:

> In the conduct of war, one must not rely on the enemy's failure to come but on one's readiness to engage him; One must not rely on the enemy's failure to attack but on one's ability to build an invincible defence.

The need to adopt a 'war mentality' or to be in a constant state of combat-readiness even in peacetime is well understood by any military general. This concept of 'combat readiness' can also be meaningfully applied to business. Such a business philosophy or orientation will constantly motivate the company to want to scale greater heights, and to seize on every opportunity to improve itself. It would always have the mentality to want to grow. In fact, the obstacle to growth would be its own resource availability and capability rather than the constraints imposed by its competitors and the environment. Unfortunately, many companies tend to become victims of their own successes. This is because when they become successful, they forget about what brought them there. They no longer become 'hungry' for growth, especially when profits are good. Instead, they are contented with only maintaining their status quo, and would only *react* when threatened by the competitors. In other words, they cease to build invincible defences around their successful businesses, and instead wait for the arrival of the competitors, or worse, they hope that their competitors would not come after them!

It is important that the correct competitive posture be adopted for any company to excel. Let me illustrate with an example. When a company is not in the number-one position in any market, business or product, in terms of either sales or profitability, it would be its greatest goal to strive for the number-one position. However, what should its goal be if it has already attained the number-one position? Here, it would not be surprising to find answers like '. . . protect the number-one position', '. . . defend the number-one position', '. . . maintain the number-one position' and '. . . stay in the number-one position'. There is a fundamental flaw in such responses in that they all reflect a reactive mindset, not a proactive posture. If you are already number one, you are the leader, and you should lead! Thus, the more appropriate answer should be to *distance oneself* as far as possible from the rest of the competitors. It must be pointed out that any time you are within sight to your nearest competitor, you become vulnerable. This is because you are providing the most logical reason and target for the competitors to catch up, or even overtake you. However, if the gap is very large, it becomes almost impossible to catch up. In fact, the gap itself would demoralize any competitor!

The attitude of not having a combat-ready mindset has, in fact, caused many American and European companies to adopt a complacent posture during the 1970s and 1980s despite the fact that Japanese companies were fast gaining market shares on them. These Western corporate giants actually began from a position of strength after the Second World War, and they were leaders in many world markets and products. Unfortunately, their great success caused them to be complacent, and many failed to take a proactive stance, and made little effort to build strong defences. For example, instead of investing more into research and development, and expanding their market shares, many of them became lethargic and were more interested in short-term profits and dividends. By slowing down their innovation process, and by not paying attention to building up their market shares, they were literally throwing open invitations to their lesser-known Japanese competitors. By adopting such a reactive posture, these Western giants made themselves vulnerable, and as history has shown, many of them have become victims of their own successes. It was not until recently that these Western companies like those in the automobile industry became more aggressive and combat-fit to take on the Japanese (Taylor, 1992; Rapoport, 1993a). In addition, there were also strong calls for US industry to be more aggressive in research and development investments (Faltermayer, 1993).

Among many well-known multinational corporations, IBM is an example of how an industry giant has failed to be proactive and combat-fit at all times. Clearly, IBM overwhelmingly dominated the computer industry, especially the mainframe market, for almost four decades. In fact, its mainframe computers were its cash cow. Unfortunately, IBM failed to capitalise on its dominance to further distance itself from the rest of its competitors. Instead, it became complacent and lost its zeal for innovation. Worst of all, it failed to realise that the industry was moving towards personal computers. As a result, it was forced into a very defensive position (Dobrzynski, 1993).

ACHIEVING RELATIVE SUPERIORITY AT THE POINT OF CONTACT

In military combat, one of the most important factors to ensure success is to understand the principle of *relative superiority at the point of contact*. In war, it does not matter how large a force you have at home or how rigorous the troops have been trained (although better training would improve their combat-readiness and effectiveness). Rather, what matters most is what happens at the point of contact—that is, the side who can gain relative superiority at the point of contact will win. In fact, Sun Tzu underlined this concept when he said:

> The strength of an army does not depend on large forces. Do not advance basing on sheer numbers. Rather, one must concentrate the forces and anticipate correctly the enemy's movements in order to capture him.

In fact, the above statement reflects what we commonly call 'niching' in business. Sun Tzu went on to elaborate what he meant by achieving relative superiority, and how a small force can take on a larger one if it can exploit the principle underlying point of contact:

> The enemy must not know where I intend to attack. For if he does not know where I intend to attack, he must defend in many places. The more places he defends, the more scattered are his forces, and the weaker is his force at any one point.

He went on to say:

> If he [the enemy] prepares to the front, his rear will be weak; if he defends the rear, his front will be fragile. If he strengthens his left, he will weaken his right; if he strengthens his right, he will weaken his left. If he tries to prepare for everywhere, he will be weak everywhere.

Thus, no one can be invincible—whether it is an army or an organisation. There are bound to be weak spots among the mightiest of armies and the strongest of business organizations. Even the mighty Japanese companies can become vulnerable, as shown by the slowing down of their economy in the early 1990s (Schlender, 1992, 1993a). The challenge for the smaller force (company) is to concentrate its entire force against a fraction of the larger force at those weak spots where superiority can be attained. As such, even small companies can find their places in any competitive environment, so long as they can develop their unique expertise and cater to specific market niches. In fact, it is tautologous to state that almost all large companies, including the multinational corporations (MNCs), began by being small. Almost all of them began with some kind of niching strategy before pursuing growth and expansion relentlessly.

Relative superiority at the point of contact can also be achieved if one learns to choose battlegrounds carefully. In the words of Sun Tzu:

> Therefore, those who are skilled in warfare will always bring the enemy to where they want to fight, and are not brought there by the enemy.
> To be certain to succeed in what you attack is to attack a place where the enemy does not defend or where its defence is weak. To be certain of holding what you defend is to defend a place the enemy does not attack or where the defence is invulnerable to attacks.

Note that Sun Tzu's principles on the choice of battlegrounds have been applied to business as well. For example, the Japanese are renowned for their clever choice of battlegrounds in their economic conquest of the world (e.g. Ohmae, 1982, pp. 240–41). In the earlier years, they deliberately avoided head-on confrontation with the Western corporate giants. For example, in exporting, they deliberately selected markets that the Americans were not interested in or had ignored completely—like South-east Asia. Even when they gained strength, and were ready to penetrate the Western markets, they spared no effort in understanding the characteristics of their battlegrounds. In fact, Kotler *et al.* (1985, p. 49) documented how Toyota skilfully exploited the beachheads (frontiers) they captured on four key West Coast cities in the USA—Los Angeles, San Francisco, Portland and Seattle—in their penetration of the American automobile market.

Despite the fact that many Japanese companies are now very strong and capable of head-on competition, they are still known to enter markets that are ignored by their competitors. In addition, they have continued to invest heavily in understanding the characteristics of their markets. For example, it is widely known that Japanese firms are very active in new economies like Vietnam and Myammar, and even in Eastern Europe.

In products, the Japanese have also deliberately sought out neglected and unfilled market segments. For example, in automobiles and consumer durables, the small-size segments were ignored completely by American and European manufacturers. Japanese manufacturers concentrated their entire initial efforts in making small cars, small television sets, mini hi-fi components, desktop photocopiers, etc. Today, they have built up so much expertise and many skills in these areas that are unrivalled by the Western corporations.

Even in the design and styling of products, the Japanese manufacturers would enter areas where the Western corporate giants were reluctant to do so. For example, while American automobile manufacturers are still debating today on the viability of cars with right-hand drive to cater for other overseas markets, the Japanese companies have already done so for more than 40 years! In fact, in making the changes, the Japanese manufacturers would even go into the minute details of adjusting and shifting all the necessary gadgets within the car to accommodate different driving positions—something that even the leading German and European car makers like Mercedes, BMW, Saab, Volvo, Citroen and Renault have failed to do.

In choosing areas ignored by the competitors, the Japanese have also gained themselves several distinctive advantages. First, as these were areas ignored by the rest, the Japanese manufacturers had all the opportunities and time to improve themselves without being threatened by their stronger Western counterparts. Second, as there was no competition, they were given, by default, unlimited access to exploit the market(s) available. Even in instances where there was competition, they tended to be weak and scattered, and this allowed the Japanese companies to concentrate their entire force against a fraction of those of the competitors. Finally, as a result of having been given an unrestricted scope for building up their market shares in specific product areas, they have developed enough expertise and strengths to challenge the leaders. A good example is that of the automobile industry. Today, Toyota, Nissan and Honda have begun to launch assaults on the luxury car markets with models like the Lexus, Cima and Legend.

It must be pointed out that Japanese companies began from a position of *weakness*, not strength. In fact, the whole nation was almost destroyed after the Second World War, and the efforts to rebuild the country and its industries were almost insurmountable. When Japanese products first appeared in the international arena they were known to be of inferior quality, cheap and imitated items. Today, Japanese products have become synonymous with high quality and reliability. Among many reasons for its success, the ability to choose battleground carefully, and the application of the principle of relative superiority at the point of contact are definitely two of the contributing factors.

Of course, Japanese companies are not the only ones who had exploited the principle of relative superiority. In the publishing industry, World Scientific Publishing Co. Pte Ltd. (WSP), a company based in Singapore, started off by publishing conference proceedings—an area ignored by larger publishers because of the small market. In doing so, WSP was put into contact with scientific authors who provided strong editorial support for their publications. Subsequently, WSP decided to focus on publishing high-level textbooks—largely graduate level text—that depend on editorial strengths that it has built up over the years. This was an area ignored by the larger publishers, who tended to concentrate on the large undergraduate textbook market. WSP deliberately avoided head-on competition with the larger publishers as it lacked marketing strengths. Its forte was in editorial work, not marketing. Thus, by concentrating on technical and scientific publications, WSP has today built up a very strong niche in an area which the larger publishers find difficult to exploit.

ROLE OF INTELLIGENCE

Without doubt, intelligence plays a pivotal role in the conduct of war. Generals develop their combat strategies based on intelligence gathered on the enemy, weather and terrain. According to Sun Tzu:

> The reason why the enlightened ruler and the wise general are able to conquer the enemy whenever they lead the army and can achieve victories that surpass those of others is because of foreknowledge.

What is interesting is his view on how the foreknowledge or intelligence should come from:

> This foreknowledge cannot be elicited from spirits nor from the gods; nor by inductive thinking; nor by deductive calculations. It can only be obtained from *men* who have knowledge of the enemy's situation.

Thus, there is a need to rely on *human intelligence* to actively collect, store, analyze and utilize information for the development of effective strategies. There is no scope for superstitious practices or hunches when it comes to planning for war. The importance of using human intelligence can be supported by the fact that Sun Tzu expounded on the use of five different types of secret agents for gathering information on the enemies (see Wee *et al.*, 1991, pp. 237–44).

Business espionage should be condemned and frowned upon (Beltramini, 1986; Pooley, 1982; Waller, 1992; Labich, 1992c). However, to pretend that business espionage does not exist would be an exercise in futility and naivety. If anything, industrial espionage is rife and commonly practised in the business world (Nelan, 1993).

Besides espionage, it is important to point out that there are many 'above-board' methods of gathering market and competitive information that could be used for the development of business strategies—for example, surveys, industrial studies, market studies and trade missions (Eells and Nehemkis, 1984). In today's business environment—where competition is rife, consumer tastes are fast changing and information technology becoming more widespread— the need to rely on intelligence for effective decision making has become more eminent (Brock, 1984; Gordon, 1982; Attanasio, 1988; Bergeron and Raymond, 1992). Many scholars have even argued for systematic ways of collecting and analysing information on their competitors and the markets (Sammon *et al.*, 1984; Fuld, 1985; Gilad and Gilad, 1988; Gilad, 1989).

In the Asia–Pacific region, it is worth noting that many companies still lack organized intelligence in developing their corporate strategies. Instead they still rely on hunches and guesses in their decision making. Some of the more superstitious chief executive officers (CEOs) and bosses even call in geomancers and temple mediums/priests for consultation in strategic decisions! There is nothing wrong in trying to evoke the spiritual dimension for business decisions. However, over-reliance on such practices at the expense of good and available market information and data would be sheer commercial stupidity.

It is also worth noting that many Japanese companies are known to pursue market intelligence relentlessly. For example, the Japanese general trading companies (GTC), the Ministry of International Trade and Industry (MITI) and the Japanese External Trade Organization (JETRO) have each established worldwide networks of intelligence systems. Together with Japanese companies, they form a formidable market intelligence force unrivalled by any other country in the world. Even the smaller companies are known to depend on the mainstream companies and government-related agencies for information.

According to de Mente (1992), author of more than 20 books on Japan, including *Japanese Etiquette and Ethics in Business* (1960) and *How to Do Business with the Japanese* (1962), knowledge flows unfettered in Japan. Japanese tend to treat the search for and utilization of information as an ongoing activity. This is very different from Westerners, who tend to seek and utilize just enough information to get by or to accomplish immediate short-term goals. Interestingly, the Japanese treatment of information in business is very similar to that for the conduct of war, where information and intelligence are extremely important for decision making.

As a further observation, Japanese executives are known to be highly religious but not superstitious. For example, their corporate ceremonies are filled with spiritual rituals and are accompanied by rich customs and traditions. However, when it comes to decision making, they rely heavily on market intelligence. They are never clouded by superstitions and hearsay. In contrast, many Chinese businessmen in South-east Asia (including Hong Kong) are highly superstitious, but not religious. In other words, they tend to believe in the spiritual realm—more often without substantiation—and rely less on using market information and data. Yet in their daily lives and corporate rituals, religion does not appear to play a major role.

SHAPING AND FLEXIBILITY

Sun Tzu used a very simple and common medium, water, to illustrate the need to be flexible in combat:

> The guiding principle in military tactics may be likened to water. Just as flowing water avoids the heights and hastens to the lowlands, an army should avoid strengths and strike weaknesses.
> Just as water shapes itself according to the ground, an army should manage its victory in accordance with the situation of the enemy. Just as water has no constant shape, so in warfare there are no fixed rules and regulations.

Thus, the wise general is someone who is able to apply the principle of flexibility to take advantage of the changing circumstances in war. Note that one of the most remarkable statements is that there are no fixed rules and regulations when it comes to execution of plans. In other words, the general has the ultimate authority to decide what he deems most appropriate, given the situation that confronts him.

The principle of flexibility in business can best be illustrated by Japanese companies. For example, Japanese production systems are known to be very flexible. To begin with, they rely heavily on subcontracting systems which are geared towards flexibility in many ways. First, it cushions the impact of falling demand and orders, as the burden (such as problems of retrenchment of workers) is passed to the subcontractors. Second, it allows the buyer to source from multiple suppliers, and hence the possibility of obtaining supplies at lower prices. Third, it creates competition among the subcontractors, which inevitably raises quality and service standards. Finally, competition among the various suppliers also tends to increase the overall efficiency and productivity of the production system.

Going beyond purchasing, the Japanese shopfloor is organised in a very flexible manner to capitalize on changes in product designs, order sizes, and so on. To complement such a system, Japanese workers are trained to perform more than one function and their job rotation system ensures that their level of competency is not affected.

At the final product stage, Japanese products are known to be shaped according to the demands of the markets that they are selling to, even though the market size may be small. For example, while the United States ignored the markets in South-east Asia in the 1960s and 1970s, the Japanese courted this part of the world enthusiastically with products that were designed specifically for them. Despite their huge successes today, the Japanese have continued to be flexible in their product offerings to newer markets in the Asia–Pacific region. For example, when China needed cars after that country had opened up aggressively in the 1980s, the Japanese were prepared to do 'reverse engineering' in order to sell the Chinese cheap, large and efficient cars. In contrast, the Western companies were reluctant to do so. The results of such flexible policies are very telling by the size of Japanese market shares in these countries. In the words of Kotler *et al.* (1985, p. 254):

> Flexibility has been the visible trademark of the Japanese. They have not engraved their strategies in stone. They have not become so committed to a specific strategy that they have been blinded by it. Rather, they remained committed to broad strategic thrusts, and they have demonstrated tremendous flexibility in pursuing these thrusts ... They have continually adapted to the market and competitive environment and their evolving position within it.

In fact, as top US and European companies have begun to close the quality gap against Japanese products in recent years, Japanese manufacturers have shifted to flexible manufacturing systems and strategy as their new competitive weapon. They do this by focusing on more and better product features, flexible factories that can accommodate varying production orders and designs, expanded customer service, innovation and technological superiority (Stewart, 1992b).

Business situations are always very dynamic as they are affected by various factors—the consumers, the competitors, the government, the general public, the state of technology, the state of the economy, and so on. To compete successfully, the company must be adaptive to changes in its environment, and must not be bound by past practices or traditions. In fact, in their book, Bartlett and Ghoshal (1989) argued that the future transnational corporations, among other things, must be able to maintain organisational flexibility in order to compete effectively. Their views were supported by Stewart (1992a). For example, there are no fixed rules on how a company should go about developing its overseas markets (Bartlett and Ghoshal, 1989). If one company cannot do it alone, there is nothing to stop it joining forces with other companies with similar interests, even if they are direct competitors. Indeed, strategic alliances are becoming an important development in the conduct of business today as they can also provide for flexibility (Sherman, 1992). In fact, Toshiba, the oldest and third-largest Japanese electronics giant, has made strategic alliances a cornerstone of its corporate strategy (Schlender, 1993c). As of 1993, it had no less than 18 strategic partners in the USA, Europe, Canada, and even South Korea. In taking such a flexible approach, Toshiba has been able to enhance its global position in both technology and marketing. Besides Toshiba, many other Japanese companies have created strong partnerships by investing in sagging European rival companies (Rapoport, 1993c). In doing so, they have created additional leverages for themselves to compete in the future. Besides the Japanese, the South Koreans are pursuing similar flexible strategies in their quest for world market share (Kraar, 1992, 1993).

INNOVATION AND USE OF INITIATIVE

Innovativeness is another interesting concept advocated by Sun Tzu. This can be illustrated as follows:

> Therefore, do not repeat the tactics that won you a victory, but vary them according to the circumstances.
> He [the general] must be able to change his methods and schemes so that no one can know his intentions. He must be able to alter his camp-sites and marching routes so that no one can predict his movements.

This non-repetitiveness of tactics implies a constant search for new ways of meeting the challenges offered by the ever-changing circumstances. In addition, the use of new approaches will also prevent the enemy (competitor) from anticipating one's plans, as one becomes unpredictable through continual innovation. In essence, the strategy to be adopted should be novel and situation dependent, rather than relying on seemingly proven strategies.

It is important to note that while shaping and flexibility are more reactive in that they flow according to the situation, innovativeness is more proactive in that it attempts to dominate or control the situation: 'Thus, those skilled in manipulating the enemy do so by creating a situation to which he must conform.'

Innovation is very much desired in business. This is especially so in the present environment where technology is becoming increasingly important as a competitive edge. Here again, the Japanese firms are adept in this area. This can be illustrated by how high technology is used in Japan. Due to the limited demand for military applications in Japan, technology is always first used in the private sector for products that are easiest to manufacture. Only later are the applications extended to include the more difficult areas. In other words, Japan uses a bottom-up approach—from the easiest to the most difficult applications. Western countries, on the other hand, tend to adopt a top-down approach—that is, technology is typically first applied in the most difficult areas such as space exploration or military systems.

There are significant differences and results between these two approaches. In the Japanese bottom-up approach of using technology for business applications, the product is targeted at the consumer and the manufacturing process is relatively simple. As Japan has a large domestic market, consumption is on a massive scale. This enables economies of scale to be achieved quickly and costs of production as well as prices can be lowered accordingly. In turn, more funds can be generated and invested in more plant and equipment and product quality can be quickly established and raised.

In the Western top-down approach of using technology for sophisticated and difficult military applications, there is always a scarcity of facilities because production is on a small scale, and quality is difficult to stabilize. Thus, costs also tend to be very high which also hamper further investments. For example, fuzzy logic was invented by the Americans. Unfortunately, the top-down approach denied them the opportunity to apply it into the commercial realm. Meanwhile, many Japanese companies have used fuzzy logic in the manufacturing of air conditioners, refrigerators, vacuum cleaners, washing machines, and other consumer durables.

The need to be innovative is becoming increasingly important today. There must be a constant search for different ways of doing things. In the process, the solutions may not conform to past practices and traditions. For example, despite the setbacks faced by many Japanese companies in the early 1990s, especially in the computer and automobile industries (Schlender, 1993a,b; Taylor, 1993), they are looking for new ways to overcome their problems. In fact, some enlightened Western writers even cautioned the Western world not to rejoice over the economic woes of the Japanese companies in the early 1990s. If anything, based on how they had overcome the oil crisis in the 1970s and the rising yen in the late 1980s, Japanese companies are likely to emerge even stronger after they have resolved their difficulties in the 1990s (Stewart, 1992b; Taylor, 1993).

While innovation is a proactive, deliberate and systematic approach to problem solving, the use of *initiative* requires both the proactive and reactive dimensions. In other words, it requires the individual to be very responsive to changes in situations, as well as able to take pre-emptive actions. Thus, resourcefulness at the point of decision making is essential. In addition, the exercise of initiative is often instantaneous and an intuitive act of the individual who is faced with the decision. In the words of Sun Tzu: 'There are situations when the orders of the ruler need not be obeyed.' In fact, he illustrated this as follows:

> If the situation is one of victory, the general must fight even though the ruler may have issued orders not to engage. If the situation is one of defeat, the general must not fight even though the ruler may have issued orders to do so.

Thus the use of initiative requires the general to make decisions at the point of battle as there is little time for him to consult the ruler (who is often not on the battlefield). He must decide on the spot what his next move is to be. If the situation dictates that he should attack, he must do so, even if he had prior orders not to engage. This is because there are so many variations and changes at each step of the battle. If the general cannot exercise initiative under such circumstances and must await the orders of the ruler for each move, it is like telling your superior that you would like to have his permission to put out a fire. By the time the order to do so is approved, the ashes would be cold!

It must be pointed out that in exercising initiative, the general must advance without seeking personal fame and glory and must retreat without fear of being punished. At all times, he must have the welfare of the people and the interests of the ruler at heart. Thus, in exercising his initiative under such circumstances, he has not betrayed the trust given to him, nor should his loyalty be questioned.

> Therefore, the general who advances without seeking personal fame and glory, who retreats without fear of being punished, but whose main concern is for the welfare of the people and the interests of the sovereign, is the precious gem of the state.

The use of initiative requires the general to capitalise on the situations facing him, and to be able to exploit the resources available to him:

> Therefore, the adept in warfare seeks victory from the situation, and does not rely on the efforts of individuals. Thus, he is able to select suitable men to exploit the situation.

Initiative also extends beyond pragmatism. This is because pragmatism, to a large extent, is reactive in nature. Initiative, however, encompasses both the reactive and proactive dimensions. Other than reacting very expediently and effectively to changes in the environment, it also involves constantly looking for better ways to win:

> If the enemy provides an opportunity, quickly capitalize on it.
> Effective strategies must constantly change according to the situation of the enemy.

In the same way, a company must encourage the flow of innovative ideas and the exercise of initiative of all fronts—from the conception of product/service ideas to the actual implementation of marketing strategies. Pascale (1990) even argued for innovative ways of managing conflicts in order to stay ahead of competition, while Naisbitt and Aburdene (1985) advocated innovative human resource management and organization as the future corporate challenge. No matter what it is, it is important that at any time when opportunities arise as a result of the changing environment or other factors, the company must be capable of capitalizing on them. It must not shy away, even though the execution process may have to be modified. At times, it may also entail changes to plans that are already made.

Briefly, innovativeness and initiative are very much related to creativity. In recent years, creativity has been actively pursued by organizations and their corporate executives. This has resulted in no shortage of literature on the subject. For example, de Bono (1971) propounded lateral thinking for management, Ackoff (1978) wrote his famous book on the art of problem solving, Miller (1986) argued for the need to foster innovation at the place of work, and recently Yu (1990) proposed an integrated theory of habitual domains as the basis for forming winning strategies. Yet despite all this available literature, the books remain only academic if corporate executives are unable to translate them into actionable plans and projects for the company.

NEED TO BE ON THE OFFENSIVE IN COMBAT

While Sun Tzu acknowledged the need for strong defence, he also advocated the need for offence. If possible, one should attack plans at inception, and avoid open conflicts. However, if open combat is inevitable, the best way to win is through attacking:

> Invincibility in defence depends on one's own efforts, while the

opportunity of victory depends on the enemy. It follows that those who are skilled in warfare can make themselves invincible, but cannot cause their enemies to be vulnerable.

It is important to understand the rationale behind the need for attacking in open combat. An invincible defence can ensure that one does not lose, but cannot guarantee a victory. At best, it can only result in a draw. At worst, it can even lead to 'self-choking' and isolation. Victory can only be achieved by capturing the enemy's territory (or destroying his forces). It cannot be won by defending one's territory or troops. Indeed, the focus on attack has led to the development of niching strategies for those with smaller forces and weaker equipment. To achieve success with niching, one must constantly keep in mind that in direct confrontation, it is the relative superiority of forces at the point of contact that matters most. Thus, absolute superiority alone in numbers and resources are not sufficient in winning. What is more important is to develop and use strategies that allow the achievement of relative superiority.

The logic on attack applies to business as well. For example, strong defence of a company's market share can reduce the probability that its competitors will not steal its customers. However, its market share is unlikely to increase unless it seeks new and potential customers and those of the competitors. There is hardly any other viable option in the case of open competition. In fact, even if a company chooses not to attack, there is no guarantee that its competitors will not pursue its customers! In businesses where economies of scale prevail, the need to pursue market share (as a means to reduce costs and hence increase profits) is even more urgent and important.

This principle of attack in open combat is well illustrated by Samsung, one of the largest South Korean companies. Moving away from making imitated products, it invests over US$2.5 billion a year into training, research and production facilities. It has also begun a deliberate policy to pursue market share in the long run by forgoing short-term profits (Kraar, 1993). Samsung is not an exception. Many other South Korean companies are pursuing similar aggressive strategies to expand their stakes in the world market (Kraar, 1992).

Moving to a more macro level, the analogy of attack can be extended to international trade among nations. Over the last two decades, the successes of countries like Japan and the newly industrialized economies (NIEs)—namely Hong Kong, Singapore, South Korea and Taiwan—have been largely due to their attacking strategies in international trade (e.g. Kraar, 1992). They have opted for an export-oriented strategy as the engine for economic growth rather than relying on domestic factors like developing import substitution industries. The results are well known.

Ironically, when threatened with the export offensive strategy of Japan and the NIEs, many Western European countries, the USA and Canada have begun to embark on defensive strategies (Smith, 1992; Rapoport, 1992, 1993b). They have used various measures to protect their domestic markets, and have devoted relatively less attention to make their industries more competitive and export-oriented (Smith, 1992). Without doubt, their protective measures will ensure that they will not lose further foreign exchange. However, with equal certainty, they are unlikely to earn the needed foreign exchange! Fortunately, many Western companies have begun to go on the offensive in recent years (Taylor, 1992; Faltermayer, 1993; Kirkpatrick, 1993; Rapoport, 1993a).

FOCUS ON THE HEART, NOT THE MIND

Underlying the use of military concepts and strategies is an important fundamental principle—the need to focus on the heart, and not on the mind of management. This is because in war, the general cannot rely on material benefits to motivate his troops. Instead, he has to appeal to their sense of national pride and loyalty. He appeals to their emotions and feelings, and uses the moral cause as justification for aggression. For this reason, the general even joins his troops and, if needed, drinks from the same coffee mug and eats from the same mess tin. In doing so, he wins their hearts, which is very important for building up comradeship and team spirit—ingredients so essential for winning wars. Indeed, no shrewd general would think of motivating his soldiers in combat with extra pay or bonus!

While it is very easy for anyone to comprehend the need to focus on the heart in the management of an army for war, it is harder to translate that into management of businesses. If any, many Western companies tend to develop policies that appeal to the mind rather than the heart. There are fundamental differences between these two approaches, as shown in Table 5.2. Managing the heart is more an art rather than a science. For example, there is a need to take a long-term perspective and the employee's contributions have to be viewed over a lifetime. To appeal to the heart, there is a need for strong social interactions, and the CEO has to adopt a much more personal and people-centred approach. When the heart can be won over, the employees are likely to be highly loyal and less likely to be lured

Table 5.2 The heart and mind of management

The heart (feelings and emotions)	The mind (logic and reason)
(1) Social orientation	(1) Task-orientation
(2) Personal and people-centred	(2) Impersonal and systems-driven
(3) Takes a long-term perspective	(3) Breeds short-term mentality
(4) Builds loyalty and group values	(4) Develops self-interest and individualism
(5) Contributions assessed over one's lifetime	(5) One's worth depends on economic value
(6) Reliance on psychic rewards	(6) Focus on tangible benefits
(7) Expertise not vulnerable to external exploitation	(7) Expertise can be bought and sold
(8) Management more an art	(8) Management more a science

away by higher perks offered by the competitors. In other words, they will find satisfaction in working for the organization as they tend to rely more on psychic rewards. The heart approach facilitates the cultivation of group values, which in turn, favours the development of team building and team work.

In general, Japanese and many Asian companies tend to focus more on managing the hearts of their employees. In contrast, Western companies, largely due to their cultural influences, tend to focus more on managing the minds. They do this largely by higher salaries and perks. If special expertise is needed, they will not hesitate to 'head-hunt' for it, and this includes hiring the CEO. For example, IBM hired a new CEO in 1993 as it was felt that there was no senior executive within the existing organization capable of doing the job. Interestingly, despite the seemingly elaborate 'head-hunting' exercise, the computer industry did not appear to give IBM's new CEO much respect (Dobrzynski, 1993). In short, the Western approach tends to treat management more of a science, and adopts a much more 'clinical' approach in the way the organization is handled.

In business practice, the heart and mind are not mutually exclusive. Rather, my arguments are that the Japanese and Asian companies tend to pay more attention to the heart while the Western companies tend to be more mind-driven. There is nothing wrong with being more mind-driven so long as a healthy balance can be maintained. For example, if teamwork is necessary to achieve success, then there is a need to inject more heart into the organization. This is where I find much of the recent literature on team building and teamwork lacking. While many of these works tend to expound on the importance and contributions of teamwork and team building, they tend to treat the subject in a rather 'clinical' manner (e.g. Dyer, 1987; Johansen *et al.*, 1991; Katzenbach and Smith, 1993). Little attention is given to building up social bonds within the team—that is, focusing on building up the heart. Ironically, when one traces back into history, it was Mayo's (1933) classic Hawthorne experiment that clearly demonstrated the emergence of the team idea in an organized work setting—one that operated with the heart. In that well-documented Hawthorne experiment, the group maintained high productivity over a five-year period largely because of mental rewards resulting from a strong team spirit. The leader of that group managed by the heart, not the mind! In fact, Mayo's works were very much supported by McGregor (1960) when he wrote on *The Human Side of Enterprise* and Likert (1961), who authored *New Patterns of Management*. Perhaps it is timely for Western executives to revisit some of these classic works to rediscover the need for the heart in management.

CONCLUSION

The analogy between war and business is a fruitful exercise, but it is too often taken for granted. For example, in the conduct of war, *leadership* is crucial. In fact, a general is carefully trained over many years and only attains his rank based on his military accomplishments. He is never 'parachuted' into the army as his stars must be earned through the rank and file. In addition, it is a military practice to rotate generals, depending on the war mission at hand. It is no wonder that Sun Tzu's writings are largely focused on the general and his strategies.

Ironically, in the world of business, little attention is paid to the training of leaders. If anything, it is quite typical for a company to be plagued with succession problems. Worse still, even when a corporate general is doing well on the job, he is often allowed to carry on as if in perpetuity until the company gets into serious trouble. In fact, this is the typical case of many American companies, as illustrated by the removal of Robert C. Stempel as Chairman of General Motors in late 1992.

Of course, there are limits to the analogy between war and business in that the former is an extreme situation, demanding exceptional responses and a suspension of normal life. War, after all, involves killing and being killed, and often allows for various forms of behaviour, espionage and control of the media, for instance. These activities are unlikely to be tolerated in peacetime. Even allowing for the notion of a 'just war' one may feel that a war mentality is not necessary or desirable for a successful business life. Yet it is equally difficult to deny that many military concepts can be applied meaningfully in business. In particular, they help to develop a mentality among corporate executives to win business wars. Thus, Sun Tzu's *Art of War*, a treatise highly regarded by many Asian corporate strategists, may provide some inspiration in this direction.

REFERENCES

Abegglen, J. C. and Stalk Jr, G. (1985) *Kaisha: The Japanese Corporation*, New York, Basic Books.

Ackoff, R. L. (1978) *The Art of Problem Solving*, New York, John Wiley.

Attanasio, D. B. (1988) The multiple benefits of competitor intelligence. *The Journal of Business Strategy*, May/June, 16–19.

Bartlett, C. A. and Ghoshal, S. (1989) *Managing Across Borders: The Transnational Solution*, Boston, MA, Harvard Business School Press.

Beltramini, R. F. (1986) Ethics and the use of competitive information acquisition strategies. *Journal of Business Ethics*, **5**, 307–11.

Bergeron, F. and Raymond, L. (1992) Planning of information systems to gain a competitive edge. *Journal of Small Business Management*, January, 21–6.

Brock, J. J. (1984) Competitor analysis: some practical approaches. *Industrial Marketing Management*, **13**, 225–31.

Chandler, A. D. Jr (1962) *Strategy As Structure*, Cambridge, MA, MIT Press.

de Bono, E. (1971) *Lateral Thinking for Management*, London, McGraw-Hill.

de Mente, B. L. (1992) In Japan, knowledge flows unfettered. *Singapore Straits Times*, 30 March.

Dobrzynski, J. H. (1993) Rethinking IBM. *Business Week*, 4 October, 44–55.

Dumaine, B. (1991) The bureaucracy busters. *Fortune International*, **123**, No. 13, 17 June, 26–34.

Dyer, W. G. (1987) *Team Building: Issues and Alternatives*, Reading, MA, Addison-Wesley.

Eells, R. and Nehemkis, P. (1984) *Corporate Intelligence and Espionage*, New York, Macmillan.

Enricho, R. and Kornbluth, J. (1987) The other guy blinked: how Pepsi won the cola wars. *World Executive Digest*, April, 44–8.

Faltermayer, E. (1993) Invest or die. *Fortune International*, **127**, No. 4, 22 February, 16–22.

Fuld, L. M. (1985) *Corporate Intelligence: How to get it, how to use it*, New York, John Wiley.

Gilad, B. (1989) The role of organized competitive intelligence in corporate strategy. *Columbia Journal of World Business*, Winter, 29–35.

Gilad, B. and Gilad, T. (1988) *The Business Intelligence System*, New York, American Management Association.
Gordon, I. H. (1982) Competitive intelligence—a key to marketplace survival. *Industrial Marketing*, **67**, No. 11, November, 69–75.
Griffith, S. B. (1982) *Sun Tzu: The Art of War*, Oxford, Oxford University Press.
Henderson, B. (1979) *Henderson on Corporate Strategy*, Cambridge, MA, Abt Books.
Johansen, R., Martin, A., Mittman, R., Saffo, P., Sibbet, D. and Benson, S. (1991) *Leading Business Teams*, Reading, MA, Addison-Wesley.
Katzenbach, J. R. and Smith, D. K. (1993) *The Wisdom of Teams: Creating the High-Performance Organization*, Boston, MA, Harvard Business School Press.
Kirkpatrick, D. (1993) Could AT & T rule the world? *Fortune International*. **127**, No. 10, 17 May, 18–27.
Kotler, P. and Singh, R. (1981) Marketing warfare in the 1980's. *Journal of Business Strategy*, Winter, 30–41.
Kotler, P., Fahey, L. and Jatusripitak, S. (1985) *The New Competition*, Englewood Cliffs, NJ, Prentice-Hall.
Kraar, L. (1992) Korea's tigers keep roaring. *Fortune International*, **125**, No. 9, 4 May, 24–28.
Kraar, L. (1993) How Samsung grows so fast. *Fortune International*, **127**, No. 9, 3 May, 16–21.
Labich, K. (1992a) Airbus takes off. *Fortune International*, **125**, No. 11, 1 June, 22–28.
Labich, K. (1992b) Europe's sky wars. *Fortune International*, **126**, No. 10, 2 November, 24–31.
Labich, K. (1992c) The new crisis in business ethics. *Fortune International*, **125**, No. 8, 20 April, 83–6.
Lazer, W., Murata, S. and Kosaka, H. (1985) Japanese marketing: towards a better understanding. *Journal of Marketing*, **49**, No. 2, 69–81.
Li, S. J., Yang, X. J. and Tang, J. R. (1984) *Sun Tzu's Art of War and Business Management*, China, Kwangsi People's Press (translated).
Likert, R. (1961) *New Patterns of Management*, New York, McGraw-Hill.
Lorange, P. (1980) *Corporate Planning: An Executive Viewpoint*, Englewood Cliffs, NJ, Prentice Hall.
Lorange, P. (1982) *Implementation of Strategic Planning*, Englewood Cliffs, NJ, Prentice Hall.
Lorange, P. and Vancil, R. F. (1976) How to design a strategic planning system. *Harvard Business Review*, **54**, No. 5, September–October, 75–81.
Mayo, E. (1933) *The Human Problems of an Industrial Civilization*, Division of Research, Graduate School of Business Administration, Harvard University, Boston, MA.
McGregor, D. (1960) *The Human Side of Enterprise*, New York, McGraw-Hill.
Miller, W. C. (1986) *The Creative Edge: Fostering Innovation Where You Work*, Reading, MA, Addison-Wesley.
Naisbitt, J. and Aburdene, P. (1985) *Re-inventing The Corporation*, New York, Warner Books.

National Economic Commission (1985) *Classical Chinese Thoughts and Modern Management*, Economic Management Research Institute, China, Yunnan People's Publishing (translated).

Nelan, B. W. (1993) A new world for spies. *Time*, 5 July, 28–31.

Ohmae, K. (1982) *The Mind of the Strategist: The Art of Japanese Business*, New York, McGraw-Hill.

Ohmae, K. (1989) Planting for a global harvest. *Harvard Business Review*, **67**, No. 4, July–August, 136–145.

Pascale, R. T. (1990) *Managing On The Edge: How the Smartest Companies Use Conflict to Stay Ahead*, New York, Simon and Schuster.

Pooley, J. (1982) *Trade Secrets: How To Protect Your Ideas and Assets*, Berkeley, CA, Osborne, McGraw-Hill.

Rapoport, C. (1992) Getting tough with the Japanese. *Fortune International*, **125**, No. 9, 4 May, 30–35.

Rapoport, C. (1993a) Europe takes on the Japanese. *Fortune International*, **127**, No. 1, 11 January, 14–18.

Rapoport, C. (1993b) Europe's slump. *Fortune International*, **127**, No. 9, 3 May, 22–27.

Rapoport, C. (1993c) Japan to the rescue. *Fortune International*, **128**, No. 9, 18 October, 30–34.

Ries, A. and Trout, J. (1986) *Marketing Warfare*, New York, McGraw-Hill.

Sammon, W. L., Kurland, M. A. and Spitalnic, R. (1984) *Business Competitor Intelligence*, New York, John Wiley.

Saporito, W. (1992) Why the price wars never end. *Fortune International*, **125**, No. 6, 23 March, 20–25.

Schlender, B. R. (1992) How deep a slump, and which way out? *Fortune International*, **126**, No. 14, 14–18.

Schlender, B. R. (1993a) Japan: hard times for high tech. *Fortune International*, **127**, No. 6, 22 March, 18–23.

Schlender, B. R. (1993b) PC wars in Japan. *Fortune International*, **127**, No. 14, 12 July, 14–18.

Schlender, B. R. (1993c) How Toshiba makes alliances work. *Fortune International*, **128**, No. 8, 4 October, 42–7.

Sherman, S. (1992) Are strategic alliances working? *Fortune International*, **126**, No. 6, 21 September, 33–34.

Sherman, S. (1993) The new computer revolution. *Fortune International*, **127**, No. 12, June 14, 20–40.

Smith, L. (1992) A dangerous fix for trade deficits. *Fortune International*, **125**, No. 9, 4 May, 96–97.

Stewart, T. A. (1992a) The search for the organization of tomorrow. *Fortune International*, **125**, No. 10, 18 May, 53–58.

Stewart, T. A. (1992b) Brace for Japan's hot new strategy. *Fortune International*, **126**, No. 6, 21 September, 24–32.

Stripp, W. G. (1985) Sun Tzu, Musashi and Mahan: The integration of Chinese, Japanese and American strategic thought in international business. *Proceedings of the Inaugural Meeting of the Southeast Asian Region Academy of International Business*, Hong Kong, The Chinese University of

Hong Kong, pp.109–18.

Sullivan, J. J. (1992) Japanese management philosophies: from the vacuous to the brilliant. *California Management Review*, **34**, No. 2, Winter, 66–87.

Taylor III, A. (1992) U.S. cars come back. *Fortune International*, **126**, No. 11, 16 November, 24–53.

Taylor III, A. (1993) How Toyota copes with hard times. *Fortune International*, **127**, No. 2, 25 January, 18–22.

Waller, D. (1992) The open barn door: U.S. firms face a wave of foreign espionage. *Newsweek*, 4 May.

Wee, C. H. (1989) Planning for war and business: lessons from Sun Tzu. *Pointer*, Singapore, January–March, 3–20.

Wee, C. H. (1990) Battlegrounds and business situation: lessons from Sun Tzu. *Singapore Business Review*, **1**, No. 1, 24–43.

Wee, C. H., Lee, K. S. and Hidajat, B. W. (1991) *Sun Tzu: War and Management*, Reading, MA, Addison-Wesley.

Yu, P. L. (1990) *Forming Winning Strategies: An Integrated Theory of Habitual Domains*, Berlin, Springer-Verlag.

Zellner, W. (1992) The airlines are killing each other again. *International Business Week*, 8 June, 30.

6

A SEARCH FOR A NEW MANAGEMENT PARADIGM IN THE POST-COLD WAR ERA: THE END OF JAPAN'S MIRACLE?

Gen-Ichi Nakamura

Gen-Ichi Nakamura Associates

INTRODUCTION

Since the end of the cold war, several advanced countries have been suffering from a long economic recession which, according to the IMF's *Revised World Economy Outlook for 1993*, is expected to result in low, zero or negative economic growth in those countries. Japan, who joined the 'advanced countries club' on 22 September 1985, has not been an exception.

In the face of this long-term economic recession, a number of Japanese managers, senior or junior, regard it as a trough of a business cycle on the one hand, and indulge in an endless 'cost-reduction competition' on the other.

In contrast to the above approach, a small number of insightful Japanese managers perceive it as just the visible part of a very large iceberg with most of it under the water as a 'major restructuring at a global level in the post-cold-war era'.

This chapter is divided into the three sections. In the first, using the second approach, we will discuss strategic implications of the

International Review of Strategic Management, Volume 5
Edited by D. E. Hussey © 1994 John Wiley & Sons Ltd

invisible and submerged parts of a large iceberg for managers and
for Japanese managers in particular. In the second section, we will
discuss a new management paradigm which can be referred to as
management by creation (MBC hereafter). The major purpose of
MBC is to search for the creation of diverse values for diverse
stakeholders and, through this process, ultimately for the creation of
the firm's *raison d'être* in society at large. In the third section, we will
pinpoint several psychological barriers for typical Japanese
managers when they try to perceive strategic implications and to
shift to a new management paradigm.

IMPLICATIONS OF INVISIBLE AND SUBMERGED PARTS OF THE ICEBERG IN THE POST-COLD-WAR ERA

Four Points of Discussion

In this section we would like to draw the attention of the reader to
the following four points of discussion:

- New US–Japan relations
- Japan, quo vadis?
- The collapse of the iron triangle
- The reversal of priorities

New US–Japan relations

During the long-lasting cold war these two economic giants enjoyed
basically amicable relations on the principle that 'the two enemies of
the enemy are assumed to be friends'. In this connection, Alvin
Toffler reportedly (*Nikkei*, 11 August 1993) gave an in-depth insight
into the previous existence of a 'tacit agreement' developed by the
US government and the Japanese Liberal Democrat Party (LDP)
government which has lasted for 38 years (1955–93). That agreement
was, according to him, on the barter trade between US military bases
located in Japan and Japan's entry into the large and affluent US
market.

   This tacit agreement was generally favorable for the USA in the
first and second decades, particularly because products exported
from Japan to the USA were regarded 'cheap and deficient'. In the
third decade, however, the competitive edge which Japan had
deliberately developed in terms of QCD (quality, cost and delivery)
within the whole context of TQC (Total Quality Control) gradually

began to function so well that the US advantage changed to become an equilibrium.

The fourth decade began to see the US disadvantage in terms of the end of the cold war versus Japan's aggressive entry into US markets leading to the collapse of 'a tacit agreement' between the two economic giants. In this connection, as predicted rightly by Toffler, it was natural to see the end of the Japanese LDP's hegemony in July 1993.

The fundamental issue for the two economic giants in the post-cold war era, therefore, will be how willingly and skilfully American and Japanese leaders can collaborate with each other in order to effectively construct and manage a new economic and political friendship in the absence of the enemy.

Japan, quo vadis?

The end of the cold war has created two types of 'new cold war', one between white and yellow capitalism (as coined by the author) and the other between Western (Christian) and non-Western (Confucian and Muslim) cultures. The first phase of the former has already been recognized during the third and fourth decades of the Japanese LDP government. During these two decades, major Japanese firms made aggressive inroads into US and EC markets and the Japanese LDP government remained reluctant to open Japan's market as symbolized by the issue of rice-liberalization.

The second phase of the former has been gradually recognized since the beginning of the 1980s. During the last decade the East Asian region (the ANIEs, the ASEAN countries and China), in economic collaboration with Japan, began to enjoy a medium to high economic growth based on their interdependence (Nakamura, 1992a). Some economists referred to the thrust of this region as a 'driving force of world economy' in the 1980s and as the 'economic center of the world' in the 1990s, respectively.

The latter has been described by Professor Hutchinton in *Foreign Affairs* (Summer 1993) in terms of the increasing conflict between the two religiously different regions. To be more specific about the Confucian and Muslim connection, a new trend is emerging i.e. mental and military alliances between two different major religions such as Confucian and Muslim, including those of China with Pakistan and of North Korea with several Middle East countries.

If these two types of 'new cold war' happen in the future, an emerging issue for Japan will be how to find a new direction for its pendulum which, as shown by Figure 6.1, has continued to swing between the Orient (the East) and the Occident (the West) in the last 125 years since the Meiji Restoration.

The last decade has shown two different types of negative responses to Japan from the Occident as well as from the Orient, presenting the country a new dilemma. On the one hand, the Western ally under the Christian flag has found a considerable difference between white and yellow capitalism particularly after the Plaza Agreement as well as between two sets of political and societal orders. On the one hand, many countries in the Orient have unpleasant memories of Japan's 40 years (1905–45) of militarism. In summary, there still remains the possibility that Japanese history will repeat itself in terms of becoming an island, as shown by Figure 6.1.

The collapse of the iron triangle

The defeat of Japan's LDP in the general election in July 1993, as a by-product of the end of the cold war, has begun to reveal the fact that this was just the first of a series of priorities to be reversed by Japan. One of the most remarkable political and economic phenomena has been the collapse of what Western journalists call the 'iron triangle', as shown in Figure 6.2. On the one hand, as some economists argue, the unity of the triad was so strong and efficient until 1985 that the 'iron triangle' or 'Japan Inc.' made a significant contribution to the birth of a new economic giant in the East Asian region. On the other, successful interdependence under the 'iron triangle' in the last 38 years steadily nurtured self-corruption and escalated to the Kanemaru scandal in March 1993. At this writing, no-one knows how long will be the list of national and local politicians as well as top and middle executives to be arrested. An increasing distrust by the Japanese people in politicians, and senior LDP politicians in particular, has contributed to an accelerated reversal of value priorities which were dominant until recently.

The reversal of priorities

As mentioned above, the post-cold war era has begun to reveal a series of priority reversals in Japan. Some explanation of the five major issues may be in order.

(1) Firm > employee/people
——→ employee/people > firm
——→ increasing distrust of employee as a consumer in the firm at large

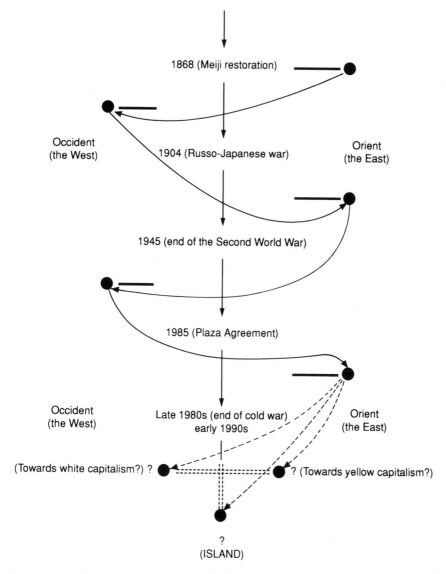

Figure 6.1 The swing of Japan's pendulum

Up to the collapse of the 'bubble economy', the value was shared, explicitly or implicitly, among Japanese business executives that 'What is good for the LDP is good for a firm, and what is good for a firm is good for employees'. As Japanese top managers began to recognize the arrival of an economic recession, a number of Japanese firms began to indulge in a 'cost-reduction competition', including a massive lay-off of middle managers and white- and blue-collar workers. Not surprisingly, employees who, believing in the long-cherished 'lifetime employment system' and who had devoted most of their life to their firms, began to feel that they were betrayed. Their distrust in these firms has escalated to a distrust in firms at large.

(2)   Firm > consumer
———→ consumer's distrust in firms at large
———→ 'silent revolt' by consumer

During the last 38 years of LDP government, both Japanese government and bureaucrats developed a series of policies and administrative guidances (*gyosei shido*) favorable to large firms, as shown in Figure 6.2, to the disadvantage of Japanese consumers. The dominant values introduced allowed the iron triangle to function efficiently. The collapse of the bubble economy in the early 1990s followed by the Kanemaru scandal in March 1993, however, revealed a long list of firms who had indulged in various kinds of immoral

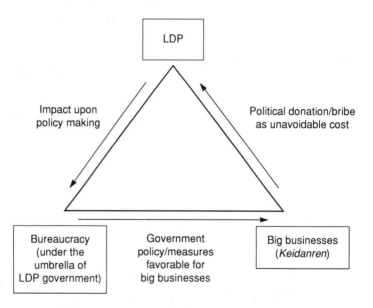

Figure 6.2   The collapse of the Japanese iron triangle (1955–93)

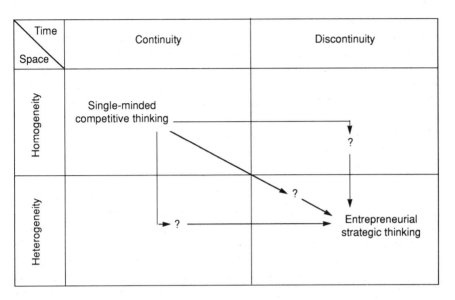

Figure 6.3   From competitive to strategic thinking

and criminal behavior. As a natural repercussion, Japanese consumers' general distrust in firms, and of large firms in particular, has reached an unprecedented high level, leading to a 'silent revolt' in terms of a deliberate reluctance to purchase medium- or high-priced products.

(3)   Large firm > medium and small firm
——→ entrepreneurial (once) medium-sized and small firm > bureaucratic and self-corrupted large firm

During the last 38 years of LDP government, Japanese government and bureaucrats, in collaboration, developed a series of policies favorable to large firms to the disadvantage of medium-sized and small firms. Ironically, the post-cold war era has begun to see a new trend towards two extremes. At one extreme, a slowly increasing number of entrepreneurial (once) medium-sized and small firms, taking advantage of value priorities being reversed began to enjoy high sales growth and profits. Nintendo and Sega Enterprises are just two of these firms staffed by highly entrepreneurial top managers. At another extreme, many bureaucratic and corrupt large firms have found themselves in loss situations. One of the common denominators of this second group runs as follows. Top managers within these firms became so successful in the upper-left quadrant of Figure 6.3 that, at the time of the change in global geopolitics, their success model in the past has not allowed them to develop a new way of strategic thinking in the lower-right quadrant of Figure 6.3. Their mentality seems to deserve the author's coined phrases such as 'strategic autism syndrome' and 'strategic dementia syndrome'.

(4)   Manufacturer > wholesaler and retailer > manufacturer
——→ wholesaler and retailer
——→ price revolution

During the last 38 years of LDP government, the Japanese government and bureaucrats developed a series of policies favorable for manufacturers to the disadvantage of wholesalers and retailers. This basic attitude is symbolized by the fixed-price sales system in the Japanese cosmetic industry. As a result, the former enjoyed much stronger bargaining power than the latter up to the end of the 1970s. The 1980s, however, began to see a fundamental shift in the bargaining power between the two supported by mass consumption and mass distribution. To be specific, the bargaining power of major supermarkets became relatively stronger than that of typical manufacturers. In addition, the bargaining power of some wholesalers has become much stronger in the early 1990s than in the 1980s as a result of their effort to rationalize the physical distribution system. The new deregulation policy of Hosokawa's Eight-Party Administration has been reinforcing the superior bargaining power of wholesalers and retailers. It is natural, therefore, to see a slowly increasing number of these taking advantage of their closer proximity to consumers to develop a novel price policy. For example, three aggressive companies such as Aoki International, Aoyama Trading and Kawachiya have been using the reversed value priority as a business opportunity to become the leaders of a 'price revolution'.

(5)   Quality of product > quality of life
——→ quality of life > quality of product (beyond TQC)

As discussed above, an increased number of Japanese manufacturers began to take advantage of TQC in developing a stronger competitive edge *vis-à-vis* their American counterparts since the late 1970s. As is well known, the new competitive situation has resulted in a series of US–Japan trade frictions, first in the manufacturing sector and second in the service sector. As far as the US–Japan trade friction is concerned, it has been expanding to almost the whole business sector, including highly advanced technologies and agricultural products. As far as the geographical area of Japan's friction is concerned, the late 1980s and the early 1990s began to see not only EC–Japan but also South Korea–Japan and Thailand–Japan frictions, just to name a few. Apart from trade friction, over-emphasis of TQC within Japanese firms, Japan manufacturers in particular, coupled with a typical 'me-too' attitude of deliberate market-share competition has resulted in the following five subissues beyond TQC:

- TQC activities have generally led mediocre Japanese firms to 'over-engineering' and 'over-service', resulting in a decreased level of customer satisfaction.
- Over-emphasis on TQC by typical Japanese manufacturers has resulted in their emphasis on 'product identity' to the detriment of 'corporate identity'. Top managers within those companies have been imbued with a notion that 'the aggregation of a partial optimum leads to a corporate optimum'.
- The QCD concept within the whole context of TQC has led mediocre Japanese firms to over-emphasis on 'customer satisfaction' to the detriment of 'other stake-holders' satisfaction'.
- TQC activities have generally led mediocre Japanese firms to an over-emphasis on 'quality of product' to the detriment of employees' 'quality of life' as symbolized by longer working hours than those of advanced countries.
- Many Western firms, American ones in particular, have been making selective use of TQC (including QCD) to successfully implement their entrepreneurial strategy. In contrast, a number of their Japanese counterparts have been suffering from a 'TQC panacea syndrome', resulting in large losses.

In summary, the time has come for Japanese managers to shift to 'a new management paradigm beyond TQC'.

A NEW MANAGEMENT PARADIGM: MANAGEMENT BY CREATION (MBC)

Four Points of Discussion

As mentioned above, the major purpose of a new management

paradigm is to search for the creation of diverse values for stakeholders and, through this process, ultimately, of the firm's *raison d'être*. In this section the author would like to draw the attention of the reader to the following four points of discussion:

- Evolution of the management paradigm in Japan
- Framework of management by creation (MBC)
- Three levels of seven kinds of value
- Alignment of seven kinds of value

Evolution of the management paradigm in Japan

Figure 6.4 illustrates the three evolutionary stages of management paradigm in Japan (Nakamura, 1992a). In contrast to Paradigm 1 (Management by 'Across-the-Board Growth') and Paradigm 2 (Management by 'Selective Growth'), Paradigm 3 (Management by Creation) is characterized by creation.

The author was intrigued by his own insights into strategic management being practiced in two distinguished firms such as Kao (Nakamura *et al.*, 1989) and Canon (Yamashita *et al.*, 1991) to develop a new MBC hypothesis in collaboration with his colleague, Professor Tatsuya Yamashita. These two firms have the three common

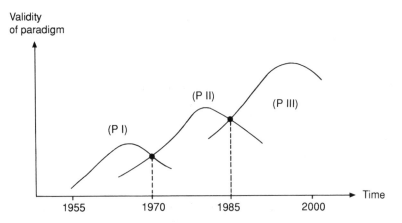

Figure 6.4 Evolution of the management paradigm in Japan. PI = the first paradigm of management by 'across-the-board growth'; PII = the second paradigm of management by 'selective growth'; PIII = the third paradigm of management by 'creation'

denominators of the existence of entrepreneurial top managers, positioning of philosophy-driven management as the core of strategic management and the creation of unique, heterogeneous and novel values through SWAN (Seeds, Wants and Needs) cycle management (Nakamura, 1990).

The original concept by MBC was developed in 1991 and has been elaborated partly by the author's empirical applications to the real world at the TPOs of his own consultations, in-house training and open seminars and partly through a series of ongoing discussions between the two and with other colleagues of the JSMS (Japan Strategic Management Society)

Framework of management by creation (MBC)

Table 6.1 shows the static framework of MBC in which two different

Table 6.1 Static framework of management by creation (MBC)

Standpoint of strategic management	Unique, heterogeneous and novel values created through MBC and offered to stakeholders	Mark
Corporate standpoint (S1 + S2 + S3): corporate posture	Creation of different, relevant values with aligned levels offered to different stakeholders	V_0
Partial standpoint (S1): strategy posture	Creation of relevant values offered to customers	V_1
	Creation of relevant values offered to society at large	V_2
Partial standpoint (S2): system posture	Creation of different, relevant values added offered to different interest groups	V_3
	Creation of relevant system values (generation of cash) to be invested in the future growth of the firm	V_4
Partial standpoint (S3): structure posture	Creation of relevant values offered to individual associates as stages for their own professional self-actualization within the firm	V_5
	Creation of relevant values offered to organization itself as group of individual associates who develop and implement strategies (S1) effectively	V_6

partial values to be created for and supplied to two different stakeholders are identified for each component of three S3 (S1 + S2 + S3) of strategic management (Nakamura, 1992b). These six different partial values—for customers, for society at large, for interest groups, system values (generated cash as source of investment in the further creation of values in the future), for individual associates and organizational values—are integrated into one corporate value or a firm's *raison d'être* in society at local, national, regional, international, global or transnational levels.

Three levels of seven kinds of value

In each of seven kinds of value, three qualitative levels such as low, medium and high can be identified. The underlying criterion of qualitatively assessing three levels of creation is simple. The qualitative levels of mediocre, homogeneous and existing values offered by a firm is 'low' at one extreme. That of unique, heterogeneous and novel values created by a firm is 'high' at another extreme, with 'medium' located between the two.

Alignment of seven kinds of value

Table 6.2 illustrates the dynamic framework of MBC in terms of alignment or misalignment between six different partial values at three levels. The three levels of those six different values are illustrated in Tables 6.2–6.7. The author was intrigued first by Ansoff's alignment model (Ansoff, 1979) and second, by the reported failure of the IBM group in 1991 to develop this alignment model of MBC.

The solid line in Figure 6.5 represents 'internal alignment'—a good fit at whatever level between six different partial values offered or created by a firm. In contrast, the dotted line stands for 'internal misalignment'—a misfit between six different partial values offered or created by a firm.

For a firm to develop an 'external alignment' to obtain a passport for survival in a given corporate environment, it is essential for it to develop an 'external alignment' with its corporate environment at the level required by the environment. Given the fact that, as discussed in the previous section, the turbulence level of the corporate environment in the post-cold war era has been and will be higher, Japanese firms should be willing and skilful to move to a new management paradigm (MBC) and develop 'both external and internal alignments of creation' at the medium level at least, and,

Table 6.2 Three levels of value for existence (*raison d'être*) (S1 + S2 + S3)

Attribute	L	Level M	H
Level of social responsibility consciousness	Low	Reasonable	High
Coverage of value	Interest group	Interest group–stakeholder	Stakeholder
Level of creating and offering six partial values	Low	Reasonable	Relatively or very high
Level of understanding/ acceptance/trust/ support	Far below the reasonable level by interest group	Reasonable level by interest group–stakeholder	Relatively or very high level by stakeholder
Societal trust in the firm	Target for 'societal distrust' in the firm	Access to a 'passport for regional citizen'	Access to 'Passport for a global citizen'

Table 6.3 Three levels of value for customers (S1)

Attribute	L	Level M	H
Appeal to	Customers' needs	Customers' needs	Customers' wants
Approach	Passive	Active	Creative
Performance level of products/ services	Conventional Homogeneous Existing	Conventional + partial improvements	Unique
		Homogeneous + partial improvements	Heterogeneous
		Existing + partial improvements	Novel
Observance of TQC (including QCD—Quality, cost, delivery)	Low level of QCD	Medium–high level of QCD	Beyond QCD (Reasonable price for excellent quality)

Continued overleaf

Table 6.3   Three levels of value for customers (S1) *(continued)*

Attribute	L	Level M	H
Interrelations with other values	No considerations to value for society	Some considerations to value for society	Considerations for co-existence with value for society
	Unfavorable for value creations in S2 + S3	Immune to value creations in S2 + S3	Favorable for value creations in S2 + S3

Table 6.4   Three levels of value for society at large (S1)

Attribute		L	Level M	H
Slogan		What is good for the firm is good for society at large	The firm and society at large are close interrelated	What is good for society at large is good for the firm
Contribution to societal activities	Individual level	None	None	Corporate associates being encouraged by the firm to commit themselves to societal activities
	Company level	None	Willingness to support societal activities in proportion to the level of resultant current profit	Willingness to support societal activities within the range of planned budget
Attitude		'Paying corporate tax is more than sufficient	Fund for societal activities being regarded as 'profit dividend'	Fund for societal activities being regarded as 'societal cost'

Table 6.5   Three levels of value added and system value (cash generation) (S2)

Attribute	L	Level M	H
Value added Attitude	Self-interest	Co-existence with interest group	Co-existence with stakeholder
Coverage of value allocation	Interest group	Interest group	Stakeholder
Level of added value and its allocation	As small as possible	Reasonable	Sufficient
System value Attitude	Self-interest	Co-existence with interest groups	Co-existence with stakeholders
Level of cash generation	Low: too far below to satisfy major interest group	Reasonable (not sufficient to satisfy high expectation level of stakeholder)	Sufficient to continuously develop MBC and to satisfy high expectations of stakeholder
Reliance on external cash source	High	Reasonable	Minimum–none

Table 6.6   Three levels of value for individual associates (S3)

Attribute	L	Level M	H
Slogan	What is good for the firm is good for the people	The firm and the people are closely interrelated	What is good for an individual associate is good for the firm
Individual associates encouraged by the firm to commit to professional self-actualization	None–low	Selectively	Sufficient

continued overleaf

Table 6.6   Three levels of value for individual associates (S3) *(continued)*

Attribute	L	Level M	H
Respect to individual dignity and quality of life	None	Selectively	Sufficient
Target area for above self-actualization	None	Within the firm	Both within the firm and in society

Table 6.7   Three levels of value for the organization itself (S3)

Attribute	L	Level M	H
Attitude	Boss versus people	Individual as equal partner	Individual as equal entrepreneur
Organizational view	Organizational hierarchy	Organizational network	Group of individual associates
Expected roles to be played	Top managers as decision makers and people as	Vertical interaction	Each individual associate expected to play both decision maker's and implementor's roles
Individual behavior	Passive	Active	Dynamic and creative
Characteristic of individual	Homogeneous	Major–homo-geneous, minor–hetero-geneous	Heterogeneous

hopefully, also at the high level. Figures 6.6 and 6.7 illustrate the alignments of Kao in the Japanese context and of Canon in the global context, respectively.

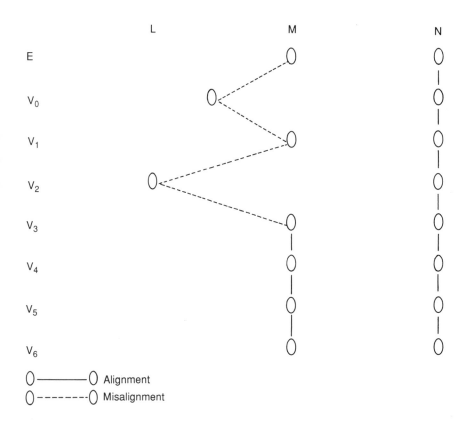

○─────○ Alignment
○-------○ Misalignment

Figure 6.5 Alignment of MBC between seven kinds of values

PSYCHOLOGICAL BARRIERS FOR TYPICAL JAPANESE MANAGERS

In this section we would like to develop a tentative conclusion by pinpointing several psychological barriers for typical Japanese managers when they try to perceive strategic implications and to shift to a new management paradigm. As far as strategic syndromes are concerned, there seems to be no international border between advanced Western countries and Japan in the sense that Japanese managers have been suffering from the same strategic syndromes as their Western predecessors. These include:

- Chinese restaurant syndrome
- Delegation/abdication syndrome

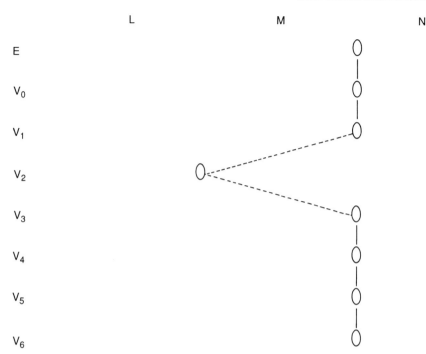

Figure 6.6   Alignment of MBC in Kao in the Japanese context

- Gresham's law syndrome
- Oedipus complex syndrome
- One-man show syndrome
- Paralysis by analysis syndrome
- Perfunctory meeting syndrome
- Pie-in-the-sky syndrome
- Separation syndrome
- Strategic myopia syndrome

The above strategic syndromes are well known and self-explanatory. Therefore, we would like to pinpoint a new type of emerging strategic syndromes from which typical Japanese managers, senior or junior, have been suffering. These include:

- Autism syndrome
- Dementia syndrome
- Information filter syndrome
- 'TQC panacea' syndrome

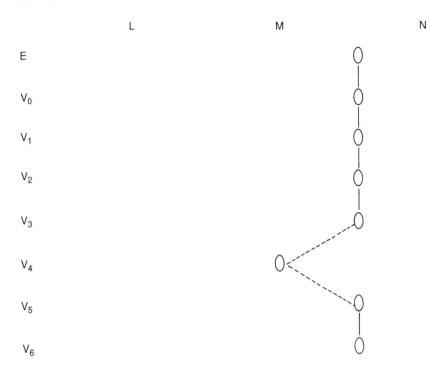

Figure 6.7 Alignment of MBC in Canon in the global context

These strategic syndromes have been discussed above. The common denominator perceived by the author among these four syndromes is that they were cherished by mediocre Japanese firms in the era of the two traditional management paradigms which made a significant contribution to Japan's success from 1955 to 1985. In other words, Japan's experience of long-lasting economic recession has been offering evidence for the validity of the phrase 'Success breeds failure'.

For mediocre Japanese firms to overcome these built-in syndromes, they will have to deal with a series of unprecedented strategic challenges in each area of strategic management (S1 + S2 + S3) as well as in the whole context.

Strategic challenges in the area of strategy S1 include:

- Development of strategy at the highest level of aggressiveness (Nakamura, 1990, 1992a; Nakamura *et al.*, 1989; Yamashita *et al.*, 1991)
- Effective use of supporting strategies (Nakamura, 1992a)

- Creation of unique, heterogeneous and new values for customers and society at large (Tables 6.3 and 6.4)

Strategic challenges in the area of system S2 include:

- Change of long-cherished seniority system
- Change of long-cherished lifetime employment system
- Change in general meetings including more openness to stockholders and society at large
- Change in board meetings, including invitation of external board members and the introduction of an earlier retirement system
- Effective use of SWAN cycle, including management speed (Nakamura, 1992b)
- Creation of unique, heterogeneous and new values added and system values (Table 6.5)

Strategic challenges in the area of structure S3 include:

- Leaning and meaning of traditional organizational structure
- Effective use of spin-off strategy including organization of subsidiaries
- Effective use of 'pot-lid' type of organizational structure (Nakamura, 1991)
- Effective use of plural corporate life system (Nakamura, 1991)
- Effective use of multi-functional/multi-divisional CEO system (Nakamura, 1991)
- Effective development of in-house executive training programs particularly for top managers with special focus on a shift from competitive to strategic thinking (Figure 6.3)
- Effective use of 'shortened space-time distance (STD)' (Nakamura, 1991)

Strategic challenges in the area of strategic management as a whole (S1 + S2 + S3) include:

- Top managers' perception of the highest level of environmental turbulence in the post-cold war era (or the end of Japan's miracle)
- Top managers' recognition of urgent and crucial need for a shift of the management paradigm (Figure 6.4)
- Top managers' willingness and skilfullness in effectively constructing a new paradigm of 'management by creation (MBC)' (Tables 6.1–6.7)
- Top managers' willingness and skilfullness in developing

'planned continuity of entrepreneurship through planned discontinuity of presidency' (Nakamura, 1991)
• Effective positioning of philosophy- and vision-driven management and MBC at the core of strategic management.

By way of a tentative conclusion, Japanese firms, in general, will have to take a long and hard road to an unprecedented challenge of becoming 'non-Japanese firms'.

REFERENCES

Ansoff, H. I. (1979) *Strategic Management*, New York, Macmillan.
Nakamura, G.-I. *et al.* (1989) *Kao: Non-Rival Management* (in Japanese), Diamond Publishing Co.
Nakamura, G.-I. (1990) New dynamics of strategic management in the global context of the 1990's. In Hussey, D. (ed.), *International Review of Strategic Management*, Chichester, John Wiley.
Nakamura, G.-I. (1991) A new breed of dynamic management. In Hussey, D. (ed.), *International Review of Strategic Management*, Vol. 2, Chichester, John Wiley.
Nakamura, G.-I. (1992a) Development of strategic management in Asia/Pacific region. In Hussey, D. (ed.), *International Review of Strategic Management*, Vol. 3, Chichester, John Wiley.
Nakamura, G.-I. (1992b) Invitation to SWAN cycle management (in Japanese). *Strategic Management Review*, **17**, No. 1.
Yamashita, T., Nakamura, G.-I. *et al.* (1991) *Canon* (in Japanese), Diamond Publishing Co.

7

THE WATCH INDUSTRY: A STRATEGIC ANALYSIS

Chiara Bentivogli

Banca d'Italia

Hans H. Hinterhuber

University of Innsbruck

and Sandro Trento

Banca d'Italia

OVERVIEW

The watch industry presents us with a typical example of the way in which shifts in competitive advantage occur. Historically, the predominance of each watch-manufacturing centre has been repeatedly challenged. Despite the position of outright leadership which the Swiss watch industry enjoyed for several hundred years, this industry nevertheless had to yield its prime position in the market to the Japanese. However, the 1980s saw the Swiss regain their hegemony in the watch industry. The idea that once they have entered a particular market Japanese firms are invincible was shown to be untenable. The aim of this study is to indicate the strategies which competing firms have used either to establish leading positions in the market or to regain dominant positions previously lost to the competition.

International Review of Strategic Management, volume 5
Edited by D. E. Hussey © 1994 John Wiley & Sons Ltd

The method of analysis employed in this study involves an examination of competitive advantage. The study is intended to exemplify certain general points about competitive strategy so that readers who are not primarily involved in the watch industry will, nevertheless, find the study useful.

The results of the study will also be of interest to those involved in the watch industry. These results provide a comprehensive view of the forces which have determined the development of an important industrial sector. These forces may, as they evolve in the future, play a definitive role in that sector. Our findings are also of wider theoretical and practical relevance since they indicate how firms which compete globally can regain lost positions and gain sustainable advantage.

THE BACKGROUND TO THIS STUDY

Over the last few years a certain view of the Japanese as competitors has gained widespread acceptance. This view may be summarised in the frequently expressed conviction that once Japanese firms have entered a particular market they are then invincible. This view seemed to have been confirmed by observing trends in the watch market up to the end of the 1970s. However, in the past ten years, the Swiss watch industry, which most people had thought of as a lame duck, has been able to regain a leading position in world markets.

The watch industry presents a typical example of a shift occurring in the nature of the factors which determine competitive advantage. What follows is a description of the development of the watch industry, indicating the strategies which the competing firms have adopted in response to changing circumstances. This work is intended to provide a case study of an industry. Readers who will, for the most part, not be involved in the watch industry may nevertheless derive many useful insights from the study.

THE GEOGRAPHICAL LOCATION OF THE WATCH INDUSTRY—A CHANGING PICTURE

Over the last few hundred years the geographical centre of the watch industry has shifted considerably. In no case, other than that of Switzerland, was it possible for a country to maintain a position of any importance in the industry once new competitors had appeared on the scene. It is a characteristic of watch production that the industry can take root in many different geographical environments. This fact certainly made it easier for leadership in the industry to shift from one country to another.

Southern Germany was the first centre of watch production. In the sixteenth century this region was one of the most important commercial centres in Europe. During this period German industry benefited from the existence of a large internal market composed of the numerous minor states into which the country was divided at that time. During the sixteenth century Italy closely resembled Germany in that it too was divided into very many minor statelets. However, unlike Germany, Italy has no watch industry. Landes (1979) is of the opinion that this fact might be explained by reference to the different degree of importance which is attached to the concept of time in the two societies.

At the close of the first quarter of the seventeenth century France was able to wrest the position of market leadership in the watch industry from Germany. The French were able to retain their leading position in the market for around fifty years, their success being attributable to their expertise in the production of expensively and intricately enamelled watches. This period of French leadership in the market did not, however, last long. Towards the end of the seventeenth century, British watch manufacturers conquered the market. Their competitive advantage was based on their ability to produce watches which, in comparison with the products of their rivals, were manufactured with greater precision and kept better time. Watches produced in the first half of the seventeenth century were not conspicuously reliable. Even a good watch typically lost or gained half an hour in the course of a day. It was not until 1680 that the minute hands were introduced—before this time, watches kept time so inexactly that minute hands would have merely been an irrelevance.

At the time when Britain achieved its position of leadership in the watch industry, the country was already a leading naval power. This provided a natural impetus for the development of technical innovation in the field of chronometry since both naval and merchantile marine interests were vitally interested in improved methods of time-keeping. The watch industry played an important role in the British Industrial Revolution. In the watch industry, workers acquired skills in precision engineering and these skills could be transferred to other industrial sectors which then also flourished (Cipolla, 1967, p. 108; Mokyr, 1985, p. 76).

During the eighteenth century France kept losing market share. In 1718, a royal watch factory was established in Versailles. English craftsmen were engaged in the hope that they would be able to inject renewed dynamism into the French watch industry. However, these efforts largely failed: English manufacturers were able to retain their leading position in the market. A factor contributing to their success was their use of the techniques of task specialisation and division of labour. A factor which contributed to the eclipse of the French watch industry was the revocation of the Edict of Nantes in 1685. This meant that Huguenot watchmakers, who had been the mainstay of the French watch industry, left the country.

It was only towards the end of the eighteenth century that Switzerland achieved global dominance in the watch industry. At this time certain Huguenot watchmakers established the first workshops in the valleys of the Jura mountains in Switzerland. Here they found a cheap and comparatively well-trained labour force (Landes, 1979). In contrast to other watch-producing countries, the Swiss watch industry was, from the very beginning, geared towards the export market. The limited opportunities offered by the home market meant that exporting was a necessity. This exposure to foreign competition may perhaps explain the efforts which Swiss watch manufacturers made to achieve very high standards in both product quality and product appearance.

Historically, countries which have begun to lose market share to competitor nations have tended to underestimate the competences of their new competitors. In the eighteenth century British watchmakers considered that the technical quality of their watches could not be surpassed. The level of technical excellence was, they believed, the sole determinant of the extent to which a given product would be able to maintain its degree of competitive advantage. Unfortunately, the needs and wishes of the customer disproved this assumption. Swiss watchmakers were able to produce watches which were not only technically superior to those of their British competitors but even looked better as well. Similar developments have occurred more recently, as will be shown in the discussion which follows.

THE WATCH INDUSTRY IN THE SEVENTIES

For many years as many as 80% of all the watches produced in the world were made in Switzerland. Only by making vigorous use of tariff barriers were foreign competitors able to retain significant market share in their own home markets (Oberender, 1988, p. 58).

Figure 7.1 shows developments in world production of watches and watch movements during the period 1982–92. Tables 7.1(a) and

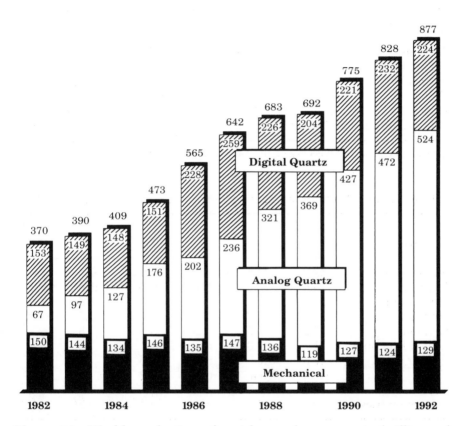

Figure 7.1 World production of watches and movements (millions of pieces). In 1992 the estimated world production of watches and movements reached a total of 877 million units indicating an increase of 6% compared to 1991 figures.

Analog quartz products (hands display) totalized 524 million units (+ 11%), maintaining their leading position in total production. Digital quartz watches (LCD display) production decreased of 3.5% to 224 million units. Mechanical time pieces registered a worldwide production progression of 4% to 129 million units.

Estimated value of world production reached a total of SFr 14.6 billion, representing a slight increase of 4% compared to 1991. (See also Table 7.2.) (*Source:* Federation of the Swiss Watch Industry)

Table 7.1(a)   World production (volume) of watches and movements (%)

Countries	Years 1960	1970	1975	1980	1985	1990	1991	1992
Switzerland	44.8	44.3	34.4	29.4	15.3	13.1	15.9	16.5
Japan	7.2	13.9	13.9	29.3	37.4	44.4	46.6	42.5
Hong Kong	—	—	2.6	19.7	20.1	21.9	20.5	20.0
France	5.7	6.4	7.7	7.7	4.2	3.2	2.5	1.8
Germany	8.0	4.9	4.3	2.2	0.6	0.4	0.3	—
United Kingdom	2.9	1.3	2.8	1.1	—	—	—	—
Former USSR	—	—	—	—	9.0	5.7	4.8	—
China	—	—	—	—	8.8	9.1	—	—
USA	9.7	11.3	12.2	4.0	0.4	—	—	—
Other countries	21.7	17.9	22.1	6.6	4.2	2.2	9.4	19.2

Source: Federation of Swiss Watch Industry (FH) (estimates).

Table 7.1(b)   World production (value) of watches and movements (%)

Countries	Years 1975	1980	1985	1990	1991	1992
Switzerland	47.2	44.5	35.6	55.1	52.8	54.7
Japan	24.4	38.0	29.8	21.5	25.6	22.1
Hong Kong	n.a.	n.a.	4.1	8.5	8.6	8.4
France	8.4	7.7	3.1	3.0	2.5	2.6
Germany	5.3	3.8	1.3	1.8	1.8	—
United Kingdom	1.7	1.0	n.a.	n.a.	—	—
Former USSR	n.a.	n.a.	n.a.	3.5	—	—
China	n.a.	n.a.	n.a.	5.2	—	—
USA	12.0	3.2	2.4	n.a.	—	—
Other countries	0.8	1.8	25.9	1.4	8.7	12.2

Source: Federation of Swiss Watch Industry (FH) (estimates).

7.1(b) present a breakdown in percentage terms, first, of the volume of watch production (Table 7.1(a)) and second (Table 7.1(b)), of the value of watch production achieved by the different countries. Figure 7.2, helps to explain why a breakdown by value and by volume produce such divergent pictures. With the exception of Swatch, the Swiss watch industry has concentrated on the high-price segment of the market and has allowed Japanese competitors to take over the low-price one.

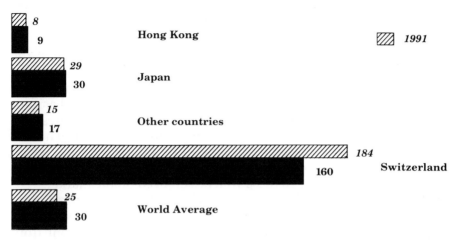

Figure 7.2 Average export prices of watches in 1990 (in Swiss francs). (*Source:* Federation of the Swiss Watch Industry)

As long as the watch remained a mechanical instrument the decisive factors in watch production remained precision and craftsmanship. These qualities were typical of the Swiss watch industry and were the result of centuries of experience in the area of precision engineering. In fact, there had been no radical changes in the techniques of watch production for several centuries.

Such improvements as a reduction in the size of the casing, the achievement of greater precision, the development of waterproof watches and the introduction of automatic winding mechanisms had occurred. However, the basis of the Swiss watch was the same mechanism which Swiss craftsmanship had developed over the course of several centuries.

In 1960 the Swiss engineer Max Hetzel invented the 'Stimmgabeluhr' (Bulova Accutron). The Swiss watchmakers, however, arrogantly dismissed Hetzel's invention as a fad which was not only unworthy of the highly sophisticated traditions of Swiss craftsmanship but was also likely to prove short-lived.

In fact, Hetzel's invention was not significantly different from the traditional mechanical watch. The transfer and regulatory mechanisms remained the same. However, shortly after Hetzel's invention, in 1962, the Centre for Electronic Watch Research was founded. The centre had as its aim the development of the quartz watch and the first quartz watch in the world was created here. This watch was the prototype for a series of products which were brought onto the market in 1970 under various names (Brauchlin-Wehrli, 1991, p. 83).

The beginning of the 1970s heralded a veritable revolution in the watch industry. Electronic watches were being brought onto the market at prices so low that it was clear that the mass consumer was being targeted. These new watches functioned on the basis of semiconductor technology and quartz crystals. Digital figures and liquid crystals replaced the hands of the traditional watch. The fact that all the parts of these watches could be mass produced, which thereby kept production costs to a minimum, explains the exceptional success which these watches enjoyed on the market.

The assembly of the traditional mechanical watch requires great manual dexterity and a high proportion of direct skilled labour hours. For this reason, it was not generally possible to profit from economies of scale by increasing the average size of the manufacturing units. However, in the manufacturing of electronic watches savings can be realised not only through economies of scale but also by taking advantage of the effects of the learning curve (Figure 7.3).

After decades during which very little had changed in the watch market, the late 1970s saw an ever-increasing number of new market entrants attempting to achieve an ever more rapid penetration of the market. Firms like the US company Texas Instruments entered the market for low-priced watches in 1975. Seiko began to market its quartz watches in 1969. The Casio Computer Company, however, waited until 1974 before it launched its product on the market. Producers from Hong Kong were comparative laggards and waited until 1976 before launching their own offensive in the electronic watch market.

By 1975, the Swiss share of world watch production in volume terms had shrunk to 34%. By 1970, Japan had already overtaken the United States in terms of volume of watches produced (Table 7.1(a)).

US firms failed to take advantage of the lead which they enjoyed over other nations in respect of semiconductor technology. This lead could have been used first to seize the watch market from the competition and then continue to dominate it. In 1975, Stewart Carrel, the director of the consumer goods division of Texas Instruments Inc. said, 'There is no doubt that the digital quartz will bring the watch business back to the United States.'

In the mid-1970s the prospects for the Swiss watch industry looked gloomy with the exception of the small market niche represented by mechanically driven luxury watches.

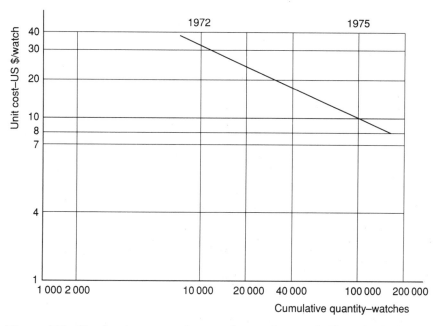

Figure 7.3 Production costs for an electronic watch (based on figures from the Samson Science Corporation)

AN ANALYSIS OF THE COMPETITIVE FORCES AT WORK WITHIN THE INDUSTRY

The situation within the market for watches will be analysed using the model proposed by Porter (Porter, 1983, p. 60; Oster, 1990, p. 108). We shall, however, extend the model by adding two additional factors which serve to determine the behaviour of firms in the given market. These two additional factors are 'state interference' and 'the behaviour of worker and workers' organisations' (Figure 7.4) (Hinterhuber, 1992, p. 81). Figure 7.5 presents the oligopolistic structure of the watch industry.

Substitute Products

There is basically no other product which can substitute for the watch in its basic time-measurement function. However, the watch market is segmenting. In the luxury watch segment the position of

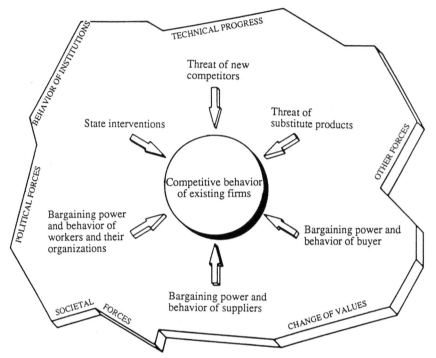

Figure 7.4   Model of competitive analysis

the watch as a lavish status item is being increasingly threatened by gold and jewellery products. The status and prestige which the watch imparts to the customer are most significant in the high-price segment of the market. Finally, at the other end of the market spectrum, the multi-functional digital watch comes into competition with pocket calculators, personal organisers and other micro-electronic devices which also possess a time-display function. In this market segment the significant factor is the degree of time-keeping accuracy.

Demand

Traditionally, the watch industry experiences seasonal fluctuations, and 45% of watch sales take place in the last quarter of a given year. Until the 1970s, watches were usually purchased as gifts to mark

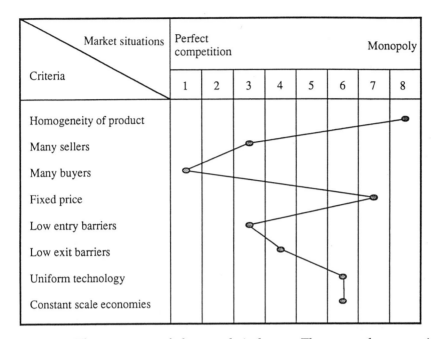

Figure 7.5   The structure of the watch industry. The more the curve is located in the right half of the figure, the more the hypothesis of perfect competition in the watch industry is invalidated

special occasions—celebrations, birthdays, passing an examination, and so on.

The watch market can be divided into three categories on the basis of price (Brauchlin-Wehrli, 1991, p. 91):

Segment C: Cheaper watches selling at prices under 120 Swiss francs; watches in this category account for more than 80% of all watches sold in volume terms and 30% in value terms.

Segment B: Watches retailing at prices between 120 and 700 Swiss francs.

Segment A: Watches retailing at prices ranging from 700 to 5000 Swiss francs; watches in this category account for around 2% of all watches sold in volume terms but represent 25% of all watches sold in value terms.

Segment AA: This segment includes luxury watches retailing at over 5000 Swiss francs. They are produced for an exclusive clientele.

The name on the watch is a crucial factor in establishing its global brand image.

Segments A and AA are dominated by mechanically driven watches. In the other categories electronic watches predominate. Figure 7.2 gives the average export prices of watches from selected countries.

In the course of the 1970s the watch industry acquired two new groups of customers. The first consisted of children who were able to buy cheap watches decorated with pictures of cartoon characters. The second group was represented by the newly rich inhabitants of the Middle East oil-producing countries. Purchases of watches from this area gave the Swiss watch industry a badly needed fillip at a time when the industry was already coming under pressure from Japanese competition.

Demand

At the beginning of the 1970s, in the wake of the revolution which had been unleashed by the coming of digital watches, the US electronics industry became one of the main producers of components (from digital display units to integrated circuits). Texas Instruments Inc., for example, entered the market as a firm which was completely vertically integrated. It was widely hoped that backward vertical integration would reduce the cost of the components, improve the quality of the product and, in this way, establish a sustainable lead over the competition.

Mechanical watches generally contain between 150 and 200 very small component parts. High-quality watches are generally made by hand. The production of mechanical precision watches requires a highly skilled labour force. The Swiss watch industry consisted of a large number of small producers of components and watch movements. In 1960, there were around 2000 such firms producing components and watch movements. By 1970, this number had shrunk to 1000, and by 1980 the number of such firms was a mere 490 (Oberender, 1988, p. 58).

The other components of a traditional mechanical watch are rubies (or other precious stones), gold watch casings and crystal, used to make watch glasses. If the watch is an exclusive luxury item then these components will represent a correspondingly greater proportion of its total cost. Watch producers deliver of between 100 000 and 500 000 component items every year. The firms that supply these items in turn guarantee the producers price reductions of between 20% and 25% provided that these same producers purchase the component items in sufficiently large volumes. Around 80% of all the watch movements produced in Switzerland in 1980, but not used in the manufacture of complete watches in Switzerland, were exported to Hong Kong. The fact that Hong Kong achieved a position as one of the world's great watch producers is partly attributable to this stream of Swiss and other foreign components.

Table 7.2 indicates the main global trends in the export of watches and watch movements over the thirty years 1960–92. The exports are given by country in terms of volume and product value.

New Competitors Enter the Market

In 1934, a Swiss law, the Statut Juridique de l'Horologerie Suisse, forbade the export of watch components and watch movements and limited the export of watchmaking machines. The conditions under which watches could be manufactured and exported were laid down in this statute, as were pricing regulations. The statute was amended at regular intervals (Oberender, 1988, p. 58). Outside Switzerland, therefore, new entrants into the watch market were restricted to competing on lower price and offered lower quality. In Switzerland itself, at least until 1961, the Statute restricted the entry into the market of new producers and limited the expansion of producers who were already established. It was not only these legal barriers which limited the chances of a successful penetration of the Swiss watch market by a prospective new entrant. The reputation and image of Swiss watches that had been built up over decades represented a formidable invisible barrier to market entry, all the more so since this reputation and image was protected by the standards for quality set up by the Confederation of Swiss Industry.

The new electronic technology effectively lowered these barriers to entry. The Swiss watch industry had established for itself a position of predominance on the basis of its historical advantage of having been the first entrant into the mechanical watch market. This advantage was undermined by the new electronic technology. At the same time, the new technology established barriers of its own against Swiss competitors in that the production of components could now profit from the economies of scale and learning-curve effects.

Generally, the electronic watch manufacturers attacked the Swiss watch manufacturers on two fronts: first, the Swiss watch manufacturers' image for reliability and precision, and secondly, the Swiss manufacturers on price. Price competition had previously

Table 7.2 World exports of watches and movements

Years	1960		1970		1975		1980		1985		1990		1991		1992		1993	
Countries	10^6 pieces	10^6 SFr	10^6 pieces	10^6 SFr	10^6 pieces	10^6 SFr	10^6 pieces	10^6 SFr	10^6 pieces	10^6 SFr	10^6 pieces	10^6 SFr	10^6 pieces	10^6 SFr	10^6 pieces	10^6 SFr	10^6 pieces	10^6 SFr
Switzerland	41	1146	71	2363	66	2720	51	2918	39	3664	42	6014	41	6046	48	6576	51	6768
Germany	4	84	3	130	3	137	4	172	5	261	9	425	10	429	8	455		
France	12	26	4	77	10	209	10	265	6	249	6	306	5	286	5	291		
Italy			1	15	1	16	1	25	1	80	4	102	3	103	4	105		
United Kingdom			1	23	2	40	7	117	10	131	4	174	4	153	5	240		
Former USSR[a]					15		22		24						79	184		
Hong Kong	1	24	6	69	16	246	126	1856	376	2204	491	2557	419	2274	337	1915		
Japan	—	16	11	276	17	834	48	1911	125	3081	257	2310	278	2727	306	2637		
USA[a]					11		3		1									
Total		1296		2953		4202		7264		9670		11888		12018		12403		6768

[a]Estimates.
Source: Federation of the Swiss Watch Industry.

been impossible because of the Swiss manufacturers' cartel. There was also another barrier to entry into the watch market which we should mention here. This was the necessity of building up an extensive distribution network so that the products could successfully be put on the market.

The Competition

The world production of watches is concentrated into three main areas: Switzerland, the United States and the Far East (Japan and Hong Kong).

Switzerland

As we have seen above, Switzerland entered the watch market at the end of the eighteenth century when British firms were still dominant. The Swiss manufacturers were successful because they produced cheaper and more sophisticated models than the British ones (Landes, 1979). Swiss manufacturers squeezed out the British producers, managed to dominate almost the whole market and remained dominant until the mid-1960s. Switzerland retained a market-leadership position based on quality, precision and prestige for more than a century.

The watch industry was for a long time characterised by a large number of small family firms. Because the industry was not affected by economies of scale or learning-curve effects there was little tendency towards a concentration of the smaller firms into larger units. The main mergers occurred in 1931 and in the mid-1960s when there was also a rash of takeovers. In this way the Allgemeine Schweizserische Uhrenindustrie (ASUAG) and the Societé Suisse de l'Industrie Horlogère (SSIH) came into being. The ASUAG was founded in response to the worldwide economic crisis whereas the formation of the SSIH, originating in a merger between Omega and Tissot, was prompted by increase in foreign competition. Swiss watch manufacturers were dominant in the middle and upper price segments, and it was in these segments that reactions to price fluctuations tended to be less extreme. Two important factors enhanced the competitiveness of Swiss firms.

(1)   Switzerland was so proud of its watch industry, which acted as an economic indicator for other areas of commercial and industrial activity, that both the government and influential Swiss banks were

ready to support domestic watch manufacturers during economic downturns.

(2) Most of the firms were family firms and were, therefore, highly committed.

In addition, there were exit barriers because the machines used in watchmaking could not easily be adapted to other purposes This made it difficult for those involved in watchmaking to divest.

Exports of Swiss watches and assembled watch movements fell from 71 million units in 1970 to 51 million in 1993 (Table 7.2). In volume terms, the number of Japanese units produced exceeded the number of Swiss units produced for the first time in 1980 (Table 7.1(a)). Hong Kong occupied the second place in the world watch production league table, accounting for 20% of all watches produced in 1992 (Table 7.1(b)). In 1972 the Swiss launched the first digital watch with LCD (liquid crystal display) on the market at a price of $2100 (Oberender 1988, p. 58). US producers of semiconductors manufactured their watches on the basis of a learning-curve effect of around 80% (Figure 7.1). The result was that prices collapsed to $10. Swiss manufacturers were unable to compete with these prices for structural reasons and their position became critical.

The US watch industry

In the 1970s the two largest US producers were *Timex* and *Texas Instruments*. Timex began to sell cheap mechanical watches at the end of the 1950s, but these were functional rather than fashionable. Timex's strategy was to produce watches that were so cheap (no rubies were used in their manufacture) that if defects developed the cost of repairing the watch would not be warranted since the purchase price of the watch was so low in any case (Oberender, 1988, p. 60). Timex needed to develop a completely new distribution network in order to be able to bring this type of watch onto the market. The company used supermarkets, electrical appliance shops and drugstores as retail outlets. At this time, Swiss watches were only sold in jewellers' shops. For this reason the Swiss did not regard Timex as a serious competitor.

At the end of the 1960s Timex had around 50% of the US market. The firm possessed facilities to produce mechanical watches without having to rely on outside suppliers. It was not until the advent of digital watches that Timex was forced to buy-in the electronic components from outside sources. During the 1970s competition in the watch industry became fiercer as new producers from Hong

Kong, Japan and the United States entered the market. Sales plummeted, and in 1979 Timex recorded a loss. To make up for the fall in contribution from its digital watches Timex increased the prices of its mechanical ones. The result of this strategy was that producers from Hong Kong were now able to enter the market not just for digital watches but also for mechanical watches. By 1983, Timex's market share had fallen to 29.3%.

Texas Instruments launched the first digital watches on the market in 1975. The firm's strategy was based on the experience it had gained in the electronics industry and had as its aim a constant reduction in the price of its watches made possible by the effects of the learning curve, estimated to be around 80%. This strategy would effectively prevent new entrants from gaining access to the market. In addition to their policy of reducing prices for digital watches, Texas Instruments also tried to weaken the position of Timex in the mechanical watch sector. This attack on Timex was pressed home with such vigour that Timex was rendered incapable of competing in the market. In 1976 Texas Instruments took its competitors by surprise by launching a plastic digital watch on the market, which retailed at only $20. A few months later, the price was reduced to $10. Millions of these watches were sold. However, many customers were disappointed at the poor quality of these watches: the control buttons jammed and the numbers were difficult to read.

Further developments in the field of integrated circuits meant that more and more functions could be built into the digital watch. However, Texas Instruments underestimated the specific needs of the customer for, for example, stopwatch functions, alarm clock functions, the facility to determine the time in different time zones, and so on. After several years in which they experienced increasing losses, Texas Instruments withdrew from the watch market in 1981.

The watch industry in Hong Kong

Manufacturers in Hong Kong began watch production in 1976 and concentrated on the production of extremely cheap watches. In 1980 Hong Kong became the world's main producer of cheap watches.

The Hong Kong watch industry, which originally assembled its products from foreign components, soon found itself able to satisfy this need from domestic sources and built up its own network of component suppliers. This was especially true in the digital watch sector with the exception of electronic components.

Watches 'made in Hong Kong' competed mainly with Timex and

with the cheaper Japanese models; they were never a threat to the Swiss watch industry. The only real damage that the Hong Kong manufacturers did to their Swiss competitors was when they produced cheap imitations of famous, prestigiously named Swiss models.

The Japanese watch industry

Basically, three large firms dominate the Japanese watch industry: Seiko, Citizen and Casio. Hattori Seiko produced his first quartz watch in 1969. Ten years later, he had, in volume terms, the largest share of the global market. To be able to compete successfully with Swiss manufacturers in the middle price bracket, Seiko and Citizen developed a complete range of mechanical and quartz watches as well as digital and analogue ones. Given the range of mechanical and quartz watches, Casio, a computer manufacturer, decided to concentrate on quartz watches and became famous for its multi-functional watches. It was the first firm to realise that the most important criterion for success in the electronic watch market was the technical excellence of the watch, and not its appearance. All Japanese producers were completely integrated when they entered the market. At the end of the 1970s Japan was the world's most important producer of watches in terms of the number of units manufactured. At this time Japanese production first exceeded Swiss production. In 1992 Switzerland accounted for around 16.5% of the world production of watches and watch movements. Japan accounted for around 42.5% of world production, being well ahead of Hong Kong, which produced 20% of the world's watches (Table 7.3(a)). Seiko and Citizen's models had gained the reputation of being high-quality quartz watches. This reputation was reinforced by a policy of constant improvement and innovation and through an extremely efficient system of customer service.

THE WATCH INDUSTRY IN THE 1980s

In the Beginning

At the beginning of the 1980s, the United States had ceased to be a significant competitor in the watch industry. Switzerland had suffered an irreversible decline in market share when compared with the previous decade. It was generally thought that the days of the analogue watch were numbered—people would soon be regarding mechanical watches as an interesting curiosity to be found only in museums.

At the end of the 1970s the Swiss watch industry was on the verge of collapse. It was not able to take advantage of new technology and was slipping hopelessly behind its competitors from Japan and Hong Kong. In 1979 Seiko acquired the Swiss watch firm Jean Bouchet Lassalle. The thinking behind this acquisition was that Seiko wished to increase its own production in the A and AA market segments. It also intended to combine the Seiko quartz watch movement with the very thin casing that the Swiss firm had developed and designed. Parallel to this development, Citizen also introduced a series of watches in the medium-price range, bearing the name 'Le Connoisseur.' This watch displayed characteristics similar to those of the Seiko-Lassalle watches.

By 1984, digital watch technology had reached maturity and the fact that the prices of these watches had collapsed meant that they were no longer profitable. By using the most modern available technology, Seiko was, by 1975, able to achieve a position of global dominance in the medium priced quartz watch sector. The days of Swiss hegemony in the medium-price segment were over. However, by the early 1980s a firm needed more than technology to achieve competitive advantage. Hong Kong manufacturers were hard to beat. 'When the yen appreciated in 1985, Seiko had enormous inventory and felt unable to meet the competition' (Eisenstodt, 1989). By the end of the 1980s Seiko recorded a loss of US $22 million on a turnover of US $2.8 million. Two factors largely accounted for this critical situation. The first of these was the upward movement of the yen. The second was the rise of the black market or, as it was sometimes called, the *gray market*. This expression was used to describe a situation whereby official distributors obtain branded goods from non-authorised suppliers. They were, therefore, able to sell these goods at very low prices. As one of Hattori Seiko's former employees—who now works for one of Seiko's competitors—put it, 'The watches had to be sold so the firm itself supplied a great part of the gray market' (Eisenstodt, 1989). The result was that the North American market was flooded with Seiko watches at prices that were so low that the owners of many official Seiko retail outlets decided that, because of this back-stabbing method of competition, they would no longer stock Seiko watches. The Lassale line was not very successful in the AA luxury watch segment where Swiss firms like Rolex, Patek Phillipe, Blancpain and so on were very strongly represented. This could be accounted for by the fact that the Lassale line had positioned itself in the upper A segment and could not, therefore, compete successfully in the luxury watch segment. The powerful fashion houses—Gucci, Dior and Cartier had now entered the AA segment and were sourcing their entire production from Swiss suppliers. This limited the sales potential of Japanese luxury models still further.

In 1982, in the face of fierce competition from the Japanese watch industry, a consortium of Swiss bankers asked the business consultant Nicolas G. Hayek, managing director of Hayek Engineering Ltd, to initiate proceedings for the liquidation of the two largest watch manufacturers ASUAG and SSIH, both of whom were heavily in debt. Hayek was opposed to the liquidation. However, although he was not the majority shareholder, he took over the directorship of ASUAG, and then in 1983 he also assumed control of SSIH and brought about a merger of these two firms. The result of this merger was called SMH (Swiss Electronic and Watch Company Ltd). Initially, the Swiss banks supported Hayek's restructuring strategy. However, it became apparent that radical measures would be necessary which would have far-reaching effects. It also became clear that large numbers of people would have to be made redundant, and that this would have political repercussions. These two factors caused the banks to shy away from involvement with Hayek's SMH company and, subsequently, to withdraw their support. In the wake of the financial restructuring, Hayek promoted the formation of a pool of shareholders which together commanded 56% of the voting rights and 51% of the capital. Today, Hayek is chairman of the board of SMH Ltd and CEO of Swatch. He represents the interests of all the shareholders who had decided to combine their voting rights in the pool and determines the operational and strategic direction of the firm. The Swiss banks financed the new firm to the tune of US $500 million, of which 10% was spent on advertising and marketing and 90% on innovations in the field of production and operations. Once the companies which had formerly belonged to the old ASUAG and SSIH groups had been reorganised into the new SMH they were further consolidated into five largely independent business areas: complete watches, components, microelectronics, production systems and services (Figure 7.6) (Capel, 1992). The business areas are divided into around 150 strategic business units, presided over by managers who are responsible for their success as 'Profit Centers.' The board of directors of the whole concern lays down the general guidelines in such matters as the allocation of resources, appointment of managers and the co-ordination of the investment programme according to preset strategic targets. The choice of the top managers is of particular importance because of its effect on the setting of central policy guidelines. Equally important is the stance which Nicolas G. Hayek has adopted in such things as company policy and corporate culture. Human resources management is decentralised.

The rapid and unexpected success of Swatch provided the basis for a renewed upturn in the Swiss watch industry. In 1960, around 44 million watches and movements were produced. By 1992 production had risen to 877 million watches and movements of which quartz watches accounted for around 80%. Measured in value terms, Swiss manufacturers had always enjoyed a clear lead over the competition in the world watch production league tables (Table 7.3(b)).

The Strategy of Swatch Ltd

In the late 1970s Dr Ernst Thomke, a director of the firm ETA which supplied the components for SMH, realised that only a new strategy could turn around the Swiss watch industry. The mainspring of this strategy would have to be technical innovation. The aim would be to become the leading player in segment C of the market by offering the broad mass of consumers a competitively priced mass-produced quartz watch. The new watch, which bore the name Swatch (SWiss wATCH), was launched on the market in 1982. It was the first watch ever to have a casing made entirely of plastic. The base which holds the watch movement in place was also made of plastic, effecting a 40% saving in costs. The Swatch consists of 51 parts. A traditional quartz watch, on the other hand, has between 100 and 120 parts. The Swatch is characterised by the use of micro-injection technology, which enables a shell to be produced from synthetic material with extreme precision. Further distinguishing features of the Swatch are that the second hand is directly powered through the quartz and that the system for holding the watch on the arm is optimally designed from the anatomical point of view (Brauchlin-Wehrli, 1991, p. 89). A very high degree of automation was introduced into the assembly stage. The materials used meant that it was possible to produce very many variations on the basic model. Moreover, the watch represents an entirely new concept. As the former marketing director Jacques Irniger put it, 'Swatch is an accessory which also tells the time' (Tully, 1984). Initially, many people criticised the product. They considered that a 'cheap and modern watch like the Swatch was not "Swiss" enough' (Dornberg, 1988).

Swatch adopted what was for the watch industry a new strategy. The Swatch marketing team tried to persuade the customer to buy more than just one watch and not merely a watch for special

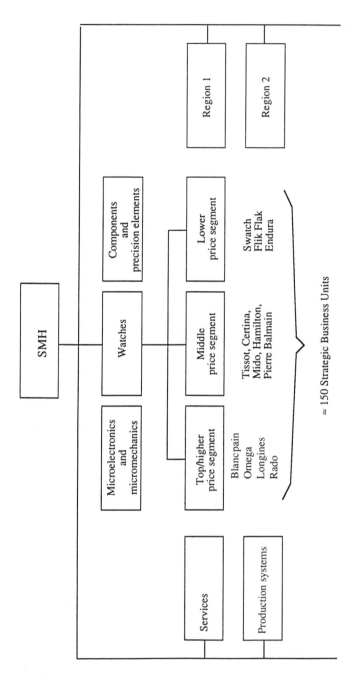

Figure 7.6   The organizational structure of SMH (adapted from Capel 1992)

occasions. Key factors in the new strategy were low prices and a constant stream of new models. These factors provided an incentive for repeat purchases and purchases of various differently designed models.

'Attack your competitor at the point where he is least expecting to be attacked' is one of Hayek's basic strategic principles. Furthermore, he added, 'the competitor is least expecting to be attacked in segment C'. The following quotations are taken from interviews which Hayek gave to the magazines and newspapers *Madame* (March 1992, pp. 68–74), *Die Welt* (14 October 1991, p. 7) and *Finanz und Wirtschaft* (16 November 1991, pp. 8–11). Some of the quotations are taken from an interview that Hayek gave to Hinterhuber in Biel on 28 February 1992 and 20 January 1994. As Hayek put it, 'We have beaten the Japanese on a battlefield which they did not expect us to choose—the cheapest price segment in the market!', 'A general cannot allow the enemy to control the whole country and content himself with withdrawing to a few fortified camps.' Similarly, 'the entrepreneur cannot abandon the low-price segment of the market and concentrate on the high-price one only' (Hinterhuber, 1993, p. 108). Hayek's strategy is first to become the main player in segment C of the market by using innovating production technology and impressive design and, second, to extend his company's leadership position in the higher price market segments with the help of know-how gained in the techniques of mass production (Figure 7.7). However, at present the Japanese producers are stronger in segment C of the market.

We can summarise the main elements of the strategy through which Swatch Ltd hopes to gain a leading position in segment C of the market as follows:

- A watch which attracts attention
- And which is of the highest quality
- At a price that everyone can afford
- A fashionable watch, the design of which is being constantly adapted
- A watch that can be worn by everyone, from managing director to manual worker
- A watch that instils in its wearer a sense of fun and 'joie de vivre.'

Decisive factors which enable these elements of strategy to be successfully implemented are:

(1) *Low costs of production:* Swatch watches are produced in fully

automated plants; production costs are around 7 Swiss francs per unit. The high level of education and training in Switzerland produces skilled production and operations managers. Their salaries are no higher than those of managers in comparable positions in other parts of the world and their skills ensure maximum utilisation of plant capacity. By international standards, the cost of capital in Switzerland is low.

(2) *High expenditure on research and development:* The more intensive the rate of technological progress, the more product development cycles must be shortened and the more important it becomes for the firm to generate innovations. The research and development section of SMH serves as a source of know-how and back-up service for watch production. Because of the know-how it has developed in the area of microchip production and in the automated manufacture and assembly of very small mechanical and electronic components, SMH is a very flexible watch producer. The company excels at minimising the time between the development of a new product and its market launch.

(3) *Constant product innovation:* Swatch Ltd is able to bring out two collections of watches every year. Each of these comprises 30 different models. Additionally, many other new watches for specific purposes are being developed. These include scuba, chrono, paging devices, ceramic watches and mechanical watches. Because of the wide range of products offered to the market—from products which emphasise high quality to those the key selling points of which are low prices—Swatch Ltd was able to increase its share of world market in the low-price segment in 1991 by over 10% in volume terms.

(4) *Original design:* The design laboratory in Milan is keen to ensure that Swatch is not just a cheap watch. It should be an expression of a feeling or a philosophy—joie de vivre, colour, humour, attention arousal, these should be emotions conjured up by a Swatch. This should go hand in hand with high quality and low price.

(5) *Brand strengths:* In value terms, SMH, which has leading brands in all price segments, has more than 10% of the world market share. Thanks to Swatch, SMH was able, for the first time, to establish a brand name in the lowest price segment. Generally, the better known a brand is and the larger the proportion of market share accounted for by international sales, the larger the amount of achievable contribution. The stronger the international presence and brand name, the more savings can be achieved in the area of advertising and public relations. The effects of

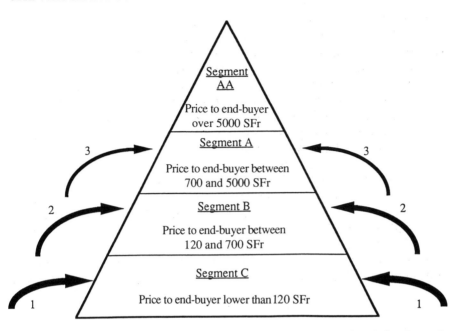

Figure 7.7 The strategy of SMH. 1: The guiding principle of the Swatch strategy is to occupy and consolidate a leading market position in the low-price segment, using both technology and design as competitive weapons. 2, 3: The cash-flow surplus and technological know-how stemming from mass production are utilized by SMH to strengthen its market position in the higher-price segments

economies of scale and the learning curve also come more strongly into play under these circumstances. The positioning and strategic thrusts of SMH watches are indicated in Figure 7.8.

(6) *Excellent distribution know-how:* SMH possesses its own distribution companies in all important countries. This enables the rapid launching of new products on the market.

Swatch was actually able to build up a lasting image which was, paradoxically, based on constant change. ETA was able to sell only 235 Swatch watches in November 1982. Swatch managed to achieve a level of contribution which more than covered all the production and marketing costs. Of the total of 3.7 million watches sold in 1984, more than a third were sold in the United States. Up to 1986, more than 15.5 million Swatch watches had been sold. In 1989 the cumulative sales figure had reached 75 million. In 1992 sales exceeded 100 million. In 1987 Swatch watches accounted for around 9% of the total number of watches produced in the world in the low-price segment. In 1992 the figure was 12%. Swatch watches were sold in jewellers and in large supermarkets. The product proved to be so successful that special Swatch sales departments were established in several of the major store chains. A further factor in the strategy consisted of convincing the customer that the Swatch watch was a 'cult product'. This was why each model was produced in only a limited edition (normally 100 000 units). This was done to give the impression 'that the watch was so fashionable that it was actually difficult to get hold of' (*New York Times*, 12 July 1986, p. 9). On the same principle, a series of 100 highly exclusive models was developed and produced. These were given to some of the most famous personalities in the world (the list included Mikhail Gorbachov and famous rock stars).

The exceptional success of Swatch can be attributed to technical innovation and to a successful marketing policy. Large Japanese

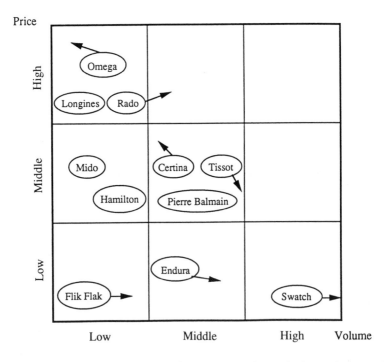

Figure 7.8 Strategic positions of SMH watches. (Adapted from Swiss Investment Research)

firms like Casio and Citizen seemed at first to be completely overwhelmed and, even today, they do not seem to have found an effective response to the Swatch strategy.

Because of the handsome profits achieved by Swatch, SMH was able to invest in other market segments. Tissot, Movado, Zenith and other Swiss brands had been bringing new models onto the market since the mid-1980s. They had created new types of watches— watches which measured the phases of the moon, multi-functional chronographic instruments, etc.). These new types of watches had achieved significant results. The Swiss watch industry, which one would have given up for lost at the end of the 1970s, now seemed to have recovered and regained its reputation. In 1986 Swiss gold watch exports actually reached the 1.5 million Swiss francs. In 1993, according to estimates from the Swiss watch federation, they were actually around 5.0 million Swiss francs.

Table 7.4 outlines the development of SMH, which was able to convert a loss of 173 million Swiss francs (in 1983) to a profit of 413 million Swiss francs in 1992 while keeping employment levels steady. The important point is, as Hayek put it, 'that the Japanese now had to run after us' (this quoted from Brauchlin-Wehrli, 1991, p. 108).

WHAT CAN ONE LEARN FROM SWATCH?

Hayek made industrial history with Swatch. His vision of industrial Europe is relevant for other branches of industry and points to the way in which old jobs can be saved and new ones created in the high-wage countries. One can summarise the main lessons that can be learned from the Swatch experience as follows:

(1) *Aggressive marketing, creativity and the willingness to take risks:* According to Hayek, 'a lot of Western managers have given up. In elite educational institutions, they acquire defeatist attitudes. They are narrow-minded bureaucrats who are not prepared to take risks and are only interested in short-term financial goals.'

(2) *Innovation and cost management:* Even in the high-wage European economies, products where direct labour accounts for less than 7% of total costs can be internationally competitive. Europe has an excellent educational system. However, the competitive advantage which this could provide seems not to be utilised to the full.

(3) *The creation of flexibly constituted empowered project teams:* Once a

Table 7.4   SMH in perspective

		1986	1987	1988	1989	1990	1991	1992
Sales	SFr. millions	1895	1787	1847	2146	2139	2373	2846
—% change		—	−5.7	+3.4	+16.2	−0.3	+10.9	+19.9
Cash-flow	SFr. millions	138	150	176	255	281	345	524
—in % from sales		7.3	8.4	9.5	11.5	13.1	14.5	18.4
Net income	SFr. millions	70	77	105	175	191	252	413
—in % from sales		3.7	4.3	5.7	8.1	8.9	10.6	14.5
Employees	No.	11 349	11 123	11 278	11 785	12 771	14 246	14 304
Sales/employee	SFr. millions	158.8	160.7	163.8	182.1	167.5	166.6	198.9
Shareholders' equity	SFr. millions	648	697	760	892	1050	1262	1575
—as % of total assets		41	43	48	52	55	58	60
Watches and movements sold		45.7	47.2	52.6	54.7	57.9	77.6	86.9
Average price	SFr. millions			30	31	29	25	28

Source: SMH.

problem has been recognised, the most important thing to do is to find the best people to solve it and to exclude those who are able to see only the negative sides of the problem and the obstacles which might prevent its solution. As Hayek puts it, 'the only people who are really useful to me are those who try to eliminate obstacles. I have no time for people who are always telling me what *isn't* possible. The crucial thing is to be clear about the main general lines of development and about the entrepreneurial vision; only then come the analysis, the Marketing Studies, the organisation and so on. Do you think,' continues Hayek, 'that Mozart did any market research before he wrote a piano concerto?', 'Let's put power in the hands of young people who think unconventionally and who are really prepared to overcome problems. We've got them and we've given them a free hand in the watch industry. We told everyone who had a new idea: "Come on, give a presentation to the boss." Let's get people who have kept their childhood fantasies. Let's not keep the super-boring over-serious people who continue with methods that were good for Switzerland 50, 100 years ago under very different conditions. Bring the young tigers to the fore! We need people who are ready to fight, who are able to take even unpopular measures and who think a little freshly and innovatively. It's not enough to constantly be reducing costs. The effect of cost-cutting measures is not just to reduce costs—in the end, there is no firm left. If we lose our production know-how, we are little better than a Middle Eastern State.' Hayek attributes the belief in the feasibility of everything that a person genuinely wants to do and which benefits the environment to the fact that 'I have been able to keep my freshness and fantasy, my dreams that I had as a young boy.' When selecting management employees, Hayek places particular emphasis on their having retained the imaginativeness of a 7-year-old child. People who are indecisive or uncommitted should not be allowed much scope in the business enterprise.

(4) *Agreeing on challenging and exceptional goals:* If a competitor offers a product at a price of 200 Swiss francs a unit, then it is not a matter of how, with a given market dimension, a particular share of the market can be reached. The crucial thing is to alter the rules of the game by agreeing on a target cost with the employees that enables the firm to offer a better product at a price of 100 Swiss francs a unit. 'We must look for new solutions,' Hayek says, 'I would be crazy if I had to explain something four times to somebody,' and so expresses in his own words the Arabic proverb: 'It's not worth talking to people who don't understand from a nod.' 'If the firm sets a goal that is practicable, challenges the employees and gives them scope, then every Swiss, young and old alike, is ready to devote his energies to the realisation of the goal, day and night. I've now got a group of 40 people working for a new car. They work Saturdays and Sundays if they have to. I don't have to tell them. They just simply produce a new and completely different car. That's an aim. They would not apply themselves as much, however, if I told them, "you must work to maintain the firm and the products that we've been making for twenty years". We are always excusing ourselves for the fact that we in Switzerland have high costs and that foreigners in Japan and Korea are cheaper. Employees do not properly apply their energies on behalf of a firm which only makes its money through financial manipulations. The product and the market are the most important things about a firm. First, we look closely at our products and then we look at the market. If I know exactly where I stand on the market with my particular product then I already know my strategy for the next five years. An example. You bring me a product that is produced in Germany and Switzerland for 100 Swiss francs but which the Japanese sell for 60 Swiss francs. What should you do? Most people immediately start to think

whether or not production should be transferred to Singapore or China or whether a licence shouldn't be got from the Japanese. Is a partnership likely and if so, with whom? The crucial factor is not giving a young work group the task of developing a new product for between 30 and 45 Swiss francs. The crucial factor is where the firm stands. If the loss of blood is too great then this must be stopped first. Strategies are of no use to the firm if it doesn't survive the next day. Only then can you begin with restructuring, reorganising and rearranging the hierarchical structure of the firm etc. Most firms begin with rearranging the hierarchical structure, without knowing where they're going. With a good team, a good product and a market you can move mountains (like with a lever) even if the organisation is weak. If you have a superorganisation without a product in a firm full of incompetents, you can't achieve much.'

(5) *Profit is only a tool:* 'I always wanted to be creative,' says Hayek. 'If I decided to do this or that thing, I never thought about how much money I'd make out of it. Money is only a tool, just as the sculptor uses a chisel.' Hayek continues: 'The market is the best measure of how good we are. We don't compare ourselves with the other Swiss firms which are only 100 kilometres away from us. We compare ourselves with champions, Japanese, South Koreans, Taiwanese, Americans, Germans and French.'

(6) *Design and proximity to the customer:* 'We orientate ourselves towards the market and make what the market wants, not what we believe to be good.' Hayek continues: 'Sometimes people in Switzerland forget that we get our money from the market and not from the CEO of the firm. Even the CEO sometimes forgets that. I often say to my employees, the person who pays us is the person who buys our watch.'

(7) *Speed of reaction:* The decisive factor for the future of an organisation is, according to Percy Barnevik, not its size but the speed with which it can react. The SMH did not buy Seiko or Citizen to be number one. 'You don't create new riches with acquisitions,' says Hayek. He closes with the words: 'The world is not just there for the Japanese, but for us all!'

THE FUTURE OF THE WATCH INDUSTRY

The watch sector at the beginning of the 1990s presents an entirely different picture to that of even 10 years ago (Figure 7.9). Then the

Swiss watch industry was on the verge of bankruptcy and all predictions spoke of an unavoidable decline. In 1990 Swiss producers had the largest market share of the world market in value terms. This was due to the success of Swatch and numerous extremely expensive watches from the A and AA segments (Tissot and Movado are insignificant in value terms). On the other hand, the mechanical luxury gold watch segment and the luxury watch segment were never really suitable for Japanese competition, in the A and AA segments, however, the Swiss watch industry seemed to find new development possibilities.

Of the American producers who stayed in the market, Timex produced its models abroad and was characterised by a constant decline in market share, especially compared with Swatch and Casio; Bulova is still in the market ('Benetton by Bulova'). In global terms, Japanese firms are still the leading players, although there are signs that they are having trouble developing a model that can react to the increased Swiss competition and the increasing pressure from Hong Kong. Seiko and Citizen floundered in the course of their attempt to take the established position on the world market away from the Swiss companies. Now, they find themselves 'stuck in the middle'— i.e. between Casio and Swatch, on the one hand, and the well-known brand names of the Swiss watch industry, on the other. Casio has remained the largest producer of multi-functional digital watches. However, according to all the evidence the days of the digital watch, as Figure 7.1 shows, are by no means over.

The 'Swatch phenomenon,' even if to a certain extent it is a question of fashion, does not at the moment show any signs of running aground. SMH has confidence, vitality and imagination. The company is in a position to alter the ground rules of the market continuously to its advantage, a fact which provides the firm with good future prospects for large-scale development. Technical innovation, which has contributed to the success of Swatch, is a decisive factor in the success of the Swiss watch industry. This is especially true if the result of Swatch is to be repeated in the middle segment of the market which, in the last 15 years, was left to Japanese competitors.

Experience shows that the leading players in the watch industry were never unsettled by the threat of new market entrants. The British producers did not take seriously the entry of Swiss firms into the market at the end of the eighteenth century. For this reason, their position in the market declined sharply. Similarly, Swiss firms were so convinced of the superior quality of their products and technology, developed over the course of centuries, that they

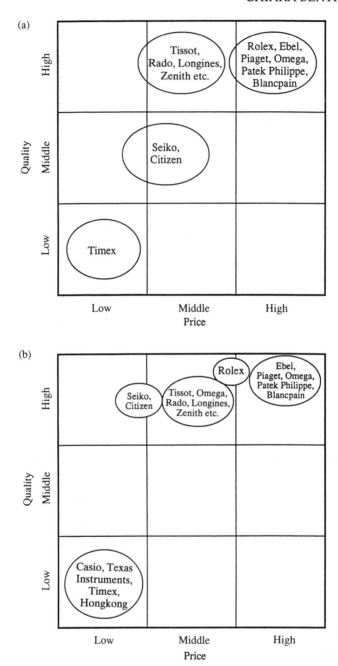

Figure 7.9 Strategic groups in the watch industry in (a) the 1960s, (b) the 1970s, (c) the 1980s and 1990s

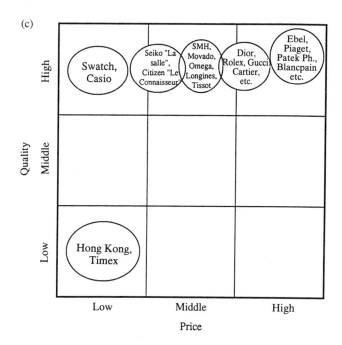

underestimated the entry into the market of firms from Japan and Hong Kong. The Swiss firms were firmly rooted in tradition, identified with their products and were therefore able to draw the right conclusions from the use of new technology for watch production. Because of these weaknesses, which the Swiss watch industry had managed to rectify at the beginning of the 1980s, a considerable proportion of market share was lost to firms from the Far East.

However, it is important to remember that the watch industry means not only technology but also design and image. At present this is a weakness of Asian producers. Producers from Japan and Hong Kong have, however, made great strides recently. The masterly combination of technology and design was the reason for the rebirth of the Swiss watch industry.

In the course of the last few decades this industrial sector has experienced a period of change and restructuring. The watch industry will never again be, as it was for decades, dominated by one country holding 80–90% of world production. It is difficult to imagine any of the three main players—Japan, Hong Kong or Switzerland—leaving the market now. The ground rules of the market could change, however, when Hong Kong reverts to China in 1997.

The future will probably be characterized by a period of consolidation unless fundamental technical innovation puts one or more of the competitors out of the race.

SUMMARY

The manufacture of time-pieces is a sector that is relatively independent of place. The dominant centre of production has shifted several times in the last few hundred years. The watch industry is a typical example of shifting competitive advantage.

After many years of unchallenged Swiss leadership, the situation changed fundamentally in the 1970s with the entry of Japanese competitors into the market. Within a few years, many players had disappeared from the market.

We have discussed the evolution of the watch industry and presented the strategies that have been adopted by different competitors over the years. In the past ten years the conviction has gained ground in the West that Japanese competitors are unbeatable once they have entered a market. Experience in the watch industry seemed to confirm this thesis until the end of the 1970s. In the past ten years, however, it has become evident that the Swiss watch industry, which was considered to be finished, could recover and grow, thereby falsifying the thesis that the Japanese, once they have entered a market, are invincible.

AUTHORS' NOTE

This chapter is partly based on a paper published by the authors in the Swiss review *Die Unternehmung*.

REFERENCES

Brauchlin, E. and Wehrli, H. P. (1991) *Strategisches Management*, Wien-München.
Cipolla, C. M. (1967) *Clocks and Culture 1300–1700*, London.
Dornberg, J. (1988) Up from Swatch. *Business Month*, March 1988, p. 24.
Eisenstodt, G. (1989) The last emperor? *Forbes*, October 2, p. 18.

Hinterhuber, H. H. (1993) *Strategische Unternehmungsführung*, 5 ed. New York, Berlin.

Capel European Research (Hrsg.) (1992) London, SMH.

Landes, D.S. (1979) Watchmaking: a case study in enterprise and change, *Business History Review* 53 (1), 1–39.

Mokyr, J. (1985) *The Economics of Industrial Revolution.*, London Allen & Unwin.

Oberender, P. (1988) *Marktdynamik und internationaler Handel*, Tübingen. p. 58.

Oster, S. (1990) *Modern Competitive Analysis*. Oxford, Oxford University Press.

Porter, M. (1983) *Competitive Strategy*. New York, Free Press

Tully, S. (1984) The Swiss put glitz in cheap quartz watches, *Fortune* 36.

Part Three

OTHER TOPICS

9

STRATEGIC TRANSFORMATION OF LARGE ORGANIZATIONS: SOME LESSONS FROM PRACTICE IN A DEVELOPING COUNTRY

T. K. Das

Baruch College, City University of New York

This chapter discusses an attempt by one of the world's largest commercial banks to transform itself in order to meet the demands of an extraordinarily rapid expansion of its branch network and business. The narration will cover the circumstances surrounding the decision to undertake a strategic transformation of the bank, the broad objectives of the transformation, the approach to achieving that transformation and some reflections on the transformation experience which might be useful in such endeavors in other large organizations. (The account given here is on the basis of the author's own involvement in the entire transformation effort as a corporate executive of the bank.)

The literature on strategic transformation has been growing in recent years (Kilmann and Covin, 1988; Levy and Merry, 1986; Mohrman *et al.*, 1989; Torbert, 1987). There is also increasing interest in looking at organizational transformation through different lenses and disciplines, such as innovation, competitiveness and entrepreneurism (Clark and Starkey, 1988; Kanter, 1983, 1989).

International Review of Strategic Management, Volume 5
Edited by D. E. Hussey © 1994 John Wiley & Sons Ltd

Without going into the various connotations of strategic transformation (Levy and Merry, 1986), it would suffice for our purpose here to conceive of it as comprising holistic, multi-level, discontinuous and comprehensive changes in corporate strategies, organizational structures and management systems. Some authors, expectedly, have focused on improving corporate management and performance against the general backdrop of transformation (Henrici, 1986; Kilmann, 1984; Mills, 1991). Much of the literature is prescriptive in nature, which raises the question of whether the insights and suggested solutions are applicable to different kinds of conditions obtaining in different organizations and cultures (Brakel, 1985). Also, there are very few accounts which relate to the particular situations in a great many of the developing countries.

Moreover, one rarely finds in the published literature comprehensive accounts of the total transformation of very large organizations (Brown, 1982; Ginzberg and Reilley, 1957). Furthermore, it is quite rare to find papers written by business executives who have been personally involved in the entire gamut of the transformation process.

This chapter is an analytical account of the strategic transformation of a very large organization, in its totality, in a developing country, by a participant executive as change agent. The strategic transformation examined here relates to the State Bank of India, the premier commercial bank in India, which currently has a network of nearly 13 000 offices worldwide and over 300 000 personnel. The chapter begins with a brief historical background for proper appreciation of the context of the transformation that is described and examined subsequently. Some of the principal lessons of the transformation experience, in all its phases and aspects, are then discussed.

BRIEF HISTORY AND OLD SET-UP OF THE BANK

The State Bank of India (SBI) has been the largest full-service bank in India since it was set up through special government legislation about 15 years before the time the strategic transformation was initiated. The legislation provided for SBI to be run as a sound business organization, even while carrying out the national policy of extending banking facilities to remote areas of a geographically vast country. Although a public sector institution, it was legislatively provided that the ministerial departments would not interfere in the day-to-day operations of the bank, or what may be termed as an 'arm's length' policy. The bank started with slightly over 450 domestic offices (along with a few overseas ones) which belonged to an erstwhile privately owned bank. Within 15 years, SBI had grown to around 2000 offices and 80 000 employees—a phenomenal rate of expansion by any standard. When coupled with substantial business diversification, and the amalgamation of certain smaller banks, it is easy to see the great pressures on management to maintain a satisfactory level of efficiency.

SBI was at the time geographically divided into seven regional groups, designated as 'Circles', each with a Local Head Office as headquarters. Each Circle controlled between 200 and 500 offices. The bank's Central Office had jurisdiction over all the Local Head Offices. There was a Central Board of Directors at the apex of the bank and seven Local Boards of Directors, one each at the seven Local Head Offices.

On the executive side, the Chairman, who was also the chairman of all the boards of directors, was the chief executive officer of the bank. He was assisted by a Managing Director and a number of senior executives with responsibility for different functional areas, such as accounts, resource development, industrial credit, investment, small-scale industries, small business, agriculture, international trade business, branch expansion, administration, personnel, premises, public relations, planning, economic and statistical research, management science, organization and methods, electronic data processing, etc. (see Figure 9.1). The Local Head Offices were each headed by an executive with the corporate title of Secretary & Treasurer. This official was assisted by a Deputy Secretary & Treasurer and a number of senior executives with functional responsibilities (see Figure 9.2). While the Central Office primarily had policy-making functions, the Local Head Offices were mainly concerned with operational aspects, although they also had a definite hand in the shaping of policies and plans insofar as they affected the regional interests.

The branches (see Figure 9.3) in a Circle were grouped together in administrative 'Districts,' which comprised about 40–50 branches situated within a particular geographical region. Each such controlling District was headed by a Superintendent, who reported to the Deputy Secretary & Treasurer. There were also other functional executives at the Local Head Office, somewhat in parallel with the departments existing in the Central Office. However, unlike the District Superintendents, who were in charge of the general administration of a specified number of branches, the functional executives had jurisdiction over all the branches in a Circle.

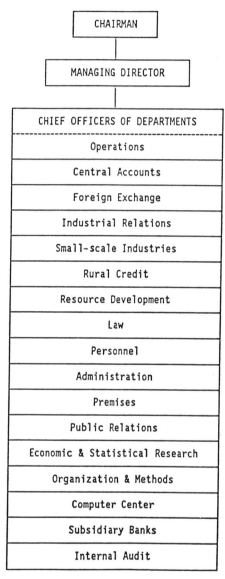

Figure 9.1   Earlier set-up of corporate headquarters

THE PROBLEM OF ADMINISTRATIVE REMOTENESS

The most crucial need of SBI was an effective system which enabled
the seniormost managers to administer and maintain control of the

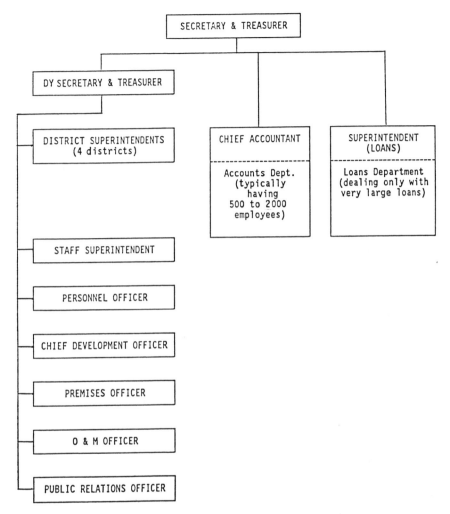

Figure 9.2   Earlier set-up of regional headquarters

rapidly expanding branch network. As the Chairman of SBI put it at the time:

> The existing organizational structure of the bank has proved inadequate in dealing with the problem of control over a large number of offices situated in remote areas. Despite the various steps taken by the bank in recent years to delegate more powers to officials at various levels, the need for decentralization and establishment of the control point as near the field level as possible is being increasingly felt.

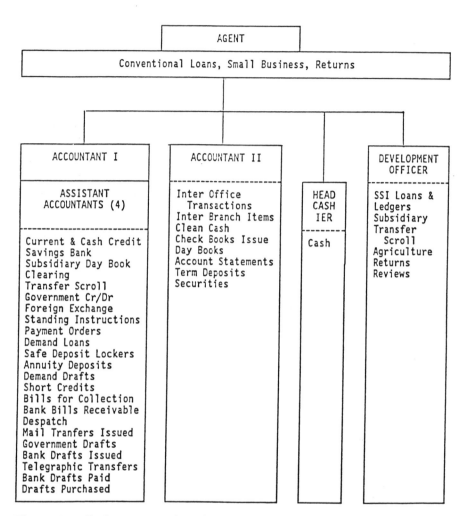

Figure 9.3   Earlier set-up of medium-sized branch

The problem clearly had several critical dimensions, besides the obvious one of managing a huge network of offices. These had to do importantly with, first, the geographical spread of the offices, and second, the inadequacy of trained personnel. A satisfactory solution had to address not only the basic question of organizational transformation but also the serious issue of reducing the remoteness of branches from their controlling authorities. This administrative remoteness directly affected the quality of headquarters control. The proper control of branches is particularly crucial in banking because of the sensitive nature of public trust in financial institutions.

Administrative remoteness, as conceived here, may be explained in terms of its three principal aspects. First, as a network of branches expands, the attention that a controlling authority can devote to the problems of an individual branch declines. The typical branch would thus ordinarily become somewhat remote, administratively speaking, than in the past. Second, as was the case of SBI, a large proportion of the new branches were being opened in relatively inaccessible areas and at great geographical distances from their headquarters. Infrastructural and communication facilities were progressively unsatisfactory in the case of newer branches. Third, the shortage of adequately experienced personnel, specially branch managers, was compelling the controlling authorities to exert more than ordinary effort to insure administrative efficiency. The net effect of these three developments was that the branches became ever more remote in administrative terms.

As economic and commercial activities were carried on all over the country, it was only natural that the bank should have branches as widely distributed as possible in order to join in these activities and cater for the business needs of individual communities. The problem was that of efficiently administering branches which were at varying distances from headquarters. Particularly when the branches were small in size, were numerous and had inadequate facilities for communication with headquarters, administrative efficiency was liable to suffer. At the time of the decision to undertake the transformation of SBI, the proportion of branches in rural interiors had exceeded one-third, and this proportion was required by national policy to steadily increase further.

Another facet of the problem of administering a large number of outlying branches was the large complement of relatively junior and inexperienced branch managers. The linkage between the managerial expertise and the degrees of freedom in corporate strategy making was well recognized (Hussey, 1988). Since this condition of limited managerial talent was unlikely to change in the foreseeable future, extraordinary efforts were made by the bank to make do with these relatively inexperienced managers through intensive administrative attention (more guidance, assistance, training, counselling). The problem of administering many units from a long distance was clearly compounded by relatively green managers and the consequential need for closer administrative attention.

Furthermore, when the ambitious growth plans were taken into account, it was clear to the management that changes had to be effected simultaneously in various areas to achieve the long-term viability of the bank. The decision was therefore made to thoroughly re-examine all aspects of the organizational functioning of the bank. It was evident that short-term or piecemeal changes of the past would have to be abandoned in favor of a change in the 'form' of the bank. A strategic transformation seemed to be the answer.

APPROACH TO STRATEGIC TRANSFORMATION

Objectives

The management of SBI decided, with the assistance of external consultants, to initiate the following steps to aid in arriving at the eventual character of the strategic transformation:

(1) Define the bank's objectives.
(2) Comprehensively study the work at branches, identifying the characteristics of their activities and the discrete task systems.
(3) Develop an appropriate management system suitable for each task system.
(4) Develop control systems appropriate for the task systems as well as the objectives of the bank.
(5) By discussing role boundaries, role expectations and role relationships among people in interacting work roles, develop an explicit understanding of the mutual demands that roles make, and of the kinds of relationships at peer and superior–subordinate level needed to perform the assigned tasks.
(6) By working in groups at higher levels of management, develop a clearer perspective of leadership roles and an understanding of the administrative policies and practices needed for effective performance of organizational tasks.

These activities and subsequent discussions over several months led the management to adopt the following critical objectives:

- Sustained profits for the bank and continued position of leadership in the banking industry.
- Deeper penetration and coverage of its markets by looking 'outward.'
- Better control system for performance and co-ordination.
- Better delegation of work so that senior management was released from routine work for more futuristic tasks.

- Clearer perspectives of objectives and tasks shared by all employees of the bank.
- Adequate flexibility of the organization to accommodate growth and rapid change.
- Development of managers, through appropriate administrative practices, who would be able to cope with the plans for rapid growth.

Building Marketing Expertise

In order to build up strong marketing expertise in the bank, the new design created the position of Development Managers with responsibility for each of the following five newly created customer segments:

(1) Commercial and institutional customers, comprising the larger units engaged in trade and industry, and including institutions such as universities, clubs and societies.
(2) Individual customers.
(3) Small-scale industries and small business customers.
(4) Agricultural customers.
(5) International banking customers.

These Development Managers were responsible for formulating policies and reviewing procedures relating to their particular market segment in keeping with Central Office directives, helping in drawing up Circle budgets and suggesting corrective action to the operations personnel.

These executives were also required to co-ordinate their thinking with the Planning Manager, who was responsible for economic analysis, corporate planning and budget review. Similar interactions were required with the Personnel Manager, the Public Relations Manager and the Law Officer. The market segment Development Managers did not have any direct authority over the Branch Managers. They were expert advisers to the operations management.

Performance Budgeting System

The management decided to introduce a performance budgeting system covering the entire bank. This was considered necessary for instituting a system of control consistent with the planned rapid growth of the bank. The system incorporated, in numerical terms, the objectives, goals and operational programs of the enterprise. It included an annual plan for each branch and covered deposits, loans, expenditures and profits in the different customer segments. A tentative budget was prepared by the Branch Manager based on general guidelines provided by the Circle management. The budget was finalized and accepted by the Regional Manager concerned on the basis of personal discussions. The final branch budgets served to form the Circle budget and the bank's annual plan was an aggregate of the seven Circle budgets.

In practice, the planning started at Central Office, where the business expectations of the bank as a whole in the forthcoming year was carefully projected on the basis of various economic trends and other factors. These planned growth levels were then communicated to the Local Head Offices who related them to the conditions obtaining in each Circle. The overall Circle expectations in each market segment were then determined (if necessary, after further consultation with Central Office) and advised to branches to serve as authoritative guidelines for the preparation of tentative budgets.

In a meeting of the top management of the bank just prior to the commencement of the budget period the allocation of performance targets among the seven Circles in various categories of business were finally decided by Central Office. It was against this final budget that the performance of each Circle was evaluated at monthly intervals. Necessary remedial action was initiated to keep in line with the budgeted levels. The performances of branches were similarly appraised at regular monthly intervals and deviations from the budget corrected by suitable measures.

The budget forms were designed to reflect past performance data of a branch and critical environmental information (such as extent of industrialization and demographic characteristics). These particulars were collected by the Branch Manager before determining his business expectations. There was also a detailed form for reporting the performance of the branch at monthly intervals. The budgetary system thus provided various executives, both at the Local Head Office and at the Branch, with a convenient document for keeping a continuous watch on the progress of actual performance in relation to pre-established operations plans. In addition, the budgetary system also provided operations personnel with a sense of direction and confidence in developing business, a certain degree of freedom in running branches and an assurance that results would necessarily be evaluated with due regard to whether or not budgeted resources were available for planned business expansion.

NEW ORGANIZATIONAL STRUCTURE

In the light of the redefined objectives of the bank and the broad thrusts outlined above, a new organizational structure was designed. A brief description follows. The subsequent sections will deal mainly with the experience of implementing the transformation process.

Set-up at Branches

The organizational set-up at branches was changed to conform to the market orientation of the bank. Instead of the traditional grouping of work according to the nature of activities and services such as deposits, loans, remittance of funds, collection of checks, and so on, the new orientation was toward the types of customers served. In other words, the bank's efforts were geared to meeting the total range of banking needs of each of the various categories of customers mentioned earlier.

In a typical large branch, there was a separate Division specifically catering for each of these customer groups. There was also a Services Banking Division looking after executor and trustee business, income-tax advisory service, etc. at branches having adequate potential for such business. The actual creation of a particular Division at a branch depended on the quantum of business available in the corresponding market segment. For instance, while most of the larger branches typically had all the five or six Divisions, the medium-sized branches had to create only one or two Divisions, depending on the nature and volume of business handled by them (see Figure 9.4). There were naturally hundreds of small branches where no formal setting-up of Divisions was warranted by the volume of business. The only changes in the latter category was in internal book-keeping and procedures (e.g. in the design and maintenance of ledgers, registers, etc.) in order that relevant data about customer segments could be generated. This served to provide complete information relating to the entire bank about each customer group for control and policy-making functions.

Every branch, of course, had an Accounts Department, which attended to all internal tasks such as book-keeping and accounts, custody of cash, etc. This Department also looked after the business operations for which no separate customer Division was constituted. The Accounts Department was in effect a common services department to all the Divisions. While the Divisions were headed by

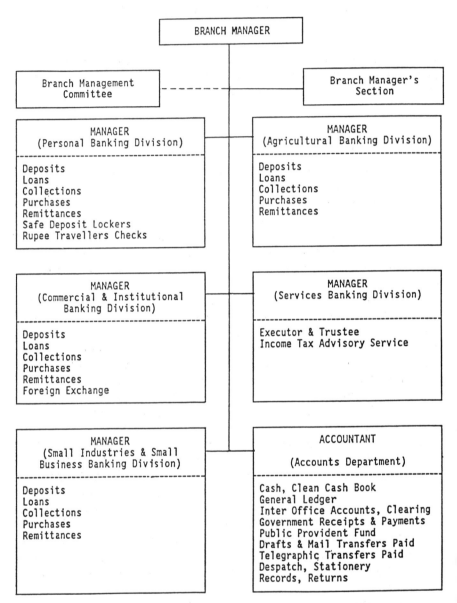

Figure 9.4 New set-up of medium-sized branch

officials designated as Managers, the head of the Accounts Department was called an Accountant. Adequate financial and administrative authority was vested in these officials to enable them to handle the major portion of their work independently. This minimized the need to refer to the Branch Manager (redesignation of the erstwhile Branch Agent). The Branch Manager, of course, continued to be responsible for the overall performance of his unit.

The following advantages would be evident in the new organizational set-up at branches:

(1) Greater thrust in business, and concentrated penetration in the various market segments by virtue of the close knowledge and specialization in the servicing of particular customer needs.
(2) Planned business development by relating it to the economic activities in the respective market segments, and assistance in the formulation of aggressive marketing strategies.
(3) Closer links with the customers for greater customer satisfaction.
(4) Development of managerial ability at levels below that of the Branch Manager.

Set-up at Local Head Offices

The following types of activities were identified for the Local Head Offices, which were the apex administrative offices of each of the seven Circles:

(1) Planning—formulating the strategy of business growth over specified periods in the context of external factors like economic trends, government policy, etc. and the optimal utilization of internal resources (personnel, premises, etc.).
(2) Promotional work—determining policies, schemes, procedures, etc. for each customer segment for exploiting business potential.
(3) Specialist services—making available expert advice to managers at all levels regarding personnel, premises, law, and public relations.
(4) Operations control—implementing and reviewing performance plans (through budgeting, described earlier), allocating manpower and other resources, and generally administering branches.

The transformation of Local Head Offices was done in such a manner that they were able to serve as an effective administrative organ for assisting branches in reaching their business goals. There was unified command of every branch, so that all instructions concerning an individual branch emanated from a single executive at the Local Head Office instead of, as previously, these being issued severally by the District Superintendent, the Chief Development Officer, the Staff Superintendent and other functional executives.

This principle was applicable not only to all operational matters (such as appraisal of business performance) but also to the allocation of resources such as additional personnel, premises, furniture, and so on. Provision was made in the new design to make adequate specialist advice available to all branches. For the first time in the bank a strong 'staff' wing was sought to be built up to carry out conscious planning and promotional work. The set-up at the Local Head Offices was designed to be appropriate for managing a Circle with up to 450 to 500 offices. Further expansions of the branch network would be accompanied, at an appropriate time in the future, by the creation of additional Circles.

To carry out its functions properly, a Local Head Office was staffed with two General Managers (both working under the Chief General Manager), in place of only one in the past. They looked after, respectively, the Operations side and the Planning & Staff side. The General Manager (Operations) had under him two or more Regional Managers, located at the Local Head Office, each of whom was responsible for all operational aspects of around 75 branches situated in a geographical region. Each Regional Manager had, apart from his own departmental set-up, three Area Superintendents whose principal job was to maintain liaison with about 25 Branch Managers through frequent visits. The General Manager (Operations) was also assisted by a team of functional executives, with titles such as Premises Officer, O & M Officer, Chief Vigilance Officer, and the Chief Inspector (see Figure 9.5).

One of the important aspects of the new organizational structure was the provision of specialist support at the Local Head Office, which was quite distinct from the operations functions. There were several new types of positions even on the operations side, but one can easily see a clear-cut operational chain of command running through the entire organization from the highest level to the lowest (see Figure 9.6).

Set-up at the Central Office

The principal tasks of Central Office were determined as planning, policy making and control of Circle performance, besides guiding Local Head Offices and sanctioning the very large credits and other capital expenditures. It was also to look after the bank's several subsidiaries, audit, investment and research activities.

The Managing Director of SBI, as in the earlier set-up, was the

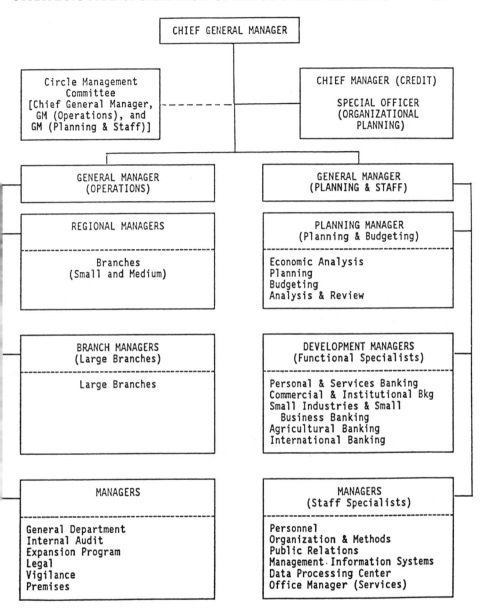

Figure 9.5 New set-up of regional headquarters

co-ordinating head for all operational functions. This helped in relieving the Chairman from ongoing operational responsibilities, and provided him with greater opportunity for concentrating on

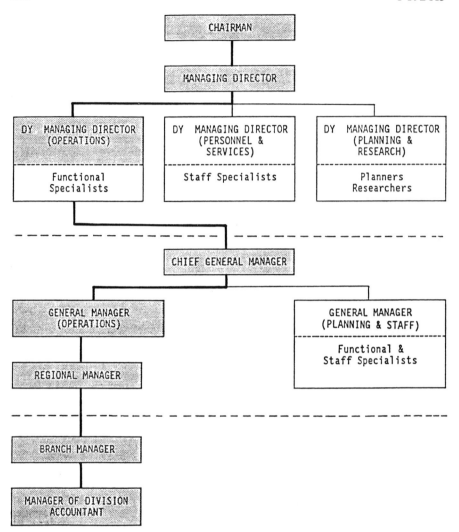

Figure 9.6 Unified chain of command in the operations wing

policy-making tasks. Three new posts of Deputy Managing
Directors were created. Each had complete functional control of,
respectively, Banking Operations, Staff & Services, and Planning &
Research. The Deputy Managing Directors had under them
various Chief Managers who were responsible for different aspects
of the bank's activities, such as individual market segments,
personnel, premises, public relations, management science,

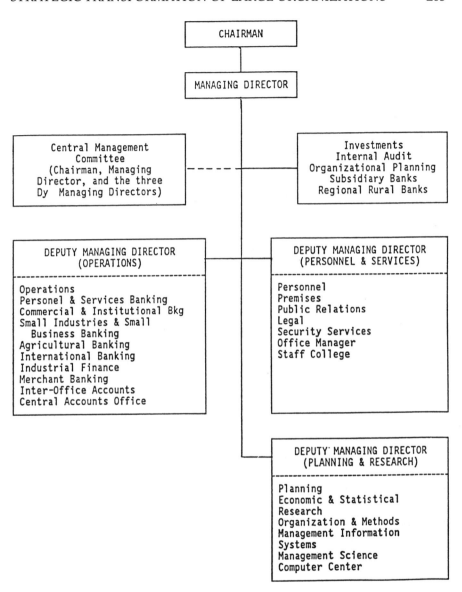

Figure 9.7 New set-up of central headquarters

economic research, and so on (see Figure 9.7). Here also, as in Local Head Offices, the operations and specialist wings were expected to constantly engage in mutual consultations for evolving realistic policies.

IMPLEMENTATION OF THE STRATEGIC
TRANSFORMATION

In this section we will lay out the overall approach to implementing the strategic transformation. The major part of the chapter will then deal, in separate sections, with the implementation efforts in three substantive areas, which were rather distinctive in this particular strategic transformation, namely, the introduction of a specialist wing, the new role dynamics and new administrative practices.

It needs no great imagination to grasp the enormity of the task of implementing the changes described above (and many other changes not covered in this brief overview) in a vast organization like the SBI. Some of the changes called for major efforts in training a large number of officials in new kinds of work, such as the performance budgeting system. Much of the success in changing over smoothly depended on how well the staff belonging to all categories appreciated the rationale of the transformation. An understanding was also needed about the basic concepts underlying the new organizational design, a recognition that different customers have different needs and so the bank's services should be tailored to satisfy these various sets of needs, the role of the functional and staff specialists, the attitudinal reorientations required in the new administrative practices, and so on. Certain changes in book-keeping and revised scales of delegation of financial and administrative authority were also required to be introduced in tandem with the comprehensive transformation.

Implementation was carried out initially in two of the seven Circles of the bank. Based on the experience, modifications were made before extending the transformation process to the rest of the bank. Considerable attention was devoted to ensure that the transformation was executed without ringing too many alarm bells. On account of the intricacies of banking work, procedural changes were kept at a minimum during the early stages.

The task of implementation was entrusted to the newly formed Organizational Planning Department at the Central Office, with a complement of specially selected executives. Similar departments were also set up at the Local Head Offices. It was left to the people at Central Office to work out the entire gamut of operational and administrative changes to switch over to the new design. The external consultants briefed the personnel concerned with this task, but the work of explaining the subject and training all the officials at branches and Local Head Offices was left to the Organizational Planning Departments.

An important advantage of this approach, whereby the bank's own executives undertook to explain the new design to the rank and file in the organization, was that the change was taken as an internal innovation, and not perceived as an 'academic' imposition from outside the bank. At various seminars of Branch Managers full explanations were given about why the changes were being made, what precisely they were and how they were to be carried out by the participants.

The seminars were conducted by a top operations executive and a representative each from the Central Office and Local Head Office Organizational Planning Departments. At these gatherings, as also in the follow up visits of the Area Superintendents soon thereafter, doubts were cleared up. Subsequently, as required by the performance budgeting system, the Regional Managers went round to all branches under their control to discuss and finalize individual budgets.

At the Local Head Offices a number of seminars were held to explain the roles of the various functionaries in the new set-up. Through role analysis exercises, the executives were apprised of their tasks and how they were to go about them. These exercises helped people in appreciating that they were required to modify their attitudes and behavior towards their superiors, peers, and subordinates in the new scheme of things. Gradually, a greater awareness of the different functions at the Local Head Office developed and new administrative practices took root.

IMPLEMENTING THE NEW SPECIALIST WING

There were, as can be anticipated in any implementation of strategic transformation of the magnitude described above, a number of significant difficulties, especially during the early stages. We discuss in this section one particular aspect of the transformation, which was distinctive in character, and illustrates the complexities of implementing substantive changes in large, functionally structured organizations. This had to do with the introduction of a specialist wing in the bank, separate from the traditional operations activities, and the consequential need to cultivate new managerial behavior patterns based on interactions between the two wings.

We discuss below the implementation experience of introducing the new operations and specialist functions in the organizational framework of the bank, with special reference to the rationale for the separate identities given to these two types of functions in the bank.

Separation of Operations and Specialist Functions

The separation of the operations and specialist (and service) functions was one of the fundamental characteristics of the new organizational design of the bank. To ensure continued planning and promotional improvements, indispensable for sustained growth and profitability, the bank needed a high-powered specialist wing at each Local Head Office. This wing was constituted of functional and staff specialists, as well as planning personnel, with the General Manager (Planning & Staff) at the head.

The General Manager (Operations) had complete charge of the operations wing, and was in a position to devote all his time and energy to the improvement of operational efficiency.

The specialist personnel had no distinct command chain of their own running through all the levels in the organization. Moreover, unlike the operations personnel, the specialists had no direct authority over the base level units (the branches): this was because, although they had some control responsibility, the function of the specialists was largely of an advisory nature. To illustrate, while the General Manager (Planning & Staff) had under his direct control the Development Managers, the Planning Manager, the Personnel Manager, etc., this command was evident only between the two levels. It did not form part of any continuous hierarchical chain covering all the other levels in the organization. In other words, the functionaries on the specialist side had their own hierarchical patterns at certain specified levels in the administrative offices of the bank. An example would be the General Manager (Planning & Staff) *vis-à-vis* Development Managers at a Local Head Office. There was no top-to-bottom, continuous hierarchical chain similar to the operational command chain.

Framework of Interaction

The considerations behind such placement of the specialist (as well as service) functionaries in the organizational structure were:

(1) To provide for a unified operational chain of command so that the operations personnel could derive the full benefits of the principle of 'one man, one boss' without let or hindrance from 'extraneous' superiors (see Figure 9.6).
(2) To provide for personnel with responsibility for specialist and service tasks, freed completely from the burden of operational routine, so that they could devote their full time and attention to

developmental and innovative aspects of the bank's activities.

(3) To provide for the continuous interaction between the specialists and the operations people. This was because, on the one hand, the operations personnel would have to depend on the people in the specialist side for expert advice and support, new programs, etc. and, on the other, the specialists could do their jobs effectively only when they could identify emerging operational problems through constant liaison with their operations counterparts.

(4) To provide for the most convenient arrangement or system in the structure for the operations and specialist personnel to meet, discuss and interact among themselves in the common endeavor of guiding and administering the branches. This was achieved by having the specialist as well as operations staff in the same office (Local Head Office) and not far away from each other, such as would happen if the operations people were to be located away from headquarters, at centers within the various Regions.

The above four aspects of the administrative set-up were in fact the principal elements of the managerial content envisaged for the Local Head Office under the new design. It was felt that for the effective performance of the total task of the Local Head Office it was necessary for each executive to constantly interact with his colleagues (discuss matters, keep in touch, exchange ideas, suggest fresh strategies, etc.). Indeed, the fundamental premise of the new managerial style was that an executive could not carry out his responsibilities properly without adopting these frequent interactions as an integral part of his method of working.

Differing Perspectives

We noted in an earlier section that a clear-cut chain of command ran through the entire operations side of the organization, but no such linkage existed for the specialist personnel. Also, unlike the operations personnel, the specialists had no direct authority over the branches, their role being primarily as advisors.

The essential difference, then, between the operations and specialist wings was based on the distinct perspectives they had of the organizational situation. The General Manager (Planning & Staff), for instance, had to function mainly on the basis of guidance and instructions from Central Office (through, for administrative convenience and propriety, the Chief General Manager). He had no authority over any official on the operations side. In fact, as we noted earlier, except for the subordinates working directly under him (Development Managers, Planning Manager, etc.), he had no line authority.

The position of the General Manager (Operations), in contrast, was vested with all the authority necessary for supervising and directing the Branch Managers and their controlling authorities, namely the Regional Managers, as well as the other functionaries at the Local Head Office on the operations side (such as Premises Officer, Chief Vigilance Officer, Legal Adviser, etc.). For instructions and guidance, all officials of the operations wing looked up to their superiors at various levels and, ultimately, to the General Manager (Operations).

In sum, while the General Manager (Operations) was directly responsible for the operations results of the Circle, the involvement of the General Manager (Planning & Staff) could perhaps be described as somewhat indirect, though, of course, of equally crucial importance in the overall Circle performance. As some would prefer to put it: 'Line tells, staff sells.' The General Manager (Operations) could 'tell' or order the operations managers and units, while it was in the nature of the position of the General Manager (Planning & Staff) to persuade or 'sell' his ideas to the operations managers.

Another way of describing the interactions is that while the operations wing channelled upward their performance results, problems and suggestions, sieved through the General Manager (Operations), the traffic on the specialist side was the filtering downward of expectations, policies and strategies through the General Manager (Planning & Staff). The meeting point was the interface between the General Manager (Planning & Staff) and the General Manager (Operations), where the two streams of seemingly different 'commodities' and 'values' were continuously and perennially intermingled, matched and combined in various alternative ways, and finally metamorphosed into a realistic and viable plan of management (with its components of market potential, organizational resources, growth targets and strategies). This process of constantly seeking a matching of (1) the expectations and specialist assistance of the General Manager (Planning & Staff) with (2) the capacity for growth and burgeoning problems of the operations managers, headed by the General Manager (Operations), can be considered as the basic objective behind the creation of the two separate wings at the Local Head Office.

Analysis of a Typical Specialist Position

At this point it would be expedient to analyze the data generated by interviews with the specialist wing personnel and others at Local head Offices. This would help both in appreciating the essential nature of a specialist's role in the bank and in understanding the kind of problems that were encountered.

The most typical specialist position was that of a Development Manager. As there were no formal job descriptions of managerial positions in the bank, it would be of advantage to recount here the major responsibilities of a Development Manager at a Local Head Office. The General Managers (Planning & Staff) who were interviewed generally agreed that the following formed (in their own words) the major *responsibilities* of a Development Manager:

(1) Acquiring thorough knowledge of the specific market segment, and keeping abreast of developments and trends therein.
(2) Providing expert help in the formulation of budgets and in reviewing performance, as also in suggesting corrective measures wherever necessary.
(3) Developing strategies and new services with a view to achieving growth of business.
(4) Identifying training needs and formulating appropriate programs.
(5) Reviewing existing systems and procedures to ensure development of business with minimum cost and with adequate safeguards.
(6) Building up of a data bank for the market segment.

The *principal difficulties* that the Development Managers faced can be understood from a sampling of the comments they made:

(1) Operations wing people are not very receptive to the new schemes developed by us.
(2) We are not always being consulted in the deployment of staff at centers sensitive in a particular segment.
(3) Training activities are not given adequate support by the operations wing.
(4) There is a tendency on the part of the operations wing to refer to us routine operational matters such as scrutiny of individual loan proposals, arrangements for the supply of special forms, etc. to branches.
(5) The operations wing often expects us to canvass for individual business proposals.
(6) Interaction of the operations wing with us is not adequate.
(7) Sometimes we are entrusted with work which has no bearing

whatsoever on our role, such as Enquiry Officer for dealing with disciplinary proceedings against an employee, etc.

(8) There should be greater co-ordination between us and the Planning Manager and the Personnel Manager, and we think the General Manager (Planning & Staff) has to bring this about.

(9) There is lack of co-ordination sometimes even among the different Development Managers.

(10) We would like more feedback from the operations wing.

(11) Our role is often not properly perceived or appreciated by our peers, or even sometimes by our seniors.

(12) We have conflict with Regional Managers over priorities of problems needing attention.

(13) We do not get much support from the operations people.

(14) The Regional Managers sometimes refer matters to us just for their convenience, shifting responsibility to us.

Analysis of a Typical Operations Position

In order to discuss the problems of interaction between the specialist and operations wings it would be useful to obtain a general idea of the nature of activities in the operations wing. The typical position in the operations wing was that of the Regional Manager. An analysis of the data collected from interviews with various persons is presented below.

As generally acknowledged (there being no job description for the position), the *responsibilities* of a Regional Manager included the following:

(1) Direction and control of branches in the Region.

(2) Achieving the budgeted levels of growth in all market segments.

(3) Development of credit to priority sector, including self-employment, Differential Interest Rates, etc. schemes.

(4) Ensuring efficient running of branches by developing managerial skills of Branch Managers.

(5) Ensuring maintenance of harmonious industrial relations.

(6) Developing proper rapport with the specialist wing.

(7) Promoting public relations.

(8) Rectifying irregularities pointed out in internal audit reports on branches.

As seen by other functionaries, however, the Regional Manager should be concerned with certain activities and priorities. We give below a sample listing the *expectations* of the General Managers (Operations) regarding the Regional Manager's role:

(1) Should fix challenging budgets for branches, and hence the Region.
(2) Tour branches more often than the current average of once a year.
(3) Ensure speedy disposal of correspondence.
(4) Increase rapport with functional specialists.
(5) Devote more time and energy to developmental functions.
(6) Throw up ideas for formulating new schemes.
(7) Control expenditure to carry out banking operations at optimum cost.
(8) Discourage direct discussions with borrowers having dealings with branches.

Co-ordination among Specialists

We had to consider also the question of co-ordination among the various functionaries working under a General Manager (Planning & Staff). Without this co-ordinating function, the suggestions emanating from the different specialists would probably be at cross-purposes, whereas the aim of the organization was to have an integrated approach in its policies, plans and procedures. In certain cases, this interaction had been found lacking.

For instance, in the case of Differential Rates of Interest schemes, more than one Development Manager was involved, although one of them was charged with the overall responsibility. In such a matter, the General Manager (Planning & Staff) would need to *ensure that the other Development Managers concerned were consulted* and that their views were taken into account. This did not always happen.

The same approach needed to be adopted, for example, when considering a proposal to transfer the work relating to loans to traders over Rs. 100000 from the Small Business market segment to the Commercial & Institutional sector. In working out the mechanics of such a proposal, it was not enough for the General Manager (Planning & Staff) to follow solely the suggestions of the Development Manager (Small Scale Industry & Small Business Banking), but also those of the Development Manager (Commercial & Institutional Banking).

This aspect of *co-ordination was particularly crucial in the case of new schemes that required a large number of trained persons.* In finalizing such schemes, the General Manager (Planning & Staff) had necessarily to examine them, as a generalist and as an experienced bank executive, from various crucial angles—whether adequate personnel were available, whether any special training would be necessary, what long-term benefits were likely to accrue from the scheme, what policy or procedural changes would be called for, etc.

Developing Co-operative Relationships

The chances of frustration in the roles of specialists, on account of low interaction levels and consequent feeling of unimportance, comprised an area demanding the special attention of the General Manager (Planning & Staff). The bank's officers in general, as a result of long managerial traditions, were not used to asking other departments for advice, except perhaps in a very limited way. Hence, if specialist advice was provided when it was not specifically sought, the operations managers had a tendency to feel unsure of themselves, as they were often embarrassed to reject or criticize the advice proffered. They apparently felt that having to receive a piece of advice, however sophisticated or specialized, implied an adverse reflection on their own competence and efficiency. The proffered assistance, again, was sometimes seen as uncalled-for interference and criticism.

These problems were expected to be tackled by the General Manager (Planning & Staff) through a *guided cultivation of co-operating relationships* between his Development Managers, etc. and the operations managers. He had to help *create an atmosphere of mutual trust and dependence* between his subordinate specialists and their operation counterparts. It would be difficult to specify here the actions which the General Manager (Planning & Staff) had to take about this climate, for the entire gamut of personnel management techniques was involved, but it seemed beyond question that the responsibility for fostering and nursing such a management environment rested with him. Without setting the stage properly, the desired interactions with the operations managers would have remained largely unrealized. Whenever any difficulty was encountered in ensuring adequate operations–specialist interactions, the General Manager (Planning & Staff) was uniquely placed to sort it out either with his counterpart, the General Manager (Operations), which would be most of the time, or with his superior, the Chief General Manager. An indifferent, wait-and-see attitude when the interactions in question were not taking place, as in certain cases at the earlier stages, could mean ignoring one important desideratum of the organizational design, which provided for and demanded these interactions. If, as we suspected, certain persons were unwilling, indifferent or unable to discharge their responsibilities in accordance with their prescribed roles, the General Manager

(Planning & Staff), as the head of the specialist wing, was required to ensure that necessary corrective measures were taken.

Significance of Long-term View of Specialists

On the part of the General Manager (Operations), it was clear that he must himself realize and *impress upon his subordinates the significance of the specialist wing* in formulating realistic policies and plans. This realization was not too evident in several cases. Merely because he sometimes had the feeling, as we could discern from our interviews, that he received all the assistance he needed from the Chief General Manager, we cannot conclude immediately that there was hardly any assistance which the General Manager (Planning & Staff) and his specialist personnel could render him. Our analysis was that the real difficulty was that some of the General Managers (Operations) were quite comfortable with taking the endless stream of tangible, workday, operational decisions, oblivious of the fact that most of these decisions were essentially routine, repetitious and had, generally, short-term consequences. However crucial these decisions appeared in the climate of immediacy, so typical of operations activities, it needed to be appreciated that the long-run implications of current business and administrative activities in a Circle had to be studied and taken into account while marking out the future path of the Circle (and the bank).

For this task, it was necessary to have an agency not so involved in the daily battlefield of operational banking. Such an agency should function in an atmosphere of objectivity, without being overly affected by the day-to-day problems, so that broader strategies could be formulated to ensure long-term growth and profitability. The need was, in other words, for someone to draw up the overall campaign plan and strategy and keep that wider framework constantly in view, and not be too concerned with sundry battle tactics and their occasional failures. This long-range perspective the General Manager (Operations), because of the intrinsic nature of his position, could have at all times. He was certain to be swayed by the shifting fortunes in the operations battlefield, if we might put it that way, losing sight of the overall campaign strategy of the Circle. The General Manager (Operations), placed as he was, had to guard against the tendency in certain cases of taking the tactical or situational planning of his operations managers for the strategic or long-range planning of the specialist wing.

It was to *provide for this long-range perspective in the administrative machinery* of the bank that the position of the General Manager

(Planning & Staff) was created. The General Manager (Operations) needed to rescue himself from the notion that his position was self-contained and adequate for taking care of Circle performance. It would be unrealistic for the General Manager (Operations) to harbor the belief that he can, single-handed, ensure sustained efficiency and growth of the Circle, combining in his role the two disparate functions of an involved operations head and a somewhat detached policy maker. In the context of the increasing volume, diversity, and sophistication of banking business, it was not possible for a single executive to do justice at once to the two different tasks we have discussed.

Interaction Pattern of General Manager (Operations)

Besides encouraging his Regional Managers to interact with the specialist wing, the General Manager (Operations) himself should, we believe, be having more frequent dialogues with the specialist. In his interactions, the General Manager (Operations) would need to be careful, however, to see that he did *not behave as a reviewing authority of specialist wing personnel.* Proper behavior in this regard had not been adopted in all cases. By way of explanation, when he discussed a subject with a Development Manager, he should only pose problems, explain difficulties, provide information, even analyze situations and suggest solutions, but he had to take the precaution that *instructions or orders were not given* to the Development Manager regarding how the latter should go about this work. That duty should be performed by the General Manager (Planning & Staff). What the General Manager (Operations) had to do was to help the Development Manager to have a critical look at the problem, so that the latter could examine the existing policies and devise new strategies. The General Manager (Operations) had to seek specialist advice; it was not for him to utilize the position of the Development Manager as a vehicle for propagating his own ideas, however valuable they may be. For, in any case, the General Manager (Operations) need not have any worry about being saddled with unproductive programs, as it was he alone who had the final say in implementing any change in operations matters. What is being stressed is that the General Manager (Operations) should not, by his behavior in the interactions with the specialist side, endanger or stifle the freedom of the latter to take a second look at problems from independent, hence perhaps different, angles. Only thus could creativity and innovativeness be fostered.

Unfortunately, all the right behaviors were not evident at the Local

Head Offices. Our analysis showed that in some cases the General Manager (Operations) was instructing (usually, verbally) the specialists, while at the same time, as if to compensate for this deviation, there were also instances of the General Managers (Planning & Staff) issuing instructions to the Regional Managers and other operations personnel. It should have been realized by the General Manager (Operations) that any attempt to condition the professional approach of the specialists by direct intervention on his part, through orders and prescriptions, would result in throttling the creativity of the specialist side. He should have been exercising his influence by feeding the specialists with the details, analyses and suggestions about operational situations; but the advice from the specialists, if it has to be really worth while, would have to be generated by the latter in an atmosphere of full professional freedom to employ their technical expertise.

Distortion of Roles

One of the consequences of a General Manager (Operations) adopting the approach mentioned above in relation to specialists, wherein the latter were almost taken under his wings and given orders, was that the dividing-line between the prescribed functions of the operations people and specialists was lost sight of and *patently operations work was passed on to the specialists*. The processing of certain credit proposals were passed on to the Development Managers, and the latter were issuing instructions to branches regarding new schemes—all at the instance of the General Manager (Operations). The *mix-up of functions naturally led to a considerable distortion of roles*, and took away from the Regional Managers some of their control over branches.

It also happened in certain instances that the General Manager (Planning & Staff), while visiting branches, acted as if he was deputizing for the General Manager (Operations)—in a few cases, with the latter's tacit approval—in the belief that the latter was badly overworked and had no time to meet the Branch Managers. It was clearly *detrimental to organizational effectiveness to hammer out such periodical informal arrangements* whereby items of work were distributed piecemeal according to the convenience of the General Manager (Operations), or any other official. It was not in the bank's interest to parcel out jobs among officials according to the daily changes in the configuration of administrative convenience. There was supposed to be, after all, a fairly stable grand design for the division of labor, so indispensable for the orderly functioning of a modern, complex organization like the bank. The General Manager (Operations), as also other categories of officials, needed to give more thought to all these issues in shaping their administrative behavior. Very few actions which distorted the prescribed roles could be justified on the ground of administrative expediency.

It was true that sometimes a particular General Manager (Operations) felt that the specialists were not doing their best in helping him attain budgeted levels of business. Such an analysis of the position was quite plausible, and naturally one would expect that he would initiate necessary remedial measures to enable the Circle to achieve the level of business budgeted. But in dealing with this matter he should *not personally take the specialists concerned to task*, but rather should be discussing it with the General Manager (Planning & Staff).

Toward Effective Interaction

We have thus far dealt with certain aspects of the existing interaction pattern between the operations and specialist wings, and have made specific comments regarding the problem areas. In terms of effective implementation, though, it was felt necessary to initiate further steps to achieve the desired kind of interaction in the bank. This resulted in a four-pronged effort.

Clarity of managerial positions

Greater clarity of managerial roles was attempted through the development of suitable job descriptions. It was necessary, we have seen, for the bank to *strive for greater clarity* of its managerial positions to minimize their ambiguous and conflictual characteristics. In the next section, we will discuss this topic in greater detail.

Counselling

Increased counselling of the managers was carried out to assist them in playing their roles along organizationally desired lines. In most of the areas where we found deficiencies in the interaction process, we noted that the General Managers had a substantive role to play. In certain respects they themselves needed to modify their behavior patterns. In other respects they, as the heads of the two wings, could wield considerable influence over their subordinate functionaries in *adopting new behaviors and cultivating co-operative relationships*. The two General Managers at each Local Head Office thus had a crucial responsibility to counsel their own wing personnel in order to fashion their attitudes, style and activities, in a manner that led to the desired kind of inter-wing transactions. Some *individual counselling* and explanatory remarks at meetings of departmental heads was found useful.

Structuring the interaction

In order to develop the organizational culture of inter-wing consultations it was decided to structure the interaction process to a certain degree. To help stabilize the consultative behavior, a *system of periodical meetings* among the functionaries was also put in place.

These meetings had *some drawbacks*. One was that the membership was rather large, from 15 to 20 in most Local Head Offices, and this appeared to be unwieldy for quick decision making. However, since our aim was to achieve more interaction among all functionaries, it stood to reason that all the persons concerned should be given a role to play in the discussion process. The more participation the meetings were able to foster, the better it was for building up co-operative relationships.

The second drawback was that about an hour of *time* was needed for the meetings by all departmental heads every week, and perhaps many more resources in terms of both preparation time and special attention. We thought, though, that by compelling the various functionaries to focus attention on these meetings, the bank would in fact be achieving its objective of ushering in a new interactive administrative culture. To that extent, therefore, the weekly time allocation for these meetings could be said to have been well justified.

The third factor had to do with regular meetings of the two wings separately. This was left to the discretion of the respective General Managers. It was felt that explicit provision for such meetings at all Local Head Offices could result in *excessive structuring*, and could even unintentionally lead to a hardening of the 'we' versus 'they' feeling among the two sets of functionaries. While some competitive spirit between the two wings could possibly enhance the quality of work, we need to remember that the extant major problem, as discussed earlier, was one of isolation and mutual indifference. Hence *a general team-building approach* with the two wings considered together seemed more appropriate at that juncture.

It should be added that the *same kind of structuring was desirable for the Central Office functionaries*. The data gathered from our interviews with the officials at Central Office were of a similar nature to those of the Local Head Offices, particularly in terms of inadequate co-ordination and consultation among the three wings under individual Deputy Managing Directors. However, this deficiency was of a less serious character. There was a more keen desire among the functionaries to *know about the important developments in other departments* with which there was no work-based contacts. It was clear that the departmental heads wanted to know from time to time about the significant policies, plans and problems of other departments at Central Office, if only to be aware of the general drift of the bank's activities and thinking. Apparently, the perusal of outgoing communications (which were circulated among all departmental heads) did not provide the information in a satisfactory manner. Hence it was necessary to institute a system of regular *weekly meetings at Central Office.* The benefits of better co-ordination, more sharing of information and a better overall view of the bank's developing thrusts in plans and policies were, it was felt, sufficient reward for the resources that were employed in terms of managerial time.

Training program

The most important instrument for bringing about a higher degree of interaction between the two wings at a Local Head Office was a specially designed training program to effect changes in perception and behavior of the functionaries concerned. This was undertaken by the bank's Staff College at Hyderabad. The College had the necessary facilities, in terms of both accommodation and expert faculty.

The program required *some outside consultants* for conducting certain special kinds of sessions. Such consultants had traditionally been employed by the bank, usually eminent professors from the two Indian Institutes of Management at Calcutta and Ahmedabad, who were experienced in organizational change and development. The program design was worked out mutually between the designated faculty members of the Staff College and the Organizational Planning Department at Central Office. The participants in the program were principally the Regional Managers and Development Managers at all Local Head Offices.

IMPLEMENTING THE NEW ROLE DYNAMICS

As we noted above, it was crucial for the bank to achieve increased clarity in the way the managers needed to behave in the various new positions in the bank. This was necessary for understanding precisely the tasks and responsibilities of each position and how each was expected to interact with other positions. In this section we will discuss how the new role dynamics in the bank were institutionalized, and describe the manner in which inter-role transactions were expected to be carried out for effective managerial performance.

Role Ambiguity and Distortion

We have seen in the previous section how there was an inadequate appreciation of the interdependence of various managerial positions in the operations and specialist wings at a Local Head Office. There was also some amount of *ambiguity and conflict in the managerial roles*, which was clearly reflected in different persons having different expectations about particular positions (Katz *et al.*, 1964). The conflicting perceptions led to a certain lack of clarity and distortion of various managerial roles. It was necessary, therefore, to attempt to evolve a mechanism for bringing about greater role clarity, covering all the managerial positions in the bank.

It will be useful to cite here some typical instances of *role distortions* that were taking place in the bank, along with our comments:

Illustration One. A Chief General Manager instructed the Regional Managers directly regarding a certain matter, ignoring the General Manager (Operations) altogether. This was because he felt that the particular General Manager was not pulling his weight and something needed to be done about the matter.

In effect, the Chief General Manager became the virtual operations head of the Circle, taking on the post meant for the General Manager (Operations). In other instances, it happened that the General Manager (Operations), in turn, bypassed the Regional managers and had dealings with the branches in the Regions. In a similar fashion, the Regional Manager had been found on occasion to ignore the Branch Manager and contact the Managers of Divisions direct.

Illustration Two. In a number of instances, a General Manager (Operations) agreed to the requests of the Regional managers to sign the 'strong' letters to Branch Managers for the purpose of pulling them up.

As the man directly in charge of a Region, the Regional Manager had necessarily to perform this chore of making the unpleasant or strict remarks against his Branch Managers. If, in the event, the General Manager (Operations) had deputized for the Regional Manager by signing the 'unpopular' communications, he did not function in the best interests of the Regional Manager and Branch Managers concerned.

Illustration Three. A General Manager (Operations), while visiting a branch directly under the Regional Manager, issued categorical instructions to the Branch Manager and other officials regarding business development, handling of an industrial relations problem, etc.

So long as there was no emergency situation—and there was none—in which rare event exceptional steps would naturally be expected, there should be no reason for the General Manager (Operations) to interfere personally in the affairs of branches under Regional Managers. His attention should be concentrated more on developing and helping his Regional Managers to become effective in managing their Regions.

Illustration Four. A General Manager (Planning & Staff), on a visit to a branch, peremptorily called together all the leaders of the employee union at the branch and enquired about any outstanding problems that they might have, without any concession to the presence of the Branch Manager.

It is clear from the examples cited above that the perceptions of various roles may be distorted by what a manager actually does. The principle of sticking to one's own area of authority and responsibility needed to be adhered to if role clarity had to be brought about in the bank; an official should not only be clear about the nature of his own role, but should also project his knowledge to the other officials with whom he interacts. This principle was not rigid or iron-clad, but whenever deviations were considered necessary, which should not be too frequent, it should be evident to the persons concerned that the principle as such was not being challenged or replaced, but that administrative exigencies had occasioned these short-cuts in the regular authority circuit. To be able to maintain a certain degree of cohesiveness and administrative discipline in a vast organization this kind of *healthy respect for task and responsibility boundaries* was considered very necessary.

Interdependence of Managerial Roles

A fundamental factor that is ignored in job descriptions is that the performance of a manager is dependent to a large extent upon the nature and quality of relationships he is able to establish with other managers. This is because *managerial jobs are interdependent and interconnected*. A manager would be very unlikely to do his job well unless he had good working relationships with at least those managers who are in some way, directly or indirectly, concerned with the performance of his job. Every job can thus be seen as part of a network or matrix of related jobs. Particularly in the bank's organizational structure, it was envisaged that there had to be a considerable amount of interactions between the various positions at the Local Head Office. It was easy to visualize the significant part which the large number of interrelationships would have in determining the standard of administrative efficiency. It follows that, to be realistic, any description of a manager's job had to take into account the *mutual obligations and expectations of other jobs*.

Exercise of Discretion

One further aspect of a managerial job which traditional job descriptions fail to mention has to do with the *exercise of discretion*. Specifically, they did not recognize or define the limits of discretion which managers were expected to adhere to. By ignoring the discretionary content in any managerial position, a job description gives, at best, only a partial view of a manager's total role. This discretionary element was really the factor which distinguishes the job of a manager from any other routine or repetitive work.

The exercise of discretion is basically the exercise of judgement, which is constituted by such personal attributes as knowledge, experience, analytical ability, intuition, etc. It was important, therefore, that the *boundaries of discretion* were outlined, so that a manager could (1) confidently exercise the discretion vested in his position and did not unnecessarily restrain him from applying his best judgement, in a mature manner, and from taking the initiative because of any ambiguities in his understanding of the range of his discretion approved by the organization, and (2) desist from any transgression of the limits of discretion permitted by the organization.

Role Analysis

In order to overcome the deficiencies of job descriptions or position descriptions noted above, the different managerial roles in the bank were analyzed. In particular, the dynamic aspects of each role were captured by recognizing that managerial jobs were interconnected, i.e. the performance of a manager was dependent not only on how he goes about doing his specified tasks but also on the nature and quality of relationships he was able to establish with the other managers in the office with whom he had to work in order to achieve the performance objectives of his role.

Role analysis discussions were held with each manager to afford a clear idea of his role, an appreciation that all the roles were interdependent, that *everyone had some obligations and expectations which must be mutually agreed upon,* and that otherwise there would be much conflict and confusion. In this manner, the *boundaries of each role became evident;* the role space of each person became clearly understood by all concerned. This gave a more realistic appreciation, when compared with traditional job descriptions, of the role as a dynamic idea, in the sense that each manager had to play his role in a dynamic fashion. Although it took some time, role analysis was eventually done for each significant position in the bank.

IMPLEMENTING NEW ADMINISTRATIVE PRACTICES

Delegation of Authority

Along with the new organizational structure and management control system, new administration practices were deemed necessary. Having regard to the vast network of branches and the wide range of business activities, a considerable degree of delegation of financial and administrative authority had to be provided at all managerial levels. Extensive delegation of authority was needed to expedite the disposal of business proposals and efficiently handle day-to-day administrative problems. The aim was that an executive should be able to attend to roughly 80% of the work by himself, without having to send matters up to the next level of financial authority. Ideally, therefore, only a small portion of an executive's tasks would be sent up to the superiors, either because the matter was not routine or because authority in excess of the prescribed limit had to be exercised in dealing with it.

Task Boundaries

An important concept inherent in the new organizational design was concerned with task boundaries. The task of each position or unit in the organization was clearly delineated, along with its responsibilities and authority, so that the relative boundaries were well demarcated. This ensured that there was no interference from superior levels, and that freedom of action was maintained at each level within set boundaries. The development of initiative and independent decision-making capacity were facilitated when the superior officers recognized the boundaries of positions below them. Of course, the controlling office had to guide and assist the subordinate office to achieve its performance targets efficiently, but in doing this any tampering with the task boundaries were to be avoided.

Face-to-face Discussions

We noted earlier that the new design stressed intensive interactions between operations management and the specialist personnel on the staff side. This mutual consultation was to be standard administrative practice. This was particularly desirable between the various Development Managers and staff specialists, on the one hand, and the General Manager (Operations) and the Regional Managers, on the other. The General Manager (Planning & Staff) was not to act as a filter for all consultative meetings nor was he expected to vet any discussions. His duty was mainly to plan and co-ordinate the activities of the various specialists under him, guide them in developing expertise in their respective functions and generally encourage frequent contacts between the specialists and operations personnel. This interaction process was also desirable to reduce paperwork and to have more face-to-face discussions as the dominant part of the administrative process.

Improving Decision Quality at Branches

The Regional Managers were the controlling authorities of all branches. As this was admittedly a challenging job, each Regional Manager was assisted by two or three officials, called Area Superintendents, who were expected to regularly visit and help the junior Branch Managers in improving their managerial performance. By discussing with the Branch Manager some of the past decisions taken by him at the branch, and by generally reviewing these and other matters, the Area Superintendent was to provide a valuable counselling service to him in developing his decision-making capabilities. The post of the Area Superintendent was also to serve as a valuable instrument to elicit useful information, based on on-the-spot study and observation, for realistic policy formulation at the

Local Head Office level. The Area Superintendent did not figure in the chain of command between the Regional Manager and the Branch Managers. He was basically a resource for the Regional Manager to address the problem of administrative remoteness discussed earlier.

Quite obviously, the kind of work required to be performed by the Area Superintendent had never been done in the bank. Before the Area Superintendents actually took up their jobs, they were put through a preparatory program, imparting the necessary counselling skills. The program included as participants all the Regional Managers, as it was felt that the relationships they built up with the Area Superintendents would have a significant impact on the quality of the latter's work. Some Branch Managers were also brought in for specific training exercises.

Before going out on a tour of branches, the Area Superintendent would typically review all outstanding issues regarding each branch. The Regional Manager gave him guidance about the manner in which he should proceed in regard to the more important matters. This detailed briefing was useful to the Area Superintendent in adopting the correct perspective while talking to Branch Managers, reflecting the Regional Manager's mind. It also helped the Area Superintendent to explain to the Branch Managers some of the rationale behind the decisions made by the Regional Manager.

On return from each tour, the Area Superintendent reported to his Regional Manager in person about the major problem areas he discussed or found at the branches, and also his analyses and suggestions on all these matters. In these face-to-face discussions the Area Superintendent was able to project in a realistic manner the state of affairs at the branches. The Regional Manager could thus form a fairly accurate idea of the branches which called for his special attention, as well as the kind of guidance and resources that each branch needed.

Decision Making by Management Committees

The new governance structure restricted the Central and Local Boards of the bank mainly to 'entrepreneurial' tasks concerned with capital resources, investment policies, the nature of activities the bank should engage in, etc., apart from certain control tasks to ensure that the objectives were being attained. This relieved the Boards from decisions relating to the operational aspects of the bank.

To enable the Boards to function in that entrepreneurial mode, much of the operations decision making was vested in newly constituted Management Committees at Central Office, Local Head Offices and the larger branches. This change was intended to *improve the quality of decisions through a sharing of responsibility in matters of major importance.* The officials in the bank had hitherto confined themselves to decision making almost wholly on an individual basis, so that the new system of working through committees was a significant departure from the normal practice. Obviously, this form of group or collective decision making was quite new in the bank.

There were five members in the Committee at Central Office comprising the Chairman, the Managing Director and the three Deputy Managing Directors, while at each Local Head Office the Committee consisted of only three members, namely, the Chief General Manager and the two General Managers. The functions of the Management Committees included the determination of growth targets, formulation of operations and personnel policies, review of performance, sanction of loans and capital expenditures up to prescribed amounts, etc. The Management Committees at the larger branches comprised the Branch Manager, the Accountant and the Managers of various Divisions. These Committees were responsible for reviewing branch performance, sanctioning loans within specified limits, evolving improved procedures, etc.

The members of these three types of Committees (Central, Circle and Branch) had to recognize that while the Committees could perform certain functions better than individuals, the reverse of this was also true, i.e. individuals could perform certain functions better than Committees. In general, Committees were effective where the quality of the output was likely to improve by a synthesis of different views, such as the overall policy area. Another useful area in this respect was significantly large business decisions, where sharing of collective responsibility was required as a precaution against excessive risk taking.

The strategy of institutionalizing this new form of collective decision making was based mainly on educating the managers about the nature and benefits of this type of decision system in the bank. The issue was divided into (1) joint decisions and (2) integration mechanisms.

As far as joint decisions are concerned, there are certain types of decisions that are better made by Committees—'two heads are better than one'. A group decision is usually better than the decision of each of the individuals in the group—more resources/experience/diverse background/ability to examine from a number of angles/less chance of individual idiosyncrasies influencing the decision/synthesis of diverse viewpoints. Our idea was eventually for the Circle

Management Committee to take over some of the executive functions of Local Board Committee—meanwhile, decisions could cover the priorities and best uses of Circle resources of personnel and similar matters. We did not want at that early stage to specify the actual functions of Circle Management Committee. Each member was expected to participate on an equal basis, divorcing himself from his executive role in the organizational structure.

The most important part of the Committee's work in the early stages was an an integrating mechanism between planning and promotion on the one hand and operations on the other. Conceptually, it was emphasized, people will work together if there is (1) a common objective, (2) sharing of information, (3) mutual dependence and (4) responsibility for task performance. Items (1) and (2) were taken care of in the new design. Item (2) had to be attained by ensuring that no information was withheld at any stage. Item (3) had to be consciously cultivated and eventually internalized. It will be observed that the General Manager (Planning & Staff) cannot succeed in achieving the bank's objectives without the assistance of the operations people. Similarly, the operations people cannot function effectively without proper planning and staff support. They may function for some time and show results in the short run. However, for sustained growth, maximum use of limited resources and the full exploitation of the business potential, the operations people cannot continue to show results without the necessary planning and staff support. To the extent that this was realized by the Chief General Manager and the two General Managers, and to the extent that they made conscious efforts to ensure that their subordinates (Planning Manager, Development Manager, Personnel Manager, on the one hand, and Regional Managers, on the other) also realized their complete mutual dependence for achieving maximum results, the Circle Management Committee could be regarded as a critical integrating mechanism in the new structure.

The same conceptual framework applied to the Branch Management Committees. It was difficult for senior Branch Managers to accept the concept of distributive leadership in the beginning. The Organization Planning Departments in the Circles had to make significant efforts to help people function on a joint basis. Here again, it was emphasized that the segment-wise division of work (which was appreciated by all) required a mechanism for integration. Otherwise each person would go his own way, and perform his portion of the task, leaving the total task to suffer. Since the Branch Manager was responsible for the total task, he had actively to foster integration at the Branch Management Committee level. The fact that we did not consider it sufficiently important to pursue this collective decision making on a priority basis had some adverse results in some branches on the two Circles where this was first tried out. In the other Circles, steps were taken to ensure that Branch Management Committees began functioning from the very beginning of the change-over. In fact, many problems of co-ordination and integration which (inevitably) arose in the initial stages of the transformation could be ironed out effectively by the Management Committees, at both Circle and Branch levels.

It was important to guard against these Committees becoming substitutes for executive decisions by the individual members. It was also critical for the Committees to differentiate between collective and individual decision making. For example, the Chief General Manager or General Manager had executive responsibility for certain tasks. These he must perform on an individual basis, without waiting for a Committee meeting. The Chief General Manager was required to resolve differences between the two General Managers under his command, and this could not be a subject for the Management Committee.

SOME LESSONS IN STRATEGIC TRANSFORMATION

Some general lessons may be stated here, arising out of the experience of carrying out strategic transformation of a very large organization. These observations are based on the author's reflections on his direct involvement as one of the senior executives responsible for the strategic transformation of the bank. Each of the points mentioned below was evident to some degree in the process of the bank's transformation, although specific details cannot be divulged here for proprietary reasons.

Long-term Staying Power

A decision about organization-wide transformation of a modern commercial bank, which is a highly complex organization, is inherently of a long-term character. It is imperative that the top management of a bank should carefully analyze the probable results of their decisions in the long run. They should prepare themselves to monitor the successive stages of organizational transformation and initiate appropriate corrective measures all through the process. It is also necessary for the management to set its short-term goals along with its long-term objectives. In a very real sense, the achievement of the planned short-term results would enhance the credibility of the long-term aims (Das, 1986, 1991). In any case, such transformation programs need to be drawn up in such a way that one can easily monitor the progress in implementation. Some concrete gains should be evident even within one or two years. For instance, a bank may wish to achieve in the long run a particular kind of market position, a certain growth rate, a specific level of profits or the development of managerial talent, it should, nevertheless, not neglect the attainment of such short-term results as, say, vigorous market thrust in a particular area, more decentralization, better administrative control and higher morale.

Executives as Change Agents

The management has to make sure that the bank can garner the requisite talent to carry through the contemplated changes. A substantial reservoir of expertise is required within the bank to ensure smooth implementation of any transformation. Outside experts may, at best, suggest some directions for change. It is the bank's own executives, at senior as well as at junior levels, who have to effect the transformation according to their own genius. The role of change agents is quite pivotal and, if a bank is to succeed in transformation itself, it must indispensably have a band of executives who can be depended upon to carry forward the transformation program. These executives must persevere in overcoming the many obstacles to be encountered in implementation, when even some top officials may seem to falter and show tendencies to let things slide back to pre-transformation conditions. If a bank lacks an adequate supply of executives with appropriate attitudes and skills to act as efficient change agents, then it would be extremely difficult to undertake any transformation.

The Cost Factor

One has to remember that organizational transformation, like everything else in this world, involves some cost. The introduction of new systems and procedures implies considerable expense. Competence in working according to past norms and styles usually becomes devalued. Some degree of resultant demoralization cannot be ruled out. The need for retraining employees in certain areas of work cannot ordinarily be eliminated. The cost to be incurred in holding seminars, etc. and distributing informational literature to explain various aspects of the changes can be quite high. Also, sometimes there is an addition to the number of personnel during the process of organizational transformation. This increase in the number of employees may not be anticipated on logical grounds at the planning stage, but the probability of being compelled to add to the complement of personnel remains fairly high in developing countries. The cost factor should therefore occupy a significant place in the calculations of the management.

Temporary Dislocation

It is inevitable that there would be a loss of efficiency and productivity during the transformation period. The organization should have the inner strength to sustain itself in the face of this temporary dislocation. Unless it can confidently weather the storm for a reasonably extended period of time, there would be the danger of the entire organizational machinery suffering a breakdown. Even if such a contingency is not apprehended, it is not unlikely that the lower standard of efficiency during the interregnum will become the new acceptable norm. In any event, temporary setbacks cannot be ruled out, but these should be seen as such, and not mistaken for permanent deficiencies or complete failures. There is no case for being overwhelmed by these initial hurdles, but the management needs to have the requisite wisdom to identify the areas in which it cannot afford to lose some ground.

Infrequent Opportunities

Organizational transformations, like major surgeries, cannot be undertaken frequently. The opportunities for further radical changes are blocked for several years. Any decision about a transformation program carries with it the added significance of precluding subsequent transformations of the same nature and dimension. History, at least here, cannot be allowed to repeat itself too often. If, therefore, the management is not deadly serious about seeing a transformation program to its successful completion, even the past efficiency would be likely to be affected because of the unavoidable dislocation.

Unrealistic Expectations

Any transformation program would most certainly generate among all ranks of the bank's personnel, and even customers and the larger public, certain kinds of expectations. It would be necessary to fulfil, even in the short run, some of the expectations that are raised while initiating organizational changes. It is probably true that some managements do get away with a lot of credit for introducing seemingly 'progressive' changes, since in the ordinary course no-one seriously assesses at a later date the long-term effects of past decisions. Unfortunately, self-criticism, self-correction and self-improvements are not virtues which are noticeable in the higher reaches of all organizations. The usually short and temporary tenures of the most senior managers preclude any possibility of the results of their shoddy decisions concerning organizational change coming home to roost while they are still at the helm of affairs. It is all the more necessary that the top managers of a bank should, as a collective body, take special care to avoid raising unrealistic expectations about the advantages of particular organizational transformations.

Visible Commitment

There is every possibility of a gradual loss of credibility in the management's commitment to an organizational transformation if adequate attention and support are not forthcoming over an extended period of time during and after the transformation. If, in the event, there is no visible evidence of commitment on the part of the senior executives at the end of the first or second year, the rank and file in the institution could become skeptical. The initial appeals of the top executives calling upon all the personnel to help usher in a new organizational era would begin to look, in retrospect, as so much empty bravado and soda-gas euphoria.

Integrated Approach

Lastly, for an organizational transformation to be meaningful, an integrated approach encompassing several areas of management needs to be adopted. For instance, the introduction of planning and budgeting in a bank may involve structural changes, besides changes in systems and procedures, administrative practices, authority structure and the management control framework. Usually, personnel policies, criteria for reward and promotion, clarification of managerial roles, training strategy and a host of other important subjects are required to be examined. Any piecemeal attempt to tackle an isolated aspect of organizational functioning would be unlikely to yield satisfactory results, and may even create some amount of confusion in the system.

CONCLUSIONS

We have touched upon some of the more important factors which bank managements should take into consideration before undertaking extensive organizational changes. There is no denying that a decision in this matter is extremely difficult to make, because of its complexity, its far-reaching consequences and its cost in terms of both money and effort. There is, in any event, no half-way house in a program of organizational transformation. If a transformation is called for, if it is feasible, if it is unavoidable for sustained corporate growth, the management would naturally have to apply its collective experience to carry it through. In doing so, however, it needs to be cautious in its approach, weighing the costs and benefits carefully before coming to a decision. Once a transformation is decided upon, though, there cannot be any half-hearted attempt at implementation. That would be almost suicidal, crippling the organization for years.

AUTHOR'S NOTE

The views expressed in this chapter are the author's and must not be attributed in any way to the bank under discussion. Parts of this chapter are based on the author's writings disseminated mostly through in-house organs by the bank for training and information purposes.

REFERENCES

Brakel, A. (ed.) (1985) *People and Organizations Interacting*, New York, Wiley.
Brown, D. S. (1982) *Managing the Large Organization*, Mount Airy, MD, Lomond Books.
Clark, P. and Starkey, K. (1988) *Organization Transitions and Innovation-Design*, London, Frances Pinter.
Das, T. K. (1986) *The Subjective Side of Strategy Making: Future Orientations and Perceptions of Executives*, New York, Praeger.
Das, T. K. (1991) Time: the hidden dimension in strategic planning, *Long Range Planning*, 24, (3), 49–57.
Ginzberg, E. and Reilley, E. W. (1957) *Effecting Change in Large Organizations*, New York, Columbia University Press.
Henrici, S. B. (1986) *Company Reorganization for Performance and Profit Improvement: A Guide for Operating Executives and their Staffs*, New York, Quorum Books.

Hussey, D. E. (1988) *Management Training and Corporate Strategy*, Oxford, Pergamon.

Kanter, R. M. (1983) *The Change Masters: Innovation and Entrepreneurship in the American Corporation*, New York, Simon and Schuster.

Kanter, R. M. (1989) *When Giants Learn to Dance*, New York, Simon and Schuster.

Katz, R. L. *et al.* (1964) *Organizational Stress: Studies in Role Conflict and Ambiguity*, New York, John Wiley.

Kilmann, R. H. (1984) *Beyond the Quick Fix: Managing Five Tracks to Organizational Success*, San Francisco, CA: Jossey-Bass.

Kilmann, R. H. and Covin, T. J. (1988) *Corporate Transformation: Revitalizing Organizations for a Competitive World*, San Francisco, CA, Jossey-Bass.

Levy, A. and Merry, U. (1986) *Organizational Transformation: Approaches, Strategies, Theories*, New York, Praeger.

Mills, D. Q. (1991) *Rebirth of the Corporation*, New York, John Wiley.

Mohrman, Jr, A. M., Mohrman, S. A., Ledford, Jr, G. E., Cummings, T. G. and Lawler, III, E. E. (1989) *Large-Scale Organizational Change*, San Francisco, CA, Jossey-Bass.

Torbert, W. R. (1987) *Managing the Corporate Dream: Restructuring for Long-Term Success*, Homewood, IL, Dow Jones-Irwin.

10

ORGANIZATIONAL CHANGE PROCESSES IN A FORCE FIELD

Paul Strebel and Liisa Välikangas

(International Institute for Management Development),
Lausanne, Switzerland

Characterizations of change abound. Change is difficult to grasp as a whole and the phenomenon itself has many dimensions (Ginsberg and Bucholz, 1990). To make some order out of the phenomenon, a typology is useful as a way of distinguishing between different types of change so they can be contrasted and treated separately. Meyer *et al.* (1990) have argued that business change can be classified best in terms of two basic types of process, continuous or discontinuous, that can occur on two different levels with respect to content, the firm or the industry. Pettigrew (1987), on the other hand, has suggested that a complete description of change should include not only process and content but also the context. For example, under what conditions, or in what context, is continuous change likely to occur versus discontinuous change?

This chapter uses a force field approach to provide the context for different change processes. The basic hypothesis is that if the change process is to successfully adapt the system to its environment, the change process must be consistent with the configuration of forces for change and resistance acting on the system.

In the first section we use the existing literature to describe four different types of change process. In the second section we use the existing literature to describe the nature of the forces for change and resistance. Then, in the third section, we employ the basic

International Review of Strategic Management, Volume 5
Edited by D. E. Hussey © 1994 John Wiley & Sons Ltd

consistency hypothesis to position the change processes in the force field. Case studies of change on the firm level are employed in the fourth section to illustrate the predicted set of force field configurations and change processes. Finally in the fifth section, we outline some managerial implications.

CHANGE PROCESSES

We start with what Meyer *et al.* (1990) call discontinuous change (metamorphosis on the firm level and revolution on the industry level) and then move on to continuous change (adaptation on the firm level and evolution on the industry level). With respect to adaptation and evolution we shall argue there are at least two different ways in which firms can adapt and industries evolve, either continuously in pursuit of progressive growth or sporadically by trial and error groping. For completeness, we also include a no-change (change-avoidance) process.

Discontinuous Change Process

Firms 'adopt stable configurations and possess inertia, but must periodically realign by undergoing rapid organization wide transformations' (Meyer *et al.* 1990, p.96). This type of change consists of radical leaps that the organization takes from one state to another in a short period of time. The driving mechanism for change is the need to survive environmental shifts including the progression through stages of a life cycle (Kimberly *et al.* 1980, Miles and Snow, 1978), changes in structural gestalts (Miller and Friesen, 1984), and technological breakthroughs (Tushman and Romanelli, 1985). These conceptions of change include the idea of a threshold under which organizations resist change and beyond which change takes place in a radical form.

On the industry level, 'industries are restructured and reconstituted during brief periods of quantum change, which punctuate long periods of stability' (Meyer *et al.*, 1990, p.97). The mechanism of change has been called quantum speciation, a term borrowed from biology (Astley, 1985). Schumpeter's creative destruction is an example of such a mechanism: technological breakthroughs make old technologies obsolete and companies dependent on them disappear while new ones mastering the new technology emerge as competitors.

Continuous Change Process

Firms 'track their environments continuously and adjust to them purposively' (Meyer *et al.*, 1990, p.95). This is essentially the evolutionary or rational adaptation described by Burns and Stalker (1961), Chandler (1962), Emery and Trist (1965) and Ansoff (1965, 1980), in which the internal structure of the firm evolves to reflect the environment. The organization internalizes or becomes like its environment to cope with it, using, for example, structural differentiation and/or integration (Lawrence and Lorsch, 1967). The driving mechanism is the tracking of the environment in pursuit of progressive development. The process is a long-term one of continuous change within the organization.

On the industry level, 'various forces propel populations of firms towards alignment with prevailing external conditions' (Meyer *et al.*, 1990, p.96). According to the institutional theorists, for example, there is a pressure to conform to the environment for legitimacy in order to gain access to resources, known as isomorphism in this tradition of research (Meyer and Rowan, 1977; Scott, 1987; Zucker, 1987).

Sporadic Change Process

Firms engage in a trial-and-error process of small incremental steps each with a short-term horizon. The steps take place periodically and do not necessarily follow a consistent direction. This results in a process of groping for the future. Typically, the goals of the firm are multiple and conflict resolution requires mediation between stakeholders.

This is quite different from the purposeful tracking that drives the continuous change process. It is rather the logical incrementalism of Lindblom (1959) and Quinn (1978). The firm muddles through environmental change as decisions are made in an *ad hoc* manner. Imperfect knowledge prevents firms from engaging in systematic long-term planning. Constrained in their choice of strategy and time horizon, it is in the best interest of management to craft strategy rather than design it (Mintzberg, 1987, 1990).

On the industry level, groups of firms with different strategies co-exist, because the evolutionary selection process is not strong (undirectional) enough to select out the winners. Rather, there is a tendency towards possibly irrelevant strategic fashions, a herd effect, which encourages a large number of competitors to move in one direction for a period of time. When this does not produce the desired results, they move in another direction.

No-change Process

Firms seek to avoid internal change by controlling critical resources. Stability can be maintained by containing and resisting change forces in the competitive environment. External intervention is used to reduce the internal need for change. Increased information and, if possible, control of the competitive environment is aimed at reducing uncertainty. This is essentially the steady-state behavior described by March and Simon (1958), Thompson (1967) and Cyert and March (1963).

On the industry level, this is the tendency towards oligopolistic practice with the firms in the industry using their collective market power implicitly, if not explicitly, to maintain and possibly extend their position within the larger macro economy.

Table 10.1 summarizes the change process characteristics as described above in terms of the driving mechanism, change activity, and time horizon for each of the four change processes.

FORCE FIELD

Kurt Lewin (1947, 1951) described personality and group dynamics in terms of vectors in a force field consisting of drivers and resistance to change. In the strategic management area, Ginsberg and Bucholz (1990, p. 454) have argued that organizational change can only be described in 'reference to a particular set of internal and external

Table 10.1 Change process characteristics

Change process	Driving mechanism	Change activity	Time horizon
Discontinuous change	Need to survive environmental shifts	Resistance; then sudden sharp jump	Immediate
Continuous change	Progressive development	Consistent adaptation	Long-term adaptation
Sporadic change	Trial-and-error grouping	Inconsistent incremental steps	Short-term periodic
No change	Defence of the existing position	Consistent maintenance of status quo	Indefinite

variables that characterize the forces for change that shape equilibrium'. More specifically, Kelly and Amburgey (1991) argue that to understand organizational change, researchers need to look at both forces driving change and resistance to it. In a preliminary paper, one of us has used forces of change and resistance in the setting of a catastrophe theory model to distinguish between different patterns of change (Strebel, 1990).

Forces for Change

For the purpose of this chapter, forces for change can be defined as variation in factors, external or internal to the firm, that cause a deterioration in performance if the firm does not adapt to them. Change forces can be conceived of in two basic forms: external and internal.

External forces for change are created by trends in the sociopolitical, economic, technological and competitive environment (Meyer, 1982). Turning points in the trends are especially important as forces of change; for example, life-cycle shifts and turning points in competitive behavior (Strebel, 1989). Turning points reflect the limits to established trends, limits to available resources (Aldrich, 1979), capacity, investment, growth and the stimuli promoting new trends, innovation (Tushman and Anderson, 1986), competitors' actions (MacMillan et al., 1985), stakeholder demands (Lundberg, 1984; Ginsberg and Bucholz, 1990), and so on.

Internal forces of change come in the form of a new CEO or manager (Kotter and Heskett, 1992), change agents who see change as necessary and pursue it vigorously converting status quo agents into supporters (Ginsberg and Abrahamson, 1991). From an organizational viewpoint these change drivers internalize the external change forces acting on the firm. The mechanisms by which such internalization may occur include feedback effects of prior performance (Oster, 1982), aspiration levels (Cyert and March, 1963) and organizational slack (Bourgeois, 1981).

The strength of a change force is given by its actual or potential impact (positive or negative) on the firm's performance (most frequently measured by market share, sales or profits). A strong change force creates a substantial decline in the performance of a company that is not adapted to it, and improvement in the performance of a company that is adapted. As such, the strength of an external force for change reflects the rate of change it causes in the environment. The sharper the turning point in the trend, or the more sudden the change in the 'texture' of the environment (Emery and

Trist, 1963), the stronger the resulting force. Environmental changes, however, may have differing impacts, affecting competitors selectively depending upon their competitive positions (Caves and Porter, 1977).

Forces of Resistance

The forces of resistance to change can be defined as those factors, internal or external to the firm, that prevent the firm from adjusting to the forces of change. Forces of resistance come in three basic forms: cultural inertia, structural inertia and strategic momentum.

Cultural inertia, for our purpose here, includes both cognitive inertia (closed mindsets) reflecting strongly held business beliefs and strategies, as well as entrenched values, behaviors and skills that are not adapted to the change forces. Cognitive inertia is due to dominant cognitive schemata, heuristics and/or biases, that prevent organizational members from perceiving the need for change (Ginsberg and Abrahamson, 1991). It is the prevailing corporate logic that conceptualizes the business in such a way that environmental signals are either ignored or misinterpreted. Cognitive bias can be explained at least in part by the tendency of managers to seek out information that confirms their preconceptions (Zaskind and Costello, 1962), and discount data that discredit them (Nisbet and Ross, 1980). The attention paid to this bias reflects its importance (Jackson and Dutton, 1988; Schwenk, 1989; Barnes, 1984; Walsh, 1980; Stubbart, 1989). However, even if the recognition of the need to change exists in principle, it may not translate into change behavior. Values and behaviors, vested interests, a lack of suitable knowledge and skills, may still prevent the firm from implementing change (Strebel, 1992). Awareness of the need to change often exists long before any action is taken to implement change (Pettigrew, 1985; Schwenk, 1988).

Structural inertia includes the organization structure, systems, technology and resources that are not consistent with the forces of change. It is embedded in the need for organizations to be stable and reproducible (Hannan and Freeman, 1984). This requires accountability and reliability. Efficiency in terms of the specialization of organization assets is required for competitive viability (Williamson, 1975) but may also constitute part of the structural inertia. Resources, tasks and authority have to be allocated, procedures and work routines standardized (Perrow, 1986). All this creates inertia that makes it difficult to change: the 'capacity to respond quickly to new opportunities presumably competes with the capability to perform reliably and accountably' (Hannan and Freeman, 1984, p. 163). The structural inertia theory suggests that, regardless of environmental characteristics, organizations are less likely to make changes in their core than in their peripheral features. Size tends to increase the emphasis on predictability, formalized roles and control systems (Downs, 1967). Furthermore, as organizations grow older they have even more occasion to formalize relationships and standardize routines (Stinchcombe, 1965).

Strategic momentum as a force of resistance comprises counterproductive strategic change driven by historical and other change drivers not relevant to the external forces of change. Organizations that have made major choices in the past develop a momentum that continues over time (Kelly and Amburgey, 1991). They tend to repeat changes experienced in the past; the choices of the past define and limit the range of choices available for the future (Boeker, 1989). As a result, the firm develops a way of doing business, a growth rate, a competitive position, a direction in which it is moving. Momentum can be explained with many of the same reasons of inertia, especially those that account for past successes. Both may become obstacles to change (Miller and Friesen, 1984). However, the difference between inertia and momentum is their relationship to the change process. Inertia pursues stability and tends to slow down any change process; momentum pursues continuity in a certain direction but may block other possible directions of change.

POSITIONING CHANGE PROCESSES IN THE FORCE FIELD

The interplay between the change processes and the force field can be most easily described by considering the interaction between the forces of change and resistance. With respect to the former, two broad bands of change force intensity can be distinguished: strong established change forces and weak emerging or declining ones. Whereas strong change forces are easy to identify with little uncertainty about their direction, weak change forces are difficult to identify with their nature and direction uncertain. This distinction is important because once change forces are strong and established, their direction is more easy to discern, thereby facilitating the shaping of the change process. However, as more players begin to align themselves with the change forces, the corresponding window of opportunity begins to close. By the same token, weaker change forces are more difficult to discern, but may present a larger window of potential opportunity.

With respect to the forces of resistance, two broad bands of intensity can also be distinguished. On the one hand, there are firms and industries with high levels of cultural and structural inertia that are essentially closed to change; on the other, there are those with low levels of cultural and structural resistance that are relatively open to change. This distinction is important because it determines the nature of the response of a firm or industry to a change force. With respect to the strategic momentum whether it is a resistance force depends on the direction of the change force. Strong momentum reinforces the change force if it is in the same direction, but creates strong resistance if it is in the opposite direction. Weak momentum generates, at most, weak resistance.

The interaction between the forces of change and resistance, with the distinction between strong and weak intensities as described above, suggests the need for at least four different types of change process to cope with: strong resistance and weak change forces, weak resistance and weak change forces, weak resistance and strong change forces, strong resistance and strong change forces. The change consistency hypothesis can be expressed in terms of four corresponding process positions.

(1) *No-change position:* No change is likely when the forces of change are weak and the resistance to change is strong. Due to the strong cultural and structural inertia, resistance to change is characterized by a high threshold below which the forces of change have no material impact. The only viable change-driving mechanism is the defence of the existing position based on the neutralization of threats for as long as possible. As long as the forces for change are significantly weaker than resistance to change, no change takes place.

(2) *Sporadic change position:* Sporadic change is likely when both the forces for change and the resistance to change are weak. The impact of the change force is uncertain and fluctuates owing to chance events. Except for some cognitive inertia associated with the uncertainty of the change force, the resistance to change is low. Under these conditions the natural driving mechanism is trial-and-error groping based on periodic, small incremental steps with a short time horizon. The fluctuating impact of the change forces results in change above the resistance threshold and no change below it. The system exhibits sporadic change.

(3) *Continuous change position:* Continuous change is likely when

the forces for change are strong but the resistance to change is weak. Since the strength of the change force exceeds the resistance threshold, there is no effective resistance. Under these conditions the change process is characterized by flexible adaptation driven by the progressive development of the change force. The strategic momentum of the system reinforces the change force. As a result, the system adapts continuously to the change force.

(4) *Discontinuous change position:* Discontinuous change is likely when increasingly strong forces for change face strong resistance. Below the resistance threshold no change occurs, despite the growing change force. The cultural and structural inertia is high and the strategic momentum runs counter to the change force. Close to the threshold, however, chance events can break the resistance. Once the change force exceeds the threshold, the resistance breaks down. The need to survive drives the change process, which is sudden and sharp characterized by a rapid collapse of the resistance. The system experiences discontinuous change.

The change consistency hypothesis can be presented in the form of a matrix (see Figure 10.1) in which the change positions are

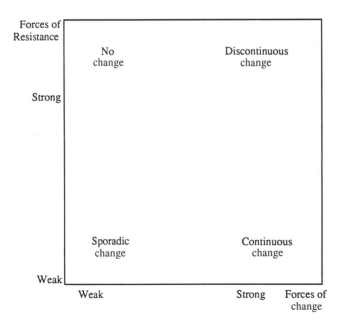

Figure 10.1   Basic change matrix

accordingly defined in terms of the strength of the forces for change and resistance.

The argument for the consistency between the four change processes and the four force field combinations rests on the ability of a particular change process to successfully adapt a firm or industry to its environment (cf. Van de ven and Drazin, 1985), by coping with the context created by a particular combination of the forces. More specifically, we suggest it depends on the fit between the driving mechanism, activity, and time horizon of the change process (Välikangas, 1992) and the context created by the forces. The basic change matrix reflects this fit. It represents the domains in the force field, corresponding to a given combination of change forces and resistance, in which the different types of change process are most likely to occur. If a firm or industry does not follow the change process indicated, the hypothesis is that they are likely to fail in their adaptation effort. If this inconsistency persists, performance deteriorates to the point where the system is no longer viable. It is in this sense that a complete categorization of change types must include the interplay between the change process and the force field.

ILLUSTRATING THE CHANGE CONSISTENCY HYPOTHESIS

To illustrate the hypothesis, the dimensions of the change process (driving mechanism, activity, time horizon) and the force field position (strengths of the forces for change and resistance) must be described in terms of observable variables. However, due to the complexity of change as a phenomenon, this poses some difficulties. With respect to the change process itself, the driving mechanism (see Table 10.1) cannot be readily observed separately from the change activities. For example, small incremental steps in different directions can be said to reflect trial-and-error groping, but the latter cannot be separately observed. The time horizon implicit in a change process also cannot be readily observed even over a period in time, because, by definition, it is a function of how long the process lasts.

Observable Change Variables

Certain aspects of the change activity can be observed. For a particular change process, the activity can be categorized into one of the four types shown in Table 10.1 by observing the nature of its movement (a sudden jump, continuous movement, stepwise movement, no internal movement) and by observing its internal consistency over time with respect to the direction of the change (consistent purposeful, or inconsistent pursuit of a change direction).

The strength of the forces for change is reflected in the rate of change in the firm's environment and the current or potential impact on the firm's performance. The potential impact on a firm's performance can be captured by the change in competitive logic (i.e. the rules of the competitive game, see Gilbert and Strebel, 1989). Thus, the strength of a change force can be categorized as strong or weak by observing the rate of environmental change (high or low), the degree of the change in competitive logic (high or low), and the change in current performance (high or low). A strong force of change is characterized by a high rate of environmental change, plus either a high impact on the competitive logic *and/or* a high impact on performance. A weak change force is reflected in a low rate of environmental change, plus a low impact on the competitive logic *and* a low impact on performance.

The strength of the forces of resistance is reflected in the degree of structural inertia as observed in the degree of organizational hierarchy, routinized systems and lack of financial resources, the degree of cognitive inertia as observed in non-dynamic strategies, the degree of cultural inertia as observed in entrenched values and behaviors, and the degree of counterproductive strategic momentum as observed in inadequate functional competencies and organizational capabilities. To get an overall categorization of the strength of the resistance forces, we take the point of view that the key is the presence or absence of those factors that are very difficult and time consuming to reverse: entrenched values and behaviors, inadequate competencies and capabilities. These factors typically require long programs of counselling, training and follow-up before they are affected. By contrast, structural inertia can be broken down by restructuring. Cognitive inertia, although more difficult to deal with, typically can be broken down by intensive communication, discussion and debate (Kotter and Schlesinger, 1979). Thus, resistance forces are taken to be weak if both the cultural *and* momentum factors are absent or consistent with the forces of change. If they are inconsistent with the change forces the resistance is strong. The set of observable change variable values predicted by the change consistency hypothesis is summarized in Table 10.2.

The discontinuous process is internally inconsistent because there is no change before the sudden jump, after which the process is indeterminate. The corresponding change in momentum is low or inconsistent with the change forces prior to the jump and

Table 10.2   Predicted change variable values

Change process		Forces for change		Forces of resistance	
Movement	Internal consistency	Rate of change in: The environment	The competitive logic/ performance	Consistency with direction of change forces:	
				Culture	Momentum
Discontinuous	Inconsistent	High	High	Inconsistent	Unclear
Continuous	Consistent	High	High	Consistent	Consistent
Sporadic	Inconsistent	Low	Low	Unclear	Unclear
No change	Consistent	Low	Low	Inconsistent	Inconsistent

indeterminate thereafter. In the case of a sporadic process, the change direction fluctuates, making it unclear whether the culture and momentum are consistent with the change forces or not. The other entries in Table 10.2 follow from the earlier discussion.

Characteristics of Case Study Sample

The cases come from the live change issues brought by the participants to the first run of the revised International Executive Program on change management held at IMD (International Institute for Management Development in Lausanne, Switzerland) from 31 May to 19 June 1992. The program was billed as one on the management of change with personalized coaching on the participants' issues. There were 25 participants from 16 countries and 13 industries ranging from telecommunications, computers and automobiles to food, oil, banking and shipping. Upon arrival, the participants handed in a short description of the change issue they were dealing with. It is this first written submission, coupled with verbal elaboration provided by participants during the program, that forms the basis of the cases described below. As such, the cases represent the state of the participants' change environment just prior to their arrival for the program. Of the 25 participants, eleven agreed to let their issues be explored for research purposes, and of these, six agreed to a follow-up visit by a researcher to check on the institutional context surrounding their change issue. These six cases are used below. Three of these happen to be from the oil and gas industry. However, each of them concerns a different aspect of change in the industry. To provide a sense of the diversity in the sample, the case studies are summarized below.

Case Study Sample

AB Pripps Bryggerier is a Swedish firm in the distribution and production of beverages. Due to legal regulation, the company has had a relatively protected position in the Swedish market. As Sweden is expected to be joining the European Union, foreign competition is expected to increase as large European producers enter the Swedish market with low prices via imports. The company faces a potential need to cut costs quickly. This is difficult, as it involves cutting administrative overhead, restructuring the organization and rationalizing the product line. A plan to close down two breweries is, nevertheless, under way. Reduction of staff, unpopular with the trade unions, is hard to justify as the company is still very profitable.

Allcomm Business Communication AG is a Swiss advertising and business-to-business communication agency, a spin-off from Ciba-Geigy where it was an internal service unit. It is foreseen that Allcomm should be profitable by the end of 1993. Allcomm seeks to grow to the size where the current number of employees (130) can be sustained. This has already led to a diversification and internationalization (through joint ventures). There is an effort to engage the whole organization to grow business and cut costs in parallel: the operational losses should be cut in half every year. At the same time, financial, personnel and customer processes and systems are being developed to meet the needs of an independent company.

British Gas Exploration and Production Ltd is the exploration and production arm of the largest fully integrated gas company in the world. British Gas was privatized in 1986. The Exploration and Production unit has embarked on a process of growth and acquisition as it became a focus for corporate investment after the privatization. With interests in 23 countries, British Gas is today among the 15 top players in the E&P business in the world. There is some concern about the reactions of the Government Office of Gas Supply in the UK as the company still has a dominant position in the British gas market (90%). The company has consequently asked the Monopolies and Mergers Commission to begin an enquiry into the related regulatory issues.

ICL Europe until recently was a British information technology supplier with a dominant position in the UK (20% of UK market for business systems). At the end of 1990 Fujitsu took a majority shareholding in the company, but exercises currently 'very arms'-length control.' However, they reinforced the long-term strategic objective of the company to grow in Continental Europe and be known as a major European supplier. The acquisition of Nokia Data in 1991 more than trebled the business on the Continent and at the same time gave a major competence in PCs. However, the merger produced additional problems in creating a 'European' culture, due to the very different approaches of the two parties. Previous efforts to promote European synergy have been set back by the strong 'local business' mentality of country managements. The need to succeed in Europe as a whole as well as in national subsidiaries is not generally shared.

Statoil Poland, the Polish subsidiary of the Norwegian state petroleum company, is in the process of establishing a presence in Poland for gasoline distribution. Restructuring and privatization of the Polish oil industry offers competitive conditions that are only emerging but offer attractive opportunities for the large oil companies. The efforts to become a major oil and natural gas provider in the Polish market and establish a Statoil branded retail network throughout Poland represent a proactive opportunity for the company. The overall objective of gaining a large market share in Poland is for the long term.

Total Budget Control is a unit of Total, the French Petroleum company. Large capital requirements have created heavy financial constraints. Cost cutting has thus been the major challenge for the Budget Control unit during the last year. An analysis of the way corporate services have been charged to subsidiaries has brought some additional revenue together with an attempt to collect the outstanding claims more promptly. To make further progress, the unit has been reorganized creating difficulties among the staff with the introduction of new customer service concepts.

Case Study Classification

To illustrate the change consistency hypothesis, the six cases will each be described further and classified with respect to the value of each of the observable change variables: change movement, directional consistency of the change process, rate of change in the environment, rate of change in the competitive logic of an industry and/or performance, consistency of culture with change forces, consistency of momentum with change forces.

AB Pripps Bryggerier has in the past enjoyed a stable competitive position in the Swedish beverage market due to the competitive shield provided by Swedish legislation on beer in particular. Sales of beer through the state-owned retail stores (which have a monopoly on selling class III beer) have been essential to the high profitability of Pripps. As Sweden is expected to join the European Union in the next few years, foreign imports are entering the Swedish market in which Pripps currently has a 44% market share in beer. The Swedes are known to have little loyalty towards Swedish beer; in fact the foreign brands are favoured. Pripps is therefore about to encounter a potential major loss of market share, in particular if its beer continues to be much more expensive than the imports (partly due to a heavy government tax on alcohol).

Pripps has embarked on a 25% cost-cutting program over the next three years. Towards that end, two breweries—in Malmö and Sundsvall—are being closed. Production is thus concentrated in the two remaining breweries in Stockholm and Göteborg. Rationalization of product lines is under consideration to meet the efficiency gains in specialization that the foreign breweries are seen to benefit from. The profit margins are also expected to fall significantly.

For Pripps the cost cutting will mean a loss of jobs. This is difficult to justify for the powerful trade unions, however, as the company is still very profitable. In the past, the company has also had a 'no-firing' policy. At the same time, reorganization of work often meets strong resistance among the employees who are accustomed to doing their jobs in a certain way. 'You can change anything as long as you do not touch the work content of people. If you do that, most people dig their heels in the sand and resist,' says one executive. The company is accustomed to fights between the management and employees, sometimes involving the trade unions. A recent example was a relatively young new boss who came to take over one of the functional departments. As he had a different management style from the previous boss, the displeased employees tried for months to get him fired, before they finally accepted the situation.

Movement: no change/discontinuous change. The recent history of the change process in AB Pripps Bryggerier implies a no-change position, secured by legislation and the government monopoly of beer distribution. Closing the two breweries represents a first move towards a possible proactive cost-netting discontinuity.
Internal consistency of the change process: consistent until the closing of

the breweries. The company has consistently built competitive strength by purchasing and developing trade marks.

Rate of change in the environment: low. Imported beer currently has only 10% market share. The change forces can be expected to grow, however, as Sweden is expected to eventually join the EU.

Competitive logic of the industry: high impact. Changes in the government monopoly on alcohol distribution as well as taxes on beer are likely to change the competition in the industry: different strengths will be needed for future competitiveness.

Performance: Currently low but increasing impact. Pripps is currently very profitable, which makes the implementation of cost cutting and laying off people a difficult task for the management.

Corporate culture: inconsistent with change forces. Corporate culture is very resistant to change. The values and behavior of employees support the stability of the work environment. Change is directly associated with 'lay-offs.'

Momentum for change: inconsistent with change forces. As changes tend to be avoided in the corporate environment and, when implemented, they become a matter of negotiations with the numerous trade unions, there is no momentum for change in the corporation.

Allcomm Group is a new Swiss advertising and business-to-business communication agency, a spin-off from Ciba-Geigy (currently Ciba) where it was an internal service unit. With a turnover of Swiss francs 21 million and 130 people, it became an independent company in January 1991. Having been an internal service unit of the global Swiss pharmaceuticals giant, the legal separation was sudden. The impact was drastic as the subsidies that an internal service unit would normally receive were cut off. The newly emerged company was expected to be profitable by the end of 1993. Although no longer providing a survival guarantee, Ciba guaranteed 100% of Allcomm's sales for its first year of independence, 90% for the second and 80% for the third.

In order to reach a break-even point by 1993 Allcomm must not only cut its costs but also develop new markets as well as acquire more business in its existing areas of strength. Due to its history, Allcomm has a strong competence in the pharmaceuticals and chemicals industry. Management believes that this know-how can be extended to business-to-business communication more generally. It is in consumer advertising where organizational capabilities need to be developed more.

In terms of its competitive strategy, Allcomm has three goals in its change program. These are cultivation of creativity and innovativeness in its services; increasing customer-orientation; and establishment of reliability and accountability of its operations. As an internal service unit, such capabilities were not focal. As an executor of requests from the corporate headquarters, a large part of the services provided were routine; cost was a non-issue. Allcomm used to charge the corporate division a lump sum for the use of its time according to a price list of hourly rates. Allcomm is now in the process of developing systems to cope with finances, customer orders, invoices and personnel administration to 'gain control' of its operations. The purpose is to create systems that can be shared by all departments in the organization.

Before Allcomm could focus on its business development, the management had to deal with the various feelings of insecurity and shock that the separation from Ciba caused among the staff. Working for a large global giant is different from working for a newly emerging communications company. Many feel their loyalty—sometimes decades of work—has been betrayed. Issues such as honoring the Ciba contracts with the cost of living salary index and pension scheme come first. There is also a cultural change: people feel they have lost their solid 'Ciba culture' and there is nothing but vague notions of 'freedom' to replace it. People were demanding: 'Who are we?' says one executive.

There have been some initiatives among the employees to initiate a new corporate culture. Allcomm 2 is such an internal initiative by a group of people that sought another approach to consumer advertising. Inside the organization, it is called the 'chaos group' due to its ability to work on its own, as it wishes. The group reports directly to the CEO. The group was given a budget with a purpose to create a certain amount of turnover in consumer advertising. Although the budget was exceeded, a return is seen in the psychological impact: The group 'helps the CEO to change things in the house'. The resistance to the freedom given to the group has been countered with reactions like that of the CEO: 'Nobody told you, you could not be like them.'

Movement: sporadic. After a discontinuous separation from Ciba, Allcomm is searching for processes that will allow it to establish a sustainable competitive position. The recent history of the change process is sporadic but potentially moving towards a continuous change, as the change forces grow.
Internal consistency of the change process: inconsistent. Some of the activities have been 'experimental.' As it is not clear how the organizational capabilities needed to become market-driven can be

established, the management has allowed some flexibility among the employees to search for the means themselves.

Rate of change in the environment: low. The forces for change are relatively low as Ciba is guaranteeing most of the sales for the first three years; however, they can be expected to grow fast as the performance pressures mount.

The competitive logic: high impact. For Allcomm the way of doing business has totally changed: the captive customer has been replaced by market competition.

Momentum for change: consistent with change forces. Some momentum for change has been established that is consistent with the change forces.

Culture: unclear. The company culture, however, is still to some extent inconsistent with an independent company, not only because the corporate identity is lacking. The employees feel they do not know what is expected from them, even if they are strongly motivated to be 'independent.' Some competencies in customer relationships are also lacking together with support systems and processes for invoicing etc.

British Gas Exploration and Production Ltd is the exploration and production arm of the largest fully integrated gas company in the world. British Gas was privatized in 1986. After the privatization, the Exploration & Production division was chosen as a target for investment. Since then, the business has become global. With interests in 23 countries, British Gas is today among the 15 top players in the E&P business in the world. The E&P division is dependent on the funds from headquarters for its growth. Today, the E&P division contributes 10% of the profit of the corporation; the target is 60% by year 2000.

There is a generation shift going on in the company. Says one executive: 'Before 1986, no active decisions could be made—they evolved through time. If somebody really pushed for one, the answer was no.' Now there is a new generation of decision makers taking over. The Board made a strategic decision after the privatization to recruit young managers to head some of the divisions evidently to stir the way British Gas operated. The organizational functioning is still very bureaucratic in British Gas, however. 'Functional silos' are one of the problems: there is a department for everything; and too many functions are duplicated across the company.

Change is taking place slowly, driven by some of the younger managers in the operational management. Says one: 'I can change this corner in this building; make it an example for others and hope that the effects will spread.' He continues 'I feel we need a different management paradigm for British Gas. So I made a presentation on the organizational pyramid turned upside down to the personnel, corporate people, and management training people. They were shocked. Someone asked one of the senior managers: "Why is he allowed to talk to us like that?" There are obvious personal reactions against tearing down an empire. But nobody was saying I was talking rubbish. I am not not the only one who knows there is something wrong in this company. I am just polarizing views and focusing their attention to what is wrong. After the presentation, I talked to people individually and they were thinking about it. Somebody even asked me: "If you had the powers, how would you restructure this company?" But I have no time to solve such a huge issue.'

Movement: sporadic. British Gas E&P is undergoing change sporadically in terms of the movement of the change process, driven by internal change agents who occasionally manage to focus attention on some of the internal problems.
Internal consistency of the change process: inconsistent. Managing change is secondary to 'doing one's job,' and this is not consistently driven in any strategic direction.
Rate of change in the environment: low. There is a lack of strong forces for change in the environment, apart from the need to be more growth oriented.
Performance: low impact. As the growth program has only started, there is no performance impact yet.
Culture: unclear. The corporate culture, values and behavior of the people are changing slowly with the generational shift, but are apparently not yet fully consistent with the need to be more growth oriented.
Momentum for change: consistent with change forces. As change forces are not clearly established, momentum for change is also low; at the same time, what little change momentum there is can be said to be consistent with the drive for growth.

ICL Europe until recently was a British information technology supplier with a dominant position in the UK (20% of the UK market for business systems), strong positions in some Commonwealth countries but with relatively minor representation in Continental ones. At the end of 1990 Fujitsu took a majority shareholding in the company, but exercises currently 'very arm's-length control.' Fujitsu reinforced the long-term strategic objective of the company to grow in Continental Europe and be known as a major European supplier. The acquisition of Nokia Data in 1991, funded entirely by ICL itself, more than trebled the business on the Continent and at the same time gave a major competence in PCs. However, the merger produced additional problems in creating a 'European' culture, due to the very different approaches of the two parties. Previous efforts to promote European synergy were set back by the strong 'local business' mentality of country managements. The need to succeed in Europe as a whole as well as in national subsidiaries was not generally shared.

However, some of the industry fundamentals are under pressure. These include the powerful role of a country manager and that of a salesman: customer needs are becoming more pan-European and service is gaining importance relative to personal selling. Companies want pan-European IT solutions, but the current country organization cannot respond to such needs effectively. Service is becoming the key, but the service people lack credibility in the industry, typically coming from lower educational backgrounds than salespeople. Most business has been local. 'We are not good at delivering pan-European solutions,' claims one ICL executive. And time is running out, because profit margins are shrinking.

The goal of the European strategy is to have a 'willingness to give and take and accept that some things will be led from another place.' Critical skills should be pooled and made accessible to everybody. 'There is a certain intellectual understanding of the need to share: a value is developing.' The change process is supported by the Fujitsu's strategic intent to have ICL as its 'Euroarm.' The CEO of ICL has been advocating a European strategy for the past seven years. Country managers are beginning to recognize the need to change. 'I hear some of my thoughts coming back from the field.' Slowly, an organizational perception of change has emerged.

Movement: sporadic/continuous. A no-change position of the past has given way to sporadic change, and potentially continuous change as the impact of the change forces becomes evident.

Internal consistency of the change process: consistent. There is gradual change towards a European strategy.

Competitive logic of the industry: high impact. ICL Europe is encountering a competitive situation in which the competitive logic of the industry is shifting towards pan-European service strategies from a previous country-based management structure.

Rate of change in the environment: high. Forces for change are high as the profit margins are eroding.

Culture: unclear. The local culture of each company is inconsistent with the change forces, but perception of the need to change is slowly developing with some values for across country co-operation developing.

Momentum for change: unclear. The company is gaining momentum for change; however, the old national momentum is still in place.

Statoil Poland is a subsidiary of Statoil, the Norwegian state petroleum company, a fully integrated oil, gas and petrochemicals group with over 12 000 employees and operations in 12 countries. Statoil is the largest producer of crude oil in the North Sea, producing 60 million tons a year. With its large production capacity, Statoil currently pursues downstream activities in new markets with good potential for growth and profitability. Developments in Eastern Europe, particularly in Poland, offer good opportunities in the context of a stagnant, even declining Scandinavian market.

Under the Communist regime, the petroleum sector of Poland was organized on the basis of horizontal integration, with crude oil production and procurement, transportation, processing and marketing each controlled by separate state entities that exercised monopoly control over their markets. It is now proposed that the industry should evolve towards vertically integrated structures, similar to the petroleum sector in the EU countries. This was an EU recommendation. The monopoly position of the Polish state will be abolished and free market competitive principles will be adopted. The estimated cost of restructuring is about $5 billion.

Statoil Poland Ltd is a major supplier of crude oil and petrol to Poland (third largest) with annual sales of $200 million. Statoil has made a preliminary co-operation agreement (letter of intent) with CPN, the previous retail monopoly for gasoline distribution in Poland. CPN has, however, made similar agreements with other oil companies such as Total, Agip and Dea. Statoil's agreement with CPN comprises establishment of a joint venture (51% Statoil owned) for the purposes of modernizing ex-CPN outlets to emerge under the Statoil brand. Statoil seeks to establish its own (100% owned) retail outlets as well, and is currently buying land for attractive retail sites. Statoil is also involved in discussions with other oil companies concerning a consortium for a takeover of the oil refinery in Gdansk: Statoil is planning to buy 10–15% of the shares in the refinery (this is part of the government imposed entry ticket to access the distribution network of oil). The long-term goal is to establish a

10–15% market share in the fuel market in Warsaw and Northern Poland.

Statoil Poland has also been building relationships with the Ministry of Industry and Ministry of Privatization (or 'Ownership Changes,' as the name implies in Polish). 'You have to be present to get to know people and establish a network when politicians come and go.' This relationship building has been an investment for being part of the privatization process. It has also implied counselling the government in possible ways of achieving the optimal solution for the privatization. There are issues that the foreign companies want to have resolved before making an investment in the sector. These include, in particular, the price and tax regime of petroleum as well as the importing of oil to Poland. Before you can start investing, you must have some clarity on these matters. 'Today, it is not profitable to operate a gas station due to a very low margin. The oil must currently be bought from a Polish refiner. We want to import our own oil.'

Movement: continuous. Early on, Statoil has been present in Poland to show commitment to the long term.

Internal consistency of the change process: consistent. Statoil's strategic intent is long-term development of market share which it has pursued for the last three years.

Rate of change in the environment: high. Statoil is encountering the radically changing environment of the Polish petroleum industry characterized by the emergence of the new vertical structures.

Competitive logic of the industry: high impact as new players continue to enter the Polish market.

Culture: consistent with change forces. The company has know-how and technology that is in demand for developing the Polish oil industry.

Momentum for change: consistent with change forces. Continuous effort has been dedicated to developing relationships with local decision-makers and counselling the Polish government in the matters related to the petroleum industry.

Total Budget Control is the budget control unit of Total, a leading international, integrated oil and gas company based in Europe with major operations in over 80 countries. The appreciation of the French franc (100% during the last ten years relative to the dollar) has made the head-office services charged from Paris appear expensive relative to what the subsidiaries could get from third parties. The new head of the Budget Control Unit is leading a drive to lower these costs which has resulted in a careful analysis of the activities of the unit.

As a result, the unit has just been reorganized in order to better serve the subsidiaries requesting services from the head office. Previously, the department operated according to a strict division of tasks. People were assigned to a particular task, charging either hourly or monthly rates for services provided by the head office to the subsidiaries.

The challenge is to convince the head-office people that there is a real market relationship between them and the subsidiaries. 'We have to put the customer first. Our customer will have only one point of reference here in the head office, and not a different person for different services.' This cannot be done unless fundamental changes are made in the way the department operates.

Getting people motivated to learn new skills and new ways of working is taking a lot of effort. Teams of four people have been formed to support change. 'We had some new open-minded people come into the teams. We developed the new concept with them. People must realize it will be good for them to do things differently. You can do this by example: by putting the right person into a critical position at the right time.'

However, major difficulties are being encountered among the staff as the new concepts are introduced. 'First they were scared of the new job, of the new language, and of the fact that they now had to do what the customer wanted rather than imposing their way of doing things. We had meetings with the subsidiaries to show the staff that what we used to do was inappropriate to their needs. We showed the benefits of a different way of working to our staff. We went into the whole process: what these head-office charges became when they got into the accounts of the subsidiaries and what their requirements were. The allocation of all charges to their proper accounts caused major satisfaction in the subsidiaries. The aim was to get people to understand *why* we did the charging. The duty of our staff is not only to have the invoicing done. It is to satisfy the customer.'

Movement: discontinuous. Relative to past organizational behavior, the change represents a sudden leap and a radically different kind of organizational behavior.

Internal consistency of the change process: inconsistent. The work routines, organization and values of the employees are shifting.

Rate of change in the environment: high. The pressure on costs is creating a high rate of change in the corporate environment of the Budget Control Unit.

Performance: high impact. The performance of the Budget Control Unit is not at all up to the new standards expected by Total's top management.

Culture: inconsistent with change forces. Although it is beginning to change, the organizational culture is still basically inconsistent with the new values and behavior required.

Momentum for change: consistent with change forces. The reorganization has initiated a momentum for change in the direction of a leaner, lower-cost approach.

Comments on the Predicted and Observed Variable Values

In general, the observed variable values in Table 10.3 conform to the predicted ones in Table 10.2 relatively well. The differences arise mainly from the dynamism of the change situations, the movement from one type of change process to another, associated with the shifting relationship between the forces for change and resistance. In the case of Pripps, although the change forces are only emerging, they are strengthening relatively fast as shown by the shifting competitive logic. The resistance to change, however, remains relatively strong and perhaps is even increasing, which is moving the firm from no change towards discontinuous change.

Although Allcomm is experiencing sporadic change it shows signs of moving towards more continuous adaptation to market forces. This is being driven by the high impact of the forces for change on the competitive logic and is reflected in the emerging change momentum within Allcomm.

British Gas is also going through sporadic change with weaker forces (than in Allcomm's case) moving it towards the continuous pursuit of growth. This migration is beginning to manifest itself internally in the emerging growth momentum accompanying the shift in management generations.

ICL is between sporadic and continuous change. The corporate culture and momentum are beginning to shift in response to the forces accompanying the rapid rate of change in the computer industry. (If the corporate culture is unable to respond sufficiently rapidly and completely, ICL could find itself confronted with discontinuous change.)

Statoil Poland shows all the signs of a continuous change process in a small entrepreneurial business unit. Total Budget Control provides a typical example of discontinuous organizational change, where the sudden jump has just occurred. As a result, momentum has been triggered in the direction of the change forces, but the culture remains inconsistent.

Table 10.3   Observed change variable values

Change process		Forces for change		Forces of resistance	
Movement	Internal consistency	Rate of change in: The environment	The competitive logic/performance	Consistency with direction of change forces: Culture	Momentum
Pripps No change/ discontinuous	Consistent	Low	High	Inconsistent	Inconsistent
Allcomm Sporadic	Inconsistent	Low	High	Unclear	Consistent
British Gas E&P Sporadic	Inconsistent	Low	Low	Unclear	Consistent
ICL Europe Sporadic/ continuous	Consistent	High	High	Unclear	Unclear
Statoil Poland Continuous	Consistent	High	High	Consistent	Consistent
Total Budget Control Discontinuous	Inconsistent	High	High	Inconsistent	Consistent

MANAGERIAL IMPLICATIONS

The basic change matrix (see Figure 10.1) can be used as a managerial tool (Strebel, 1992). It offers a framework for mapping out scenarios as well as designing reactive and proactive managerial intervention paths. The nature of these possibilities is outlined below.

Scenario Building

The players in the industry, or within the firm, are first positioned in the change matrix according to their resistance to change and the impact of the change force on them. This provides the basis for exploring different ways in which the interplay between the forces of change and resistance may evolve and how the players may move in the matrix. There are five generic scenarios that are possible corresponding to the players staying where they are, migrating to one of the other positions in the matrix or being forced out of the matrix (the system collapses).

Reactive Intervention Paths

The slower a firm is in responding to the strength of a change force, the closer it will be to discontinuous change in the upper-right corner of the change matrix (position B in Figure 10.2). In the extreme position close to the edge of the discontinuity, the managers' choice of intervention path is limited to either putting the firm through discontinuous internal change or allowing it to collapse. Further back from the edge, the manager may be able to protect the firm from the force of change, by resisting the change force, or by gaining enough time to intervene in the direction of sporadic or possibly even continuous change. Since the change matrix can also be used to categorize viable organizational structures and cultures,

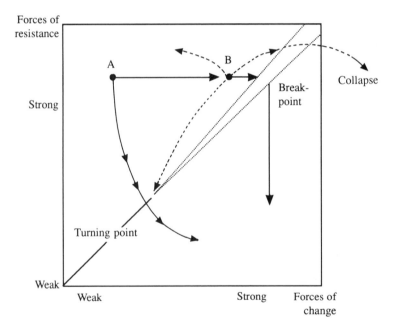

Figure 10.2   Possible managerial intervention paths
A = initial position for proactive intervention;
B = initial position for reactive intervention;
———▶ viable intervention paths;
- - - -▶ difficult intervention paths

as well as implementation styles, a rather complete description of the implementation path is possible.

Proactive Intervention Paths

The sooner the firm recognizes an emerging change force, the more time and therefore choice (position A in Figure 10.2) the manager has in selecting an intervention path to lead the company towards any of the four positions in the change matrix. Broadly, however, there are two basic paths that managers can use to move the organization from no change in the top-left corner of the matrix to continuous adaptation in the bottom-right corner: either a gradual turning point based on sporadic change opening the organization up so that it can discover and then track the change force as it develops, or a later sudden breakpoint, based on discontinuous realignment of the organization with the strengthening change force.

CONCLUSION

The positioning of change processes in a force field provides a set of propositions about what type of change is appropriate in different contexts described by the configuration of the forces of change and resistance. These propositions can be expressed in terms of a predicted set of change variable values. The actual change processes in six live case studies seem to reflect the predicted set of change variable values rather well. The main discrepancy seems to be associated with the movement of the case companies from one region of the force field to another, that is, a shift from one type of change process to another. Apart from shifting external forces, this movement also reflects the impact of managerial intervention. With respect to the the latter, the change consistency hypothesis has practical implications for the management of change in organizations. However, the analysis of the impact of managerial intervention on the change process and vice versa goes beyond this chapter. In addition, the confirmation of the validity and reliability of the change consistency hypothesis will require extensive testing.

REFERENCES

Aldrich, H. (1979) *Organizations and Environments*. Englewood Cliffs, NJ, Prentice Hall.

Ansoff, I. (1965) Corporate Strategy, New York, McGraw-Hill.

Ansoff, I. (1980) Strategic issue management, Strategic Management Journal, 1, 2, 131–48.

Astley, G. (1985) The two ecologies: population and community perspectives on organizational evolution, Administrative Science Quarterly, 30, 224–41.

Barnes, J. (1984) Cognitive biases and their impact on strategic planning, Strategic Management Journal, 5, 129–38.

Boeker, W. (1989) Strategic change: the effects of founding and history, Academy of Management Journal, 32 (3), 489–515.

Burns, T. and Stalker, G. (1961) The Management of Innovation, London, Tavistock.

Bourgeois, L. J. III (1981) Measuring organizational slack, Academy of Management Review, January.

Caves, R. E. and Porter, M. E. (1977) From entry barriers to mobility barriers: conjectural decisions and contrived deterrence to new competition, Quarterly Journal of Economics, 91, 241–61.

Chandler, A. D. (1962) Strategy and Structure, Cambridge, MA, MIT Press.

Cyert, R. M. and March, J. G. (1963) A Behavioral Theory of the Firm, Englewood Cliffs, NJ, Prentice Hall.

Downs, A. (1967) Inside Bureaucracy, Boston, MA, Little, Brown.

Emery, F. E. and Trist, E. L. (1965) The causal texture of environments, Human Relations, 18, 21–32.

Gilbert, X. and Strebel, P. (1989) Taking advantage of industry shifts, European Management Journal, 7 (4), 396–402.

Ginsberg, A. and Abrahamson, E. (1991) Champions of change and strategic shifts: the role of internal and external change advocates, Journal of Management Studies, 28 (2), 173–90.

Ginsberg, A. and Bucholz, A. (1990) Converting to for-profit status: corporate responsiveness to radical change, Academy of Management Journal, 33 (3), 445–77.

Ginsberg, A. and Venkatraman, N. (1985) Contingency perspectives of organizational strategy: a critical review of the empirical literature, Academy of Management Review, 10, 421–34.

Hannan, M. T. and Freeman, J. (1984) Structural inertia and organizational change, American Sociological Review, 49, 149–64.

Jackson, S. and Dutton, E. (1988) Discerning threat and opportunities, Administrative Science Quarterly, 33, 370–87.

Kelly, D. and Amburgey, T. (1991) Organizational inertia and momentum: a dynamic model of strategic change, Academy of Management Journal, 34 (3), 591–612.

Kimberly, J., Miles, R., et al. (1980) The Organizational Life Cycle, San Francisco, CA, Jossey-Bass.

Kotter, J. and Heskett, J. (1992) Corporate Culture and Performance, New York, Free Press.

Kotter, J. and Schlesinger, L. (1979) Choosing strategies for change, Harvard Business Review, March–April, 106–14.

Lawrence, P. R. and Lorsch, J. W. (1967) *Organization and Environment*, Boston, MA, Harvard Business School.

Lewin, K. (1947) Frontiers in group dynamics, concept, method and reality in social science: social equilibria and social change, *Human Relations*, 1, 2–38.

Lewin, K. (1951) *Field Theory in Social Science*, New York, Harper and Row.

Lindblom, C. (1959) The science of muddling through, *Public Administration Review*, 19, 79–88.

Lundberg, C. (1984) Strategies for organizational transitioning. In Kimberley, J. R. and Quinn, R. E. (eds), *Managing Organizational Transitions*. Homewood, ILL, Irwin.

MacMillan, I., McCaffery, M. and Van Wijk, G. (1985) Competitors' responses to easily imitated new products: exploring commercial banking product introductions, *Strategic Management Journal*, 6, 75–86.

March, J. G. and Simon, H. A. (1958) *Organizations*, New York, John Wiley.

Meyer, A. D. (1982) Adapting to environmental jolts, *Administrative Science Quarterly*, 27, 515–37.

Meyer, A. D., Brooks, G. and Goes, J. (1990) Environmental jolts and industry revolutions: organizational responses to discontinuous change, *Strategic Management Journal*, 11, 93–110.

Meyer, J. and Rowan, B. (1977) Institutional organizations: formal structure as a myth and ceremony, *American Journal of Sociology*, 83, 340–63.

Miles, R. and Snow, C. (1978) *Organizational Strategy, Structure and Process*, New York, McGraw-Hill.

Miller, S. and Friesen, P. H. (1984) *Organizations: A Quantum Review*, Englewood Cliffs, NJ, Prentice Hall.

Mintzberg, H. (1987) Crafting strategy, *Harvard Business Review*, July–August, 66–75.

Mintzberg, H. (1990) The design school: reconsidering the basic premises of strategic management, *Strategic Management Journal*, 11, 171–95.

Nisbet, R. and Ross, L. (1980) *Human Inference: Strategies and Shortcomings of Social Judgement*, Englewood Cliffs, NJ, Prentice Hall.

Oster, S. (1982) Intraindustrial structure and the ease of strategic change, *Review of Economics and Statistics*, 64, 376–83.

Perrow, C. (1986) *Complex Organizations, A Critical Essay*, New York Random House.

Pettigrew, A. (1985) *The Awakening Giant*, Oxford, Blackwell.

Pettigrew, A. (1987) *The Management of Strategic Change*, Oxford, Blackwell.

Pettigrew, A. (1987) Context and action in the transformation of the firm, *Journal of Management Studies*, 24 (6), 649–70.

Quinn, J. B. (1978) Strategic change: logical incrementalism, *Sloan Management Review*, 20, 7–21.

Scott, W. (1987) *Organizations: Rational, Natural and Open Systems*, 2nd edn, Englewood Cliffs, NJ, Prentice Hall.

Schwenk, C. (1988) The cognitive perspective on strategic decision making, *Journal of Management Studies*, 25 (1), 41–53.

Schwenk, C. (1989) Linking cognitive, organizational and political factors in explaining strategic change, *Journal of Management Studies*, 26 (2), 176–87.

Stinchcombe, A. (1965) Organizations and social structure. In March, J. G. (ed.), *Handbook of Organization,*. Chicago, Rand McNally.

Strebel, P. (1989) Competitive turning points: how to recognize them, *European Management Journal*, **7** (2), 141–47.

Strebel, P. (1990) Dealing with discontinuities, *European Management Journal*, **8**, 434–42.

Strebel, P. (1992) *Breakpoints, How Managers Exploit Radical Business Change*, Boston, MA, Harvard Business School.

Stubbart, C. (1989) Managerial cognition: a mising link in strategic management research, *Journal of Management Studies*, **26** (4), 325–47.

Thompson, J. D. (1967) *Organizations in Action*, New York, McGraw-Hill.

Tushman, M. L. and Anderson, P. (1986) Technological discontinuities and organizational environments, *Administrative Science Quarterly*, **31**, 439–65.

Tushman, M. and Romanelli, E. (1985) Organizational evolution: a metamorphosis model of convergence and reorientation. In Cummings, L. and Staw, B. (eds), *Research in Organizational Behaviour, 7*, Greenwich, CT, JAI Press.

Välikangas, L. (1992) *Patterns of Change in a Firm*, Licenciate thesis, University of Tampere, Finland.

Van de ven, A. H. and Drazin, R. (1985) The concept of fit in contingency theory. In Cummings, L. and Staw, B. (eds), *Research in Organizational Behaviour, 7*, Greenwich, CT, JAI Press.

Walsh, J. (1988) Selectivity and selective perception: an investigation of managers' belief structures and information processing, *Academy of Management Journal*, **31**, 872–96.

Williamson, O. E. (1975) *Markets and Hierarchies*, New York, Free Press.

Zaskind, S. and Costello, T. (1962) Perception: implications for administration, *Administrative Science Quarterly*, **7**, 218–35.

Zucker, L. (1987) Institutional theories of organizations, *Annual Review of Sociology*, **13**, 443–64.

11

CORPORATE PLANNING: AN EMPIRICAL STUDY OF UK CHARITABLE ORGANISATIONS

Matthew Gibson Lynas

Aberdeen University

and Keith Ritchie

Halliburton Plc

INTRODUCTION

The scale and scope of charitable activity throughout the United Kingdom is difficult to establish with any accuracy. Undoubtedly, charitable organisations receive and contribute significant resources in providing services to those in need. There is a growing awareness that changes in the operating environment create new and different challenges and opportunities. To survive and indeed develop the response competency of organisations, in what is an increasingly competitive environment, needs to be assessed. One aspect of such assessment clearly lies in improving organisational effectiveness through application of appropriate systems to deploy resources more effectively. Attendant on this perspective is obviously the need to develop the competencies of management in particular. This chapter examines such issues and, in particular, the role of planning.

CHARITIES IN THE UK AND ROLE OF PLANNING

By 1989 there were over 165000 charities registered with the Charities Commissioners in England and Wales. This number

International Review of Strategic Management, Volume 5
Edited by D. E. Hussey © 1994 John Wiley & Sons Ltd

continues to grow annually at a rate of about 2%. Added to this total are charities in Scotland and Northern Ireland. Financial estimates of the total money given to charities range from 3% to 5% of GNP. The Charity Commissioners estimate that in 1991 trustees controlled £16 billion every year (Jackson 1990). All these figures point to charities being involved in significant activities.

Particular challenges posed to charities in the 1990s would seem to be apparent in the success of spectacular events such as Comic Relief or ITV's Telethon. The effects of economic recession and the much-talked-about 'compassion fatigue' all suggest increasing difficulty in attracting and retaining financial support for a particular cause.

Changes in government policy are also a major factor in their views towards the provision of care in the community. This suggests an increased emphasis on private sector provision of services and markets for goods and services. The indications are therefore that consideration of strategic processes, related to attracting and effective deployment of resources, will be an increasing pressure on charitable organisations.

Related to the above assumptions we should bear in mind that there is a continuing emergence of new popular causes and enduring social problems which divert resources from one charity to another. Add to this the increasing importance of 'green' issues, the threat of Aids, famine in Africa or the intense problems of Eastern Europe, and we have some idea of the context within which charitable organisations must seek support and demonstrate accountability for utilising resources effectively.

The description of the context within which charitable organisations must demonstrate effectiveness does not end with the views expressed above. There is obviously increasing competition for resources in financial areas, in attracting voluntary effort, in lobbying for government input. This must be set against the increasing demands made on charities. The need for more effective planning systems is evident. However, it is not simply a question of considering systems and competencies. It is also a question of understanding the type of structures and culture which are needed to support and inform, respectively, the operation of effective corporate planning and strategic thinking.

OVERVIEW OF PROBLEMS RELATED TO ESTABLISHING PLANNING IN CHARITABLE ORGANISATIONS

There are a number of obvious problems which face organisations seeking to establish systematic planning. First, charities in the UK cover a wide range of areas in terms of the nature of inputs they provide. Some are national or international, others local. They range from the very large with a total income of several tens of million pounds per annum to very small with annual income of only hundreds of pounds. Many are involved in the provision of services themselves while others simply dispense resources to enable recipient organisations to provide such services (Seddighi *et al.,* 1988). It is obvious that such diversity will cause charities to have very different planning assumptions, horizons and methods of approach.

The voluntarist approach may, at first sight, appear to be in contradiction to systematic planning concepts and commitment to professional management. The literature would nonetheless indicate that there may not be as wide a difference between what is acceptable in private sector organisations and what is needed in charitable or voluntary ones (Newman and Wallender, 1983; Handy, 1990).

The adoption of business planning methods may well be seen by some to be at odds with the motivational goals of personnel who are not engaged in running a particular charity. Obviously there is an element of substance in this insofar as too 'commercial' an approach might have an effect on an organisation's goodwill and consequently be counterproductive. The mountainous problem still remains in that responses to change need to recognise first the undoubted pressures which do exist for more accountability and consequent effective deployment of resources, while at the same time recognising the likely resistances arising from perspectives such as those held about indulging too deeply in commercial activities. These are aspects which clearly go beyond a particular type of planning system and the competencies needed for more systematic support of management. They are about the management of organisational change, the challenging of assumptions and the reconciling of more structured methods, with the culture of charitable organisations.

THE PLANNING PROCESS

Research for this chapter attempts to identify types of planning processes and related criteria and to make some suggestions as to how charitable organisations may utilise concepts such as corporate planning, in their development and management.

Corporate Planning

The chapter is essentially concerned with the process described as corporate planning (Argenti, 1989). This perspective essentially regards corporate planning as a process covering the organisation as a whole. Although the processes involved in strategic thinking are recognised and might be seen to be equally concerned with a holistic view, the corporate planning perspective has been taken as a better focus of intent in this research. The term strategic planning has not been set aside entirely, for within the design of the survey questionnaires its value is implicit, in that questions are used to test whether strategic thinking processes exist as part of planning.

SOME THEORETICAL PERSPECTIVES

It is obviously difficult to consider planning in isolation without addressing the wider issues of why charities should adopt any of the techniques of management. Drucker (1990) and Handy (1990) emphasise the negative nature of the very term *management*, especially in non-profit organisations. Their implied criticism embodies the view that business management is concerned with a *bottom-line* orientation. Drucker (1990) goes on to point out that this could be a misleading perspective, as the lack of some simple measurement of goal achievement, within non-profit organisations, makes the need for effective management more pressing. In any event, it is a fairly simplistic view to assume that business goals are concerned solely, or even mainly, with profit maximisation. The removal of the profit-maximising element from any analysis of organisations, typified by their *non-profit* nature, does, to an extent, explain the difficulties experienced in developing an appropriate theory for a non-profit-making field of activity.

Both Drucker and Handy stress the need for management development within voluntary organisations. Handy summarises the case against those who adopt an unfavourable view of management, by basing their assumptions on a negative association with big business or bureaucracy. He suggests that the 'Perils of Voluntarism' comprises two elements: 'Strategic Delinquency' and the 'Servant Syndrome'. Essentially, strategic delinquency is the belief that the cause is more important than the goals. This view can be as dysfunctional as in commercial organisations, mainly because it takes a blinkered perspective that 'it is better to have taken part than to have succeeded!'

The Servant Syndrome refers to the replacement of professionalism with the belief that everyone should *muck in*. This suggests virtue in struggle and perhaps chaos, most certainly amateurism as opposed to adopting a more systematic management of resources. That this could be perceived as a selfish view on its own, perhaps diminishing impact, dissipating scarce resources, is often not recognised. Another myth is that it is not possible to prioritise or direct effort, embodied in the platitude that 'there is so much to do, you try to do it all'.

The research does not set out to dispute whether some planning goes on within voluntary organisations. It is accepted that some degree of thought is given in many organisations. The real issues lie in the implementation of formal planning processes. It is important to recognise that success will depend on aspects such as organisational structure (Chandler, 1962), on culture (Handy, 1985; Armstrong, 1990). Although these are seen as important issues for future examination the research did not explore the organisational context in any depth.

The authors do recognise that planning's role is not merely that of aiding improved performance through the development of strategy and goals but should also lead to organisational development in areas of improving communication, facilitating the sharing of problems and involving personnel in focusing on the direction of efforts (Langley, 1988; Quinn et al., 1988). Any theory which is likely to be developed in respect of planning is likely to be fairly general in nature and may not, because of the diversity in terms of size, objectives, degree of voluntary input, be necessarily applicable to every situation. It is also important to note the differences, which writers like Bryson (1988) and Argenti (1989) note, between corporate and strategic and long-range planning. Argenti identifies strategic planning as being 'issues'-orientated rather than specifying goals and translating these into what are often financial targets. It is thus more concerned with analysing the environment in which the organisation operates and the related response competences required to operate effectively in that environment. It is likely to be concerned with management of change and the search and exploitation of opportunities.

Arising from the review of literature the stress in strategic thinking is on the importance of clarifying mission for the successful implementation of the planning process. Clearly, establishing the overriding purpose of vision of the organisation can further the planning process. Argenti (1989) and Drucker (1990) are both clear that this is an essential prerequisite to the process of corporate planning. Handy, examining in particular such issues from an organisational and motivational angle, includes this particular point as being a key to developing planning. Bryson (1988) sees mission clarification as one stage in his eight-point plan which is considered later.

There are strong theoretical views on the consequences of not clarifying the mission of the organisation (Argenti, 1989; Drucker, 1990). Obviously, the concern about the lack of consensus and direction is justified if we are to consider the implementation of corporate planning in any organisation. The confusion which might well arise within voluntary organisations, particularly organisations having a number of concurrent or parallel objectives, is another reason for ensuring that there is clarity at the mission level. Such internal competition will only be tolerable if there is effective management and if such management has some supportive structure, as will be evident in the way in which interrelationships are determined. This is obviously a particular function of organisational design of effective systems, particularly those needed for planning and control of resource application.

The literature appears to draw little from the world of commerce in relation to the kind of modifications which might be required in terms of planning concepts. The emphasis appears mainly to highlight the problems of transfer into the unique environment of voluntary organisations (Drucker, 1990; Handy, 1990). Bryson (1988) suggests that certain techniques and lessons can be drawn from the private sector. In particular, analytical frameworks such as SWOT and, to some extent, the Harvard Policy Model, which allows identification of values of the various stakeholders, can be of value. Bryson also draws attention to the possible benefits of Porter's ideas on Competitive Advantage, and in particular his Five Forces Model (Porter, 1985).

The context for application of systematic planning and other *management* concepts has been referred to by Butler and Wilson (1990). The context is the combination of environment and culture and can be regarded as influential in informing the development of strategies. Awareness of both these dimensions is clearly critical in the creation of the planning process. It is of interest that, although Bryson (1988) suggests that business models are highly dependent on logical relationships and as such may not be necessarily appropriate in the *charitable context*, Butler and Wilson (1990) suggest that 'the moral—democratic, participative and altruistic' characteristics of any charity are as likely to lead to decisions being taken in a political rather than a logical form. Although the underlying theory on methods of planning used by UK charities is at this point somewhat vague and unclear, the arguments for application of more systematic approaches, such as those discussed by writers such as Argenti, need to be considered in the light of the challenges facing such organisations.

PRACTICAL PERSPECTIVES

There is a great deal of practical advice on how to plan for both non-profit-making organisations and charities. In general, the literature highlights the crucial importance of the mission statement, if a strategic perspective is to be followed. It is then assumed that appropriate strategies can be developed and policies adopted to take the charity in the direction desired. There are obvious differences of opinion on the tools and techniques to be used in the planning process. The empirical research for this study aims to identify, contrast and compare suggested approaches. One point worth noting is that the literature, whether theoretical or practical, tends to see the use of a strategic approach as being a preferred or indeed the only relevant means of planning in charities.

Gies *et al.* (1990) see the planning process as setting parameters for the discharge of day-to-day management decisions. In this sense strategic planning develops a common approach that can be based on the common value system (culture) of the organisation, thus leading to more consistent decisions. The influence of the stakeholders on the planning process is highlighted by their research. The warning which these authors give on over-use of quantitative techniques, as opposed to involvement of the stakeholders in the clarification of conflicting aims, is important. The view is that over-emphasis on quantitative techniques can assume consensus and thus discourage the exploration of the fundamental values, which are very important within organisations of a charitable kind but is equally important in developing underpinning assumptions for strategy.

Work by George (1989) and Epsy (1990) adds to the practical guidance on the process of clarifying organisational purpose and on how to develop a strategic plan. Essentially this revolves around the review of the existing situation and consideration of the option of remaining *static* as opposed to exploring opportunities for developing an organisation. This concept embodies use of analytical models and techniques with the emphasis on identification of goals. Such a process tends to emphasise the *mission* as the key to management success for any non-profit organisation (Drucker, 1990). This process orientation, by implication, involves stakeholders in the development of long-term goals. It emphasises the measurement of performance linked to a concept of *service to people*. Mission, specific tasks, measurement of achievement is therefore a consistent plea in the literature. Handy (1990) believes that measurement of achievement will often be seen in financial terms but emphasises the need to ensure that hard data are the 'servant and not the master.'

STRATEGIC PLANNING CONCEPTS

Ritchie's (1992) research finds that Bryson (1988) provides the clearest exposition of strategic planning in the sense of applicability to charitable organisations. The three steps of this process involves stakeholders in attempting a consensus on the need for and the purposes of the planning process. Bryson reverts to the 'legal charter' as confirmation of the overall scope or remit of the organisation before determining what the mission should be. Steps 4 and 5 utilise techniques such as environmental scanning or appropriate analytical models (e.g. SWOT). Steps 6 and 7 develop the key strategic areas for the future.

The final stage attempts to institutionalise the strategy by finding the means of integrating it into the organisation and gaining acceptance of the members of that organisation. This assumes that the climate into which the process is being integrated is amenable in the sense of being committed to planning as a contribution to operational effectiveness.

These practical contributions, deriving from the literature, are supplemented by more specific functional contributions. For example, Porter (1987) offers concepts within the functional aspects of marketing. Financial control is informed by writers such as Ramanthan (1982) on aspects such as fund raising.

Questionnaires developed at both pilot and main stages of this research are informed by the theoretical and practical sources which have been presented in the preceding sections. The questions aim to ascertain whether or not evidence exists of the incorporation of such practical and theoretical insights into the strategic planning processes of charitable organisations or if indeed other methods of planning, of a less conceptualised kind, are in use.

THE REALITY OF PLANNING IN NON-PROFIT MAKING ORGANISATIONS

No firm conclusions can be drawn from the limited information available on how charities in the UK plan. The research methodology for this study aims to clarify if formal processes are followed. In this sense it is limited to providing the conceptual clarification upon which to base further research. This is planned to examine the relationship of planning to performance and aims to present case work demonstrating this relationship at a later stage.

THE FIELD RESEARCH METHODS AND FINDINGS

The research involved in a pilot study with a second survey instrument developed as an outcome from this. The overall design aimed to obtain insights into the practical application of planning and the type of current processes in use in large and medium-sized charities, within the UK.

Sample

It was decided to keep the review as broad as possible and the decision was made to carry out a systematic sample of 200 out of the 400 top fund-raising charities listed in the Charities Aid Foundation's (CAF) annual publication *Charity Trends* (CAF, 1990). This source is acknowledged as being the most up-to-date database for UK charities, although the most recent data relate to 1989. By concentrating on both large and medium-sized charities it was hoped to gain some idea of current practice. Relative size was considered to be one of the features likely to determine the scope of the planning.

In evaluating sample results a split was made into large and medium-sized charities. Figures 11.1 and 11.2 illustrate the voluntary income and total income in respect of the 200 charities sampled. It will be seen from these figures that the split, into two halves, shows the relatively greater size of the top 100 sampled, in terms of total and voluntary income. It may also be noted that this could have a distorting effect on the top 15 sampled charities, each with voluntary income in excess of £10 million. The median voluntary income of the first 100 charities sampled is £1 970 000 compared to an average of £5 446 000. The second half of the sample is more evenly spread with median voluntary income £518 000 and a mean of £559 000.

The purpose of charities in the CAF's top 400 cover a variety of different areas. These are shown in Table 11.1, which uses the classification adopted by the CAF (1990). It was not possible to

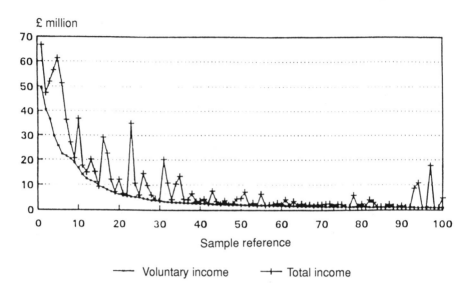

Figure 11.1 Voluntary and total income of charities sampled from 1 to 100

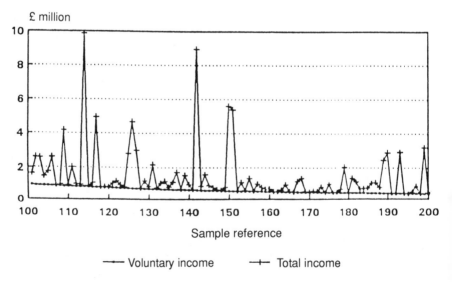

Figure 11.2 Voluntary and total income of charities sampled from 201 to 400

Table 11.1   Areas served by top 400 charities

	1–200	201–400	Total
Medicine and health	74	90	164
General welfare	49	41	90
International aid	28	20	48
Preservation of heritage and environment	8	5	13
Animal protection	11	10	21
Religious/missionary work (UK and overseas)	23	20	43
Youth	3	9	12
Arts/education	4	5	9
	200	200	400

Source: CAF (1990).

replicate the CAF classification for charities sampled given the limited information in *Charity Trends*. However, as 50% of charities were sampled, these broad areas will have been covered by the research sample. It is interesting to note that the notion of *purpose* would not seem to be a key factor in determining the relative positioning in the ranking.

Data Collection

The *pilot* study aimed to determine the nature and extent of planning in charitable organisations. In particular, it examines factors influencing the planning process. The design of the *follow-up* study was derived from a review of the literature in combination with indicators from the *pilot* questionnaire responses.

Response Rate

There were 162 replies from the 200 questionnaires distributed in the pilot study showing a high (81%) rate of return. Replies were fairly evenly distributed throughout the sample with slightly more replies in the top half (83 versus 78).

Responses to the pilot indicated that 75 organisations were willing to participate in the second-stage survey. Fifty replies were received at the pilot stage, giving a 25% overall response rate.

Interpretation

The reason for splitting the survey into two samples of 100 data sets each was designed to enable comparison between the larger charities and the medium-sized organisations in the lower half of the sample. This was in order to see whether relative size of an organisation influences the type of planning undertaken. The top half of the sample covered 100 charities out of the top 200 listed in the CAF's *Charity Trends* (1990). Voluntary income ranged from £49 million to £937 000, with total income from £67 million to £993 000. Average voluntary income of those sampled was £5 446 000 with an average total income of £9 897 000.

There is a narrower spread in the bottom range of values. The coverage is 100 organisations ranked in *Charity Trends* from 201 to 400 with a voluntary income of £559 000 and an average total income of £1 427 000. The ranges are from £924 000 to £324 000 and from £9 874 000 to £360 000, respectively (see Figures 11.1 and 11.2). It is interesting to note that in the top half voluntary income formed 55% of total, compared to 39% for those in the bottom half.

Interpretation of Processes

The responses showed that 122 (75%) of charities responding claimed that some form of formal planning took place within their organisation. A further 9% expected to adopt a similar system over the course of the year ahead (Table 11.2).

The above would indicate that some form of planning process takes place within the vast majority of UK charitable organisations. Totals of those planning or intending to plan represent 84% of the sample. Even allowing for non-repliers as *non-planners*, the total uptake is around 69% (122 + 15/200). Those who did not plan or had no intention of planning showed no common characteristics in terms

Table 11.2   Replies received and 'planners'

	Number	Percentage
Replied	162	81
Of these replies		
—those who plan	122	75
—those who expect to plan	15	9

One reply was anonymous so top plus bottom half results do not sum arithmetically to the total result.

of their sphere of operation, size or relative importance of voluntary income to total income.

If it is assumed that the two samples are independent and normally distributed, by comparing the top half with 69 (83%) planners with 52 (67%) in the bottom half a test of the difference in these proportions gives a 95% confidence level, confirming that the difference is statistically significant. It is concluded that more planning takes place in the top half of the sample among the larger charities.

Planning Horizon

The response to the question shows a slight lack of clarity in that it resulted in some multiple answers with respondents acknowledging use of both short- and longer-term planning horizons, presumably for different purposes. Table 11.3 shows the planning horizon, distribution. From this it will be apparent that the choice of planning period is fairly normally distributed with few short- or very long-term planners. Most organisations plan over 1–3 (34%) or 3–5 years (43%). It is of particular note that there is use of a horizon of 3 and more years by over 59% of the larger charitable organisations compared to 42%, within the smaller ones.

Table 11.3 Planning horizon distribution

	1–200	201–400	Total
Less than one year	8	8	16
1–3 years	20	22	42
3–5 years	35	16	52
>5 years	6	6	12
	69	52	122

HISTORY OF PLANNING IN CHARITABLE ORGANISATIONS

Table 11.4 indicates the percentage of charities which have adopted a formal system of planning. Overall planning is a relatively recent phenomenon. This would seem to be consistent with the evidence from the literature, which broadly indicates an increasing interest in planning for not-for-profit organisations. The difference between the

Table 11.4 Planning in charitable organisations

	Total (%)	1–200 Top half (%)	201–400 Bottom half (%)
Within the last 5 years	64	61	69
6 or more years	36	39	31

two proportions shown in Table 11.4 is not statistically significant at a 90% confidence level. There is therefore no evidence that size has influenced the timing of the introduction of the planning process.

Planning Factors

Table 11.5 sets out the percentage of respondents who acknowledged use of the factors within the table which assist internal and external analysis.

Planning factors considered

Each factor has been evaluated for the top and bottom half of the

Table 11.5 Percentage of respondents' acknowledgement of factor

	Total (%)	1–200 Top half (%)	201–400 Bottom half (%)	Significant difference
Internal				
Financial	100	100	100	No
Marketing	78	79	77	No
Employees	81	81	81	No
Demand for services	77	78	75	No
Organisation/management	88	84	92	N/A
Fund raising	91	88	94	N/A
External				
Social	59	66	52	Yes
Technological	60	63	56	No
Political	62	62	63	No
Economic	68	73	62	No
Other				
Present and future purpose	91	90	92	N/A

sample to see if the difference in proportions is statistically significant and to identify evidence of greater use of planning by larger charities. A normal distribution was assumed for each planning criterion. These were tested at a 90% confidence level, comparing the relative position of each top and bottom half factor (Table 11.6).

It is interesting to note that the most significant difference between the top and bottom half organisations can be seen in the use that larger charitable organisations make of external analysis of environmental factors, within their planning process (2.6 out of 4, on average, by the larger charities as opposed to average of 1.8 used by the smaller sampled charities).

One area of apparent consistency within the literature is the high average of all those reviewing *the purpose* of the charity. However, we must bear in mind that many of the organisations surveyed have a relatively short planning horizon (in some cases only one year). Of those charities not reviewing *present and future purpose*, only one large and two medium-sized ones plan for one year or less.

Most organisations still plan over a short horizon (1–3 years) although one exception indicated that they adopted a 5-year planning horizon. The converse, which clearly conflicts with general advice on planning, is that some charities review the *purpose* annually. The thoroughness of such a process is questionable and, as stated, does not accord with theoretical perspectives on the corporate planning process.

The question is whether the similarity that can be detected between very large and medium-sized organisations in the charitable sector in their use of planning factors is, in fact, deceptive. Although this study has presented statistically significant results in evaluating the perspectives of *those who plan; planning horizons; certain aspects of planning factors*, the proposition as to whether there is a distinctive difference in the approach to planning between large and smaller charitable organisations cannot be explained in any superficial way.

Table 11.6   Planning factors (average of areas covered)

	Top half	Bottom half
Internal factors—Average number of factors	5.1	5.2
External factors—Average number of factors	2.6	1.8
Purpose—Average	0.9	0.9

The conclusion here is that although Question 6 of the questionnaire attempted to identify factors which are widely considered within the planning process and offers some prospect of differentiating between the areas incorporated into that process, no significant relationships have been uncovered between size of organisation and the type of planning factors considered. There is some evidence of greater use of internal and external factors in the upper quartile (those organisations ranked 1–100). The precise significance of this result is open to interpretation. The replies of those in the second quartile (101–200) are difficult to explain, especially with regard to their use of *internal planning factors*, which are consistently below those of their larger and smaller fellow organisations.

Some Conclusions from the Pilot Questionnaire

The overall conclusion does give rise to some disappointment in the inability to establish significant differences relating to size and planning practice. There is a wealth of data which indicates that a great deal of planning is taking place in UK charities. *The pilot* provided useful information relating to who plans and on typical planning horizons. The relatively short planning periods seem to conflict with the evidence of environmental scanning and processes for reviewing the purpose of such organisations. These aspects tend, in general, to follow theoretical perspectives, as found within corporate planning literature.

Table 11.7 is an attempt to assess the degree to which organisations adopt systematic strategic processes. Basically it is a strategic planning index based on three factors. A score of one point was given for each of the following items: *plan for three or more years; review of purpose; review of more than two external factors.*

If a score of '3' is accepted as providing evidence of strategic

Table 11.7 Planning index

		1–100	101–200	201–400	Total
Index	0	2	4	4	10
	1	5	12	13	30
	2	8	8	23	40
	3	21	9	12	42
		36	33	52	122

planning based on the methodology derived from the literature, then 43% of larger charities (1–200) and 20% of medium-sized charities (201–400) seem to be following such an approach. Of the total sample, just over a third follow such an approach. Perhaps there may be some concern in the findings that in a further third the scores of 1 or 0 are thus displaying little indication of the presence of the attributes regarded as inherent in any recognised process of formal planning.

INFLUENCES IN PLANNING—INDICATIONS FROM 'SECOND'-STAGE QUESTIONNAIRE

Question 2 of the second-stage questionnaire aimed to examine the influence of certain factors considered likely to be involved when planning is initially adopted by an organisation. In particular, items likely to provide evidence of the use of private sector methods or management theory were included. Table 11.8 shows the net scores.

The overall results show that a significant contribution arises from the appointment of new management in charitable organisations and from increased demand for the services the charity provides. To an extent this confirms Butler and Wilson's (1990) hypothesis that organisational influences, rather than external factors, are key determinants of the strategy adopted. Equally, it could support Bryson's (1988) assertion that models such as Porter's have a relevance in clarifying the strategic direction of charitable organisations.

The following are summaries of key indicators:

- *Purpose (mission/goals linkage):* With one exception all respondents rated purpose highly. Generally, all charities seem aware of the

Table 11.8   Net scores for factors of influence

Factor of influence	Net score total	1–200	201–400
New management	43	21	22
Private sector	−1	−1	0
Increased demand	55	22	33
Competition	−12	−12	0
Consultants	−28	−17	−11
Textbooks	−26	−4	−22

critical importance attached to clarifying the link between mission and goals as part of the planning process. Table 11.9 illustrates this insight.

- *People:* Questions 4, 5, 7 and 9 of the questionnaire aimed to identify the extent of full-time management influence versus that of volunteers and supporters and the degree of participation of others (e.g. members) in the planning process. Virtually all respondents signified that they employed designated staff tasked with implementing and monitoring the planning process. It is not surprising that the responses were at the *weakly agree* level. A similar positive acknowledgement of a split in Roles with regard to long-term and operational planning emerges from responses to Question 9, although again this is perhaps paradoxically more marked in the bottom half.

- *Financial:* Everyone agreed on the importance of financial budgeting in their planning processes. This correlated to Q6 (i) in the pilot questionnaire. While the bottom half tended to agree that planning processes concentrated on financial aspects, the top half tended to see their planning process as being more 'issues' oriented. Question 10 (Planning is qualitative rather than quantitative) shows that both top and bottom responses favour the view that planning is qualitative rather than quantitative.

- *Areas considered in the planning process:* Question 8 of the second-stage questionnaire tried to identify areas addressed in planning and analytical concepts used in addition to those such as financial budgeting, already discussed. Specifically, the use of SWOT analysis is employed in assessing organisational responsiveness. Both large (1–200) and medium-sized (201–400) organisations expressed familiarity with the concept and acknowledged its use.

Table 11.9   The mission–goals linkage—perceived importance

		Total	Top half	Bottom half
(Q3)	Critical stage involves determining future goals			
	Strongly agree	34	17	17
	Agree	15	5	10
(Q8a)	Planning process considers mission			
	Strongly agree	30	15	15
	Agree	15	5	10

The idea of stakeholders raised queries and the largest number of 'don't knows' and nil replies. The top half seemed more familiar with the concept compared with the bottom half. Output targets rated very highly, confirming the importance of measurement of success criteria which are not necessarily expressed in financial terms. This links closely to the importance given to the demand for services. Finally, the influence of internal and external environments are seen to receive consistently positive attention, as part of the planning process. It is also worth noting that, with exception of the word *stakeholder*, respondents did not seem to experience problems with the terminology used. Overall results were generally consistent between the pilot and second-stage questionnaires.

CONCLUSIONS

The study established wide support for planning as a means of focusing on environmental issues facing charitable organisations and as a contribution to better resource allocation. The mention of planning as a contributor to improved cost effectiveness failed to elicit the same degree of unanimity.

There is evidence that the importance of organisational structure in relation to planning was recognised but was not seen to be a strongly stated awareness. Interestingly, planning was seen as making a contribution to reducing internal conflict. How this would be done without considering structural and behavioural processes is not clear!

Clearly, the pressures on services and resources are compelling reasons for organisations considering some form of planning. Some of the comments summarise the reasons why charities plan: 'It's the essential difference between success and failure'; 'It enables aims to be achieved'; 'Planning keeps control of change'. All these point to recognition in charitable organisations of the importance of planning.

Finally the objective of the research was to identify if and how UK charities plan. The first part of the question has been fairly well answered while the second part has been shown to be rather more complex and difficult to interpret. Nevertheless, fairly definite indicators emerge. The second-stage questionnaire has identified perceived key benefits—better resource allocation, decision making, cost effectiveness, aid to responding to change, reduction of conflict. It is of note that this plays down the organisational elements favoured by researchers such as Butler and Wilson (1990) in the sense that elements identified in more business-orientated literature seem to be regarded as more important to our respondents. It is perhaps not altogether surprising that the strategic planning process, widely enunciated in the literature, is more in evidence among large charities as defined in this research. It remains to be resolved as to the degree to which organisational influences are regarded as critical to the adoption and effectiveness of planning in the charitable sector.

REFERENCES

Argenti, J. (1989) *Practical Corporate Planning*, London, Unwin.

Armstrong, M. (1990) *The Handbook of Human Resource Management*, London, Kogan Page.

Bryson, J. M. (1988) *Strategic Planning and Non-Profit Organisations*, London, Routledge.

Butler, R. J. and Wilson, D. C. (1990) *Managing Voluntary and Non-Profit Organisations*, London, Routledge.

Chandler, A. D. (1962) *Strategy and Structure*, Cambridge, MA, MIT Press.

Charities Aid Foundation (1990) *Charity Trends*.

Drucker, P. F. (1990) *Managing the Non-Profit Organisation*, London, Harper Collins.

Epsy, S. N. (1990) Corporate identity and directions. In Gies, D. L., Ott, J. S. and Shafritz, J. M. (eds), *The Non-Profit Organisation—Essential Readings*, New York, Brooks-Cole.

George, P. L. (1989) *Making Charities Effective: A Guide for Charities and Voluntary Bodies*, Jessica Kingsley.

Gies, D. L., Ott, J. S. and Shafritz, J. M. (eds) (1990) *The Non-Profit Organisation—Essential Reading*, New York, Brooks-Cole.

Handy, C. B. (1990) *Understanding Voluntary Organisations*, Hammondsworth, Penguin.

Jackson, S. (1988) Charities: unto us a sum is given, *Director*, **44**, 34–7.

Langley, A. (1988) The roles of formal strategic planning, *Long Range Planning*, **21**, 40–50.

Newman, W. H. and Wallender, H. W. (1983) Managing not-for-profit enterprises. In Pearson, R. J. (ed.), *The Management Process: A Selection of Readings for Librarians*, Chicago, American Library Association.

Porter, M. E. (1985) *Competitive Advantage: Creating and Sustaining Superior Performance*, New York, Free Press.

Porter, M. E. (1987) From competitive advantage to corporate strategy, *Harvard Business Review*, **65**, 43–59.

Quinn, J. B., Mintzberg, H. and James, R. M. (1988) *The Strategy Process: Concepts, Contexts, Cases*, Englewood Cliffs, NJ, Prentice Hall.

Ramathan, K. V. (1982) *Management Control in the Non-Profit Organisation.* Chichester, John Wiley

Ritchie, K. M. (1992) *Corporate Planning by UK Charities,* University of Aberdeen and the Robert Gordon Institute of Technology, unpublished dissertation.

Seddigh, H. R., Clark, C. J. and Lawler, K. A. (1988) The structure of the charity sector in England and Wales. *Applied Economics,* 20, 335–350.

12

THE TIME PROCESSING MATRIX: A TOOL FOR STRATEGIC MANAGERS

Paul M. Lane

Western Michigan University, USA

Carol F. Kaufman

Rutgers University, USA

INTRODUCTION

It is well known that time is scheduled, used and experienced very differently in some cultures versus others. For instance, business persons in the USA are often considered to be driven by clock-determined schedules, while other cultures emphasize informal, unscheduled social time as an important component of any business relationship. On a strategic level, one may ask why some strategic plans do not recognize the differences in time cultures in the increasingly global economy.

This chapter discusses and develops the concept of time processing and later the Time Processing Matrix (TPM) as a tool for strategic managers. The area of time processing has long been overlooked as an explicit area in both the developing and implementation of strategies. Understanding the concepts of time processing through the Time Processing Matrix can help in the development of strategy and its application. Time processing will first be introduced in terms of business examples. Using these

International Review of Strategic Management, Volume 5
Edited by D. E. Hussey © 1994 John Wiley & Sons Ltd

concepts, the Time Processing Matrix will be developed and implications to strategy will be offered.

The authors suggest two major characteristics of processing. The first characteristic focuses on the variability versus the repeatability of time use. Does the time as perceived vary from the next period or do similar time blocks tend to repeat? The other characteristic deals with how time is divided by some meaningful breakpoint. For some, this is determined by the passage of clock or calendar time; by others, when the task is completed.

Processing reflects the flow and separability that can be perceived in one's concept of time and in their approach to time use. It focuses on the patterns of movement and divisibility. The original work in this area was performed by the anthropologist Hall (1959) as it applied to cultures. However, we have substantially modified and extended this work in the application to management and business from individuals to very large organizations. Both strategists and managers will find that time processing is particularly valuable in considering cultural time differences in the increasingly global context of business.

In this chapter the concepts within time processing are expanded into a new strategic planning tool called the 'Time Processing Matrix'. The matrix, which is an array of some of the key concepts in time processing, allows the strategic planner to examine and define certain relationships among repeatable and differing events, which may or may not be segmented into discrete parts. It provides a tool to help sensitize management to the different time processing styles and thus enhance the strategic process.

Returning to the question: why is it that some strategic plans do not recognize the differences in time cultures in the increasingly global economy? Corporations could easily be in more than one time-processing culture when considering their vertical or horizontal relationships. In the horizontal case, many alliances, mergers or acquisitions in the integrating Europe face important time differences, particularly in time processing. Thus, an alliance between a Finnish firm and an Italian one, would expect to cross cultural time differences. Time processing is particularly relevant in the type of cooperation required in an ongoing alliance. In the simple vertical case you would expect different time cultures, and in particular in time processing, if senior management were in northern Europe, for example, and production occurs in southern Europe for a market in the United States. The Time Processing Matrix is a tool to sensitize management to some of the differences in time between individuals, between organizations and between cultures.

Why is it that so many strategic plans end up in the desk drawer and not on top of the desk? Vertically, jobs seem to require different time styles. Top managers are needed who look at the big picture, who can develop and lead long-range strategy. As we move down the corporate ladders in almost any country in almost any area, employees are focusing on smaller and smaller pieces of the corporate activity. They may well be in jobs that encourage a time-processing style different from that of top management. For example, a laborer in a repetitive job may have no time to plan or prepare for change. Not only are there different job level differences in time processing; there are also individual differences that must be considered. These differences in functions and individuals can severely limit the impact of a strategic plan unless its implementation is structured with these differences in time processing in mind. Finally, competition may be in another processing format changing the reliability of prediction about how they will respond.

Time is well established as an important strategic variable because of its significance in the planning process (Lane and Kaufman, 1992b, 1993). Firms make judgements concerning various types of time within their operations; variables such as product life cycles, forecasting, employee schedules, compensation, and evaluation periods are all related to the firm's assumptions regarding time. Even more complex differences in time perceptions and use across national and corporate cultures underscore the importance of examining the firm's decisions and behaviors related to time, as corporations cross national boundaries in their entrance of other markets. In this chapter the focus is time processing as it applies to strategic management issues.

Time is implicit in strategy in several meaningful ways. The subtle assumptions which corporations make regarding time are likely to affect the planning horizons which they choose and the past, present, or future orientation which they enact (Lane and Kaufman, 1992a). Time processing is likely to effect the type of planning that is to be done. For instance, time within one organizational culture may be found to proceed from one well-planned, scheduled event to another, while in another organization time simply flows in response to daily life.

BACKGROUND ON TIME PROCESSING

Processing is one of the four major aspects of time considered by the authors (Kaufman *et al.*, 1991a; Lane and Kaufman, 1992b). These include: activity (Kaufman *et al.*, 1991b), orientation and horizon (Lane and Kaufman, 1992a), perceptual time use (Kaufman and Lane, 1994), and processing (Lane and Kaufman, 1994). In their work with the Time Orientation Matrix the authors discussed an important use of one of the aspects of time in considering the strategic process. In this chapter the strategic nature of processing is considered. Through examining the concept of processing carefully in relation to both functional areas of business and important strategic concepts, a better understanding can be reached of some of the problems inherent in the planning process.

Rather than simply looking forward or backward in time, processing considers how time is perceived and used while moving through a period of time. In general, three basic types of processing have been discussed: linear, in which time moves in a straight line or progression, marked by differences in events; cyclical, in which time moves through repetitive cycles, of the same or similar events; and procedural, in which all time is devoted to a particular activity until that activity is completed (Hall, 1959, 1986; Graham, 1981; Morello, 1989; Gentry *et al.*, 1991).

Processing Across Many Disciplines

Concepts regarding time processing have appeared in the disciplines in which time is studied in numerous ways and combinations. These concepts include: linear time, cyclical time, procedural time, segmented time, separable time, sequential time, circular time, and ribbon time, among others. The present chapter focuses on a subset of time-processing concepts: linear, cyclical procedural, and segmented. These specific concepts are chosen because they are likely to bear specific relevance to strategic decision making, they are thought to provide important contrasts which can affect strategic plans, and the contrast will help sensitize management to the differences in time processing.

The basic concepts that will be examined here have been developed and refined from some of the ideas put forth by Edward T. Hall (1959, 1983). Hall utilized these variations in time processing to examine cultures through an anthropological perspective. Here processing is applied to management and the strategic planning process. However, the anthropological nuances have important strategic implications as corporations cross national boundaries, and must exist and function within different time cultures.

In economic analysis, time is often considered to flow from past to future in somewhat of a straight-line pattern with no real variability across persons; that is, time is generally the same for everyone, whether at the individual or corporate levels. Hours and minutes and years basically marked the passage of time in units that everyone could count, but how that passage occurred was not really considered.

Studies in anthropology, sociology, and home economics (Hall, 1959, 1983) profiled the numerous variations in time, as it is perceived and used. Time did not necessarily flow in the same straight line for everyone; sometimes it varied, and sometimes certain repeated activities were instead the primary way of organizing time. For instance, in some cultures in which time was regulated by agricultural cycles or seasonal events, the predictability of planting, growing and harvesting crops delineated certain important 'times' in people's lives (Levine, 1988; Jones, 1988). Other cultures, with more linear timestyles structured around events which happened one after the other, instead moved away from the cyclical natural cycles to perhaps a 'Westernized' standardized time, in which cyclical time was not as apparently dominant, but variations in time events were important.

Moreover, people were found to prefer using time in different ways. Some individuals preferred to break their day into several discrete parts, with certain time blocks devoted to each activity, a limited amount for each. Others instead chose to work on certain activities until they were finished, and only then could the next activity begin.

Four Major Components of Processing

Processing has to do with how you think about your time use and the tasks you have to complete. There are four major components to processing that will be examined in terms of the processing matrix— cyclical, linear, procedural and segmented, (see Figure 12.1). Individuals or groups may view their progression through time

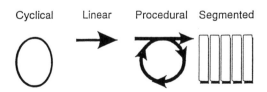

Figure 12.1 Cyclical, linear, procedural, and segmented time

using any combination of these processing types. The past and future may extend in a flowing, directed sequence; consisting of repetitive skips, or a series of activities.

The Concept of Cyclical Time

Cyclical time is found the world over. It is one of the configurations of movement that anthropologist Hall initially reported which we have extended. People are following some cyclical pattern whether in nature, in the payroll process, or of their own devise. Cyclical time, by its very nature, does not focus primarily on a future or past, but usually concentrates attention on the present use which is systematically repeated in the future. The boundaries of the cycles may well be the boundaries of the present in cyclical time processing. Examples of cyclical time have traditionally included agrarian economies dependent on the seasons, but the authors have found what appear to be cyclical patterns in many organizational settings. Many managers find themselves and their jobs tied to a daily, weekly, or monthly cycle of sales reports. Employees at all levels from executives to plant workers find themselves functioning in cyclical purchase patterns from monthly items such as mortgages and other payments, to weekly shopping trips to the hypermarket and so forth. It is quite possible that those you manage, your peers, and those you do business with may in fact be using this kind of time processing.

This is not a kind of time to be dismissed as belonging to other cultures by Western executives. It is quite possible that the vast majority of the world population are using cyclical processing in some situations or roles. The cycles that people follow come from a number of different sources. First, some cultures are cyclically based in terms of the way that they think about time. Many of the world's religions are cyclical in nature. Cycles happen for many because of their dependence on the cycles of nature, such as the tides, the seasons, weather patterns, and so forth. They may also be determined or imposed by business and government.

The Concept of Linear Time

Linear time is time stretching out in one direction or the other. While linear time could stretch in a variety of directions, typically there is the distinct impression of moving into the future and a heritage linked with the past. People using this type of time tend to think of the tripartite division of the English language as explained in

Orientation Horizon Matrix (Lane and Kaufman, 1992a, 1993). This is the time of the business culture in much of Western Europe and North America as was observed by Hall (1959, 1983) and Graham (1981). Sometimes it is also referred to as ribbon time.

Linear time use is often seen as a stream, so that work, household production, and leisure activities are laid 'end to end' to fill 24 hours. One could assert that many members of the business community conceptualize time this way. For this reason, the concept of linear time will not be belabored as it is probably familiar to most of the readership. In Figure 12.1 linear time is represented as an arrow moving from left to right, suggesting past to future. There is no conceptual reason why the arrow could not run the other direction or in both directions.

The Concept of Procedural Time

Procedural time might be defined as beginning a task with the idea of working on it until it was done. Today procedural might be defined as a task orientation. Beginning a task with the idea of working on it until it was done, does not mean that it gets completed in one session, rather, whatever time is available is used to work on that task. Thus, you can work procedurally on sections.

Representing procedural time is always difficult. We have elected to use a line with a loop in it to represent procedural time in Figure 12.1. The idea is that you can spend as much time as you need in the loop before moving on to the next task or activity. Further, the loop can represent a task orientation that suggests whenever there is time you will apply it to the task.

In Page-Wood et al. (1990), and subsequent work, people from all walks of life and all age groups have made drawings and written definitions of time that are considered to be procedural in nature. These have included half-full vessels and mazes. Many people appear to work in a procedural fashion working on one project until it is done and then moving to the next. This is not a clock-based approach to time use but rather divisions come at breakpoints or at the completion of the project.

In procedural time things are processed by what needs to be done and not by clock time. In the academic world people pursuing their dissertations, research and writing may well fit into this category. In other societies, where ritual plays an important part in life, it has been found that such events begin when things are ready, not when a certain clock time is reached. The clock orientation is not there. Further, procedural time does not necessarily treat time as a limited resource. There are a number of examples of procedural time use which may help you to understand the concept. Note that many of these tend to be tasks that you would not think of stopping, for example:

(1) *Sports:* Most sporting events, whether a friendly game of golf or a baseball game, a tennis match, polo, or croquet, are played procedurally until the winner has been determined. Other examples include chess, lawn bowling, rugby, swimming, cricket, card games, bocce, bowling, curling and horse racing (although time is measured, the winner determines when the race is finished). Olympic examples might include such events as gymnastics, running and skiing which are not over when the time is up, but when certain activities are performed at highest quality, or when one completes the desired activities within the fastest time.

(2) *Travel:* Many times when we travel on public transportation we recognize that it is a procedural task. When the door shuts on the plane before a transoceanic flight, you are there for the ride, no matter how long it takes. You may worry about being late and the problems it will cause or you can sit back and enjoy the ride. No matter what you do, all of you on that plane should arrive at the same clock time when the flight is complete. The same applies on ships, trains, buses, and so forth.

(3) *Gardening:* Many tasks in the garden are approached procedurally. We plant the seed and follow certain procedures until the crop matures. Cutting the lawn is usually started and completed, no matter how long or short a time is involved.

The Concept of Segmented Time

Segmented time is defined as dividing time use into blocks of clock or calendar time for purposes of measurement or control. The process of segmenting appears to be external to the activities being performed. The blocks are not necessarily equal. They have starting and stopping points but may vary in size. Creating and keeping track of these blocks is almost a half-billion dollar business in the United States and Europe. There are many companies with books and software that help with this process such as Denmark's Time Design, Franklin Planners from the United States, etc.

There are a number of sports games that are essentially segmented. The game is played for a number of fixed segments, and the person or team with the most points at the end of those segments

Figure 12.2   Segmented time

is the winner. Only in the case of a tie is more time allotted to the game. Such sports might include rugby and basketball.

In Figure 12.2 segmented time is represented in two ways. First, superimposed on a straight line are boxes of equal size. Second, in a cyclical pattern we show time with varying size boxes representing different size segments.

Many executives and managers around the world carry around vinyl- or leather-bound life planners that revolve around 10-, 15-, or 30-minute segments. They neatly plan their whole life around these 'clock blocks,' adding them together to make larger blocks. These life planners impose a template of equal-sized blocks which must be grouped appropriately. Not every culture or individual fits the planners as they are currently configured. This may be because they use different segments such as the Japanese use of 10-minute segments (Katzenstein, 1989) or because the typical day focus does not work for a culture such as in Spain.

The US planner with 15 minute segments between 8:00 am and 5:00 pm does not fit well in cultures that may start very early because of the heat, has lunch and a siesta before another round of business in the late afternoon and evening such as in Spain and some other Latin countries. The same is probably true of a number of other different cultures including Saudi Arabia, Tunisia, and Iran.

PROCESSING CONCEPTS APPLIED TO BUSINESS FUNCTIONS

Cyclical Time in Business

Some of the functional areas of business would appear to be largely cyclical. The planning cycle itself is such an example. Most companies follow a yearly or quarterly cycle for developing long-range plans, particularly market planning. Other areas that seem to have a strong cyclical content would be human resources and the legal department. Anyone who works in a union shop understands the importance the cycle of the contract has on the overall business. Finally, there is a great deal of discussion about cycles such as the fashion cycle and the product life cycles.

Linear Time in Business

Talks with executives often lead to an understanding of how many companies are run on tradition with a view to the past. Businesses can rely on past, present or future periods in their planning. Some types of firms choose to forecast future performance from several periods of past data. Others, such as US automakers, tend to assume that the successful past will endure long into the future. Still other firms are instead future oriented, adopting methods such as scenario planning to investigate the outcomes of alternative futures.

Procedural Time in Business

Some business functional areas seem to be primarily procedural in processing style. The creative areas fit particularly well, including the creative part of advertising, product research and development, and marketing research. Procedural processing would also appear to be an important part of some of the strategic tools available. In planning, scenario planning is very much of an iterative procedural planning process. Similarly, the idea of skimming the market in terms of price is also a procedural process, keeping the price high as long as possible.

Another example is found in multinational food-processing companies. These firms typically formulate, test, reformulate and retest new or modified products before introducing them to the overall market. Where multiple or cross-cultural tastes are considered, several ongoing formulas are likely to be tested concurrently until they receive satisfactory approval within each market.

Similarly, international negotiations may ideally target certain dates for the culmination of their dealings, but realistically they must proceed until each issue has finally come to some resolution. Such procedural complexity is thought to characterize the harmonization process of the European Single Market of 1993, in which several factors of agreement must individually be resolved before the overall unification is completed.

Procedural social time is critical in some cultures but is annoying to people from a linear segmented timestyle since it is not segmented and linear. That is, in some cultures, business persons want to form a friendship first before getting down to business. This friendship time may seem 'to go on forever' to those who are accustomed to social time after the task at hand is accomplished.

Many managers work procedurally. In many places managers speak of working on a project until it is done. In the United States, where work takes precedence, managers will talk about staying until the job is done. Conversely, in Ireland business people have described their socializing activities in the same procedural way. In Japan, Katzenstein (1989) suggests that staying until the job is done and staying past when the job is done because other people's jobs are not done is a common practice.

Segmented Time in Business

Quarterly financial reports are segments of the annual operation. Many people are forced to think in terms of the segments of the reporting cycles. Many other monthly or weekly reports represent the time-study approach to segmentation. In some cultures meetings are set with a beginning and ending time. Even if business is done before the concluding time, people will tend to continue to meet to fill the assigned segment. Often the meetings follow a prearranged agenda with planned time allowed for each subject. However, if one subject is finished short of the time allowed, the unused time may be allowed for future items. In some cultures, business associates instead may intersperse social interaction time with business discussion, with blocks of discussion time interwoven throughout their meeting times (Copeland and Griggs). In the United States it is not uncommon to invite people for a social gathering with a beginning and ending time.

The lunch break, lunch hour, and coffee break are all examples of daily segments of time within the workday set aside for specific purposes: segmented activities. As you travel around the world, you will find that there are different ways to be sure that the activities are accomplished within the allotted clock block. In Mexico cafeterias are provided for the employees in the plants to help the workers complete their lunch within the segment allotted, either by providing it for them or by providing the necessary equipment for final preparation. In the United States, Europe and now Japan 'fast food' continues to gain in popularity whether eaten in the restaurant, picked up or delivered; the idea is to enable everything to be accomplished within the segment of time allotted for lunch.

TIME PROCESSING MATRIX DEFINED

The Time Processing Matrix is a tool for managers to help them search for and examine different processing styles that may exist within their organization and in their competitive environment. The TPM's ability to help sensitize managers to look for processing differences can be particularly important in today's globalizing economy. In Europe alone there are many time-processing styles that will have to be incorporated into companies that will develop markets and production facilities across the many national boundaries. The TPM is also significant because processing style influences purchasing, consumption and disposal processes so important to the marketplace.

The two-by-two Time Processing Matrix is built on two basic concepts: pattern of movement on flow and separability of time (Figure 12.3). The horizontal axis is the pattern of movement ranging from clearly defined cycles to what appears to be linear. This suggests that the size and types of cycles can vary substantially, from those lasting for a few days like fashion to those lasting for generations. The other dimension, the vertical axis, has to do with the preference for division of time. A high preference for division would be found at the lower end of this axis and almost no preference for time division would be found at the upper end of this axis. This dimension is segmented and procedural, ranging from segmented at the bottom to procedural at the top.

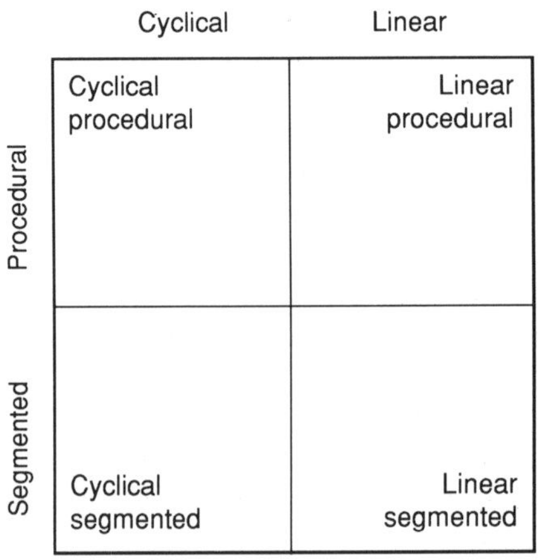

	Cyclical	Linear
Procedural	Cyclical procedural	Linear procedural
Segmented	Cyclical segmented	Linear segmented

Figure 12.3   Time Processing Matrix

The Time Processing Matrix provides for four possible combinations of time processing moving clockwise are: *linear segmented, cyclical segmented, cyclical procedural* and *linear procedural*. This matrix was created to explore the processing concepts. It can be used by managers to explore the amount of task segmentation and procedural processing. Further, it allows for the understanding of the role of cyclical and linear approaches to time in the organization. The matrix challenges the user to think through some of the different types of processing combinations that may exist in any organization. The matrix is not proposed as all-inclusive, but rather a thinking and working tool to elicit an understanding of the impact of time processing on the organization and its strategies.

Combinations of the Time Processing Matrix

Linear segmented processing

This would represent much of industrial time in northern Europe and the United States. Linear time implies the past, present and future direction with a straight arrow usually in the direction of the future. The segmented notion implies that the individual is dividing time into segments. This is the time of the time planners like the Franklin Planner, Daytimers, Time Design, etc. It is also the type of processing implicit in linear forecasting, the Product Life Cycle and the Sustainable Growth Model. For example, in forecasting, the best predictor of the future is thought to be the past, which also implies some potential for repeatability. Similarly, Beta is constructed by using performance in past periods and used to project future period performance. From the sellers point of view the JIT (Just-In-Time) and EOQ (Economic Order Quantity) are also based on estimates based on past performance in similar segments and projecting these into the future.

Cyclical segmented processing

This kind of time processing is often overlooked or not recognized in the business literature. It has been found frequently among all levels of employees when asked to draw or define time. Individuals would draw something that was clearly cyclical and repetitive that was divided into distinct parts. The cyclical part implies that people view time in repetitive cycles. The segmented portion is the perception of the individual that time is divided into segments. Many people who operate on a cyclical timestyle and function well in a *linear segmented* business society (United States, northern Europe) would be likely to use cyclical segmented time. They are cyclical and they are standardizing to the segmentation of the business system.

Time which is cyclical and segmented is characterized by distinct activities which repeat in somewhat of a predictable pattern. Thus, dividing the assessment of business performance into a four-quarter fiscal year illustrates the notion of *cyclical segmented* time, since comparable business indicators will be measured (repeated) every three months (segmented).

Finance seems tied to segments as dictated by the capital markets and cycles within those markets. Other cyclical-segmented examples include the actual schedule of advertisements and the valuation process at most companies. Similarly, a number of the marketing and strategic tools are cyclical and segmented. These include the yearly Buying Power Index in the United States, lagged effects of advertisements which carry over for several cycles, etc. In pricing strategy there are more examples: profit-oriented pricing and customary pricing. Profit-oriented pricing is an attempt to maximize the return in each period, towards a goal of the annual cycle. Customary pricing reintroduces recognizable past pricing levels in order to stimulate purchase behavior by certain segments.

It is interesting that buyers may view things differently from sellers. For example, the idea of economic order quantity may be viewed as *cyclical segmented* to the buyer. Buyers expect availability on a predictable regular basis sufficient to meet their needs. Thus, their cycles may not meet the linear projections of the seller. It is important for management to recognize these differences and that their positions on the Time Processing Matrix may be reversed based on their timestyles or time-processing cultures.

Scenario Planning is such an example. For some firms it would be part of an annual cycle of planning. For others it would be done from time to time as they look to the future and attempt a variety of planning techniques. Therefore the authors have placed it in between. As you place things on the matrix, you should feel free to locate them in far corners or toward the center as you think they occur in your environment. The usefulness of the matrix is to look for and recognize the different timestyles in the strategic planning process.

The whole planning process itself may be considered to be a cyclical segmented process in many companies. Comparisons of organizational performance are often made repetitively at certain points throughout the firm's fiscal year. However, the length of those cycles are likely to vary across countries. In addition, the amount of time given to the firm to reach certain objectives within the business cycle may be very different. For instance, performance measures for new Kentucky Fried Chicken stores in the United States would typically be evaluated within each year's cycle for the ability to earn profits on a fairly rapid basis. Their Japanese counterparts, however, are likely to be 'allowed' much poorer performance in the short term, as growth is expected to occur over a longer planning cycle, as in the film *The Colonel Comes to Japan*. Thus, while similar measures are considered, their impact within the planning cycles are quite different.

Cyclical procedural

The cyclical part implies that people view time in repetitive cycles. The procedural portion suggest that the individual or organization approaches a task with a focus on completion. This might well be the time of a person dependent on the cycles of nature or other cyclical patterns. Environmental planners in Third World nations must consider the interaction of business with the cyclical weather patterns which impact the flow of day-to-day living. While monsoons and droughts are less familiar to management in northern Europe and the United States, they are realities in numerous foreign markets, and managers must determine how to carry out business within them.

Another procedural example might be sales representatives, who periodically (cyclically) call on their accounts, but resolve to spend as much time as necessary with each account. How this is done is likely to vary cross-culturally.

In retailing there is the Wheel of Retailing, which basically implies the continual expansion and contraction in a cyclical response to customer preferences. The timing of these cycles varies in length on a procedural basis. Thus, price-discounted warehouses come into a market in response to consumer demand for low-price products. As time goes on, warehouses will tend to either specialize or evolve into more full service. As the original evolves in other directions a new set of low-price warehouses can be expected. In the United States there are several generations in the hamburger wars following this scenario. Another example is the retail revival cycle, in which products from a past period are reintroduced for as long as their popularity will endure. In the United States the revival of the 1950s period has been a big market success.

Linear procedural

Linearity implies the past, present and future direction with a straight arrow, usually in the direction of the future. It may also imply sequential in terms of working towards a satisfactory output. The procedural element suggests that the individual or organization approaches a task with the focus on completing the task in total or piece by piece as time allows. Thus, a procedural person may not be able to complete the whole task in one sitting as suggested by Hall (1959) but they will approach each piece of the task as a procedure to be done.

New product development could be *linear procedural* or *cyclical procedural*. The development of new products and testing their concepts is generally best done on a procedural basis. In some organizations like the automotive companies it is cyclical in that in each cycle there are new products and refinements. In other organizations like Pharmaceuticals the process is lengthy and linear and not necessarily related to the previous years' developments.

The *linear procedural* processing is inherent in building, creating and shaping for the future. Market investment (Lane, 1986) is such a practice where investments are made to build the market for the future. Public relations and its concerns with image building falls into the same category. The market share or penetration pricing strategy fits well here as an applied example. Just-In-Time from the point of view of the buyer and the Family Life Cycle also fit here.

TIME PROCESSING AS A MANAGERIAL TOOL

The Time Processing Matrix enables the researcher or manager to greatly expand their examination of strategic time issues, as the concepts within the processing area allow for both variability and repeatability in time, as well as segmentation through to continuous flow of time. Managerial planning concepts, such as financial analysis, return on investment, inventory turnover, and so forth are based on fundamental assumptions regarding time in the organization and time periods for strategic assessment.

For instance, variations in automobile product lines typically follow new 'models' for each chronological year, despite customer preferences and problems. Models which are favored are sometimes changed or discontinued in the effort to provide newness. The Japanese, on the other hand, tend to respond to customer difficulties in a much shorter time, retooling their assembly plants in response to consumer requirements, rather than in response to the cyclical plan to introduce new models only at an established time in the selling cycle.

The matrix allows the strategic planner to place the organizational processes and types of time use within the appropriate quadrants of this two-by-two matrix in order to diagnose the underlying time assumptions which have been made. Once the organizational strategy can be 'placed' within the matrix, matches and mismatches can be found among, for instance, time assumptions, type of time-related decisions and the time-related norms of the markets which are served.

In Figure 12.4, the Time Processing Matrix, the authors have arrayed on the matrix several commonly used models and functions categorized from their perspectives. The reader might position them differently based on the reader's timestyle, their organization and the cultures where they are doing business. These would probably change from country to country. What is desirable is to sensitize management to ask the question about how these functions relate and to understand that there are processing timestyle differences and sometimes mismatches.

Importance of Time Processing

The importance of time processing can be quickly understood if we take a look at some commonly held beliefs and practices. First, time management programs and writing tend to focus only on the idea of *linear segmented* time. This may explain to some readers who have

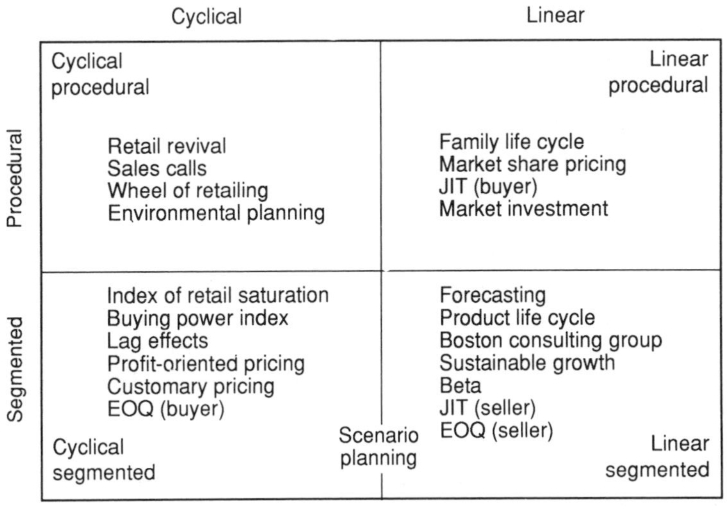

	Cyclical	Linear
Procedural	Cyclical procedural Retail revival Sales calls Wheel of retailing Environmental planning	Linear procedural Family life cycle Market share pricing JIT (buyer) Market investment
Segmented	Index of retail saturation Buying power index Lag effects Profit-oriented pricing Customary pricing EOQ (buyer) Cyclical segmented	Forecasting Product life cycle Boston consulting group Sustainable growth Beta JIT (seller) EOQ (seller) Linear segmented

Scenario planning

Figure 12.4   Managerial applications in the Time Processing Matrix

found a different location for themselves on the Time Processing Matrix why they have difficulty implementing time-management programs. It also suggests there may be even more potential for time-management programs beyond the increases in efficiency and effectiveness that they have already engendered. Time-management programs may be developed for people on different kinds of processing time.

Second, financial theory uses an approach to time that assumes that there is a past, present and future and that these are segmented into equal blocks of clock or calendar time. If the assumption of segmentation into equal blocks were to be removed, present value, future value and most other financial calculations would appear to lose their meaning. Organizations not processing on *linear segmented* time will not be likely to have a focus on the bottom line for each quarter. In other words, competitors may be competing in the same playing field with differing rules. Identifying the competitive advantage is a question to challenge management.

Third, ratio analysis, of course, has to reflect the goal of the planner, as well as the meaning and construction of the ratios within each cultural context. If performance is being assessed in the short term in a linear-time society, then the ratios will necessarily become as conventionally defined in terms of some relationship among yearly measures or several year averages. However, if the assumption of time and performance are instead considered to vary, linearly based performance measures may not provide the type of information which is a true indicator of the firm's actual status. For instance, if Ramadan affects several weeks of business in Saudi Arabia, should the business quarter in which Ramadan occurs be compared with the other three quarters within any given fiscal year? Financial models borrowed from another culture may grossly misestimate actual performance when the time-processing assumptions in the culture are not considered.

Fourth, education for business would seem to require segmentation into calendar units such as terms or semesters, but not all blocks are of equal length. It is interesting to note that some terms are as short as three weeks or three weekends at some schools and as long as 12 weeks at others. Semesters for teaching the same material can stretch to as long as 17– weeks. One of the problems with some educational systems is that they depend on those being educated conforming to patterns of movement and division that is found in their educational system. In a *linear segmented* educational system, prospective managers who do not function well in segmented clock blocks and are more procedural in nature may have trouble.

Management may well have linear and segmented timestyles but be working with employees that are basically procedural and cyclical in their timestyle. Thus, there is a clear mismatch that needs to be worked at so that they can work on teams together. A particularly good example is found in the *Going International* film series (Copeland and Griggs), popular in the United States for educating business students and managers in the vast cultural differences which can be encountered in global markets. It particularly addresses the Western ethnocentric attitude towards business, cautioning US expatriates not to impose their cultural norms in their firms on other countries. One potent example depicts a time-processing mismatch in a computer-processing department in India. An executive from the United States is shown ordering an Indian computer manager to stop the current jobs within the department to substitute the executive's emergency job. Thus, the executive, assuming a *linear segmented* system, simply infers that one segment can be substituted for another. The Indian manager, who overtly agrees to make the switch, is shown having no intention of interrupting the procedural nature of the task which is already in progress.

MANAGERIAL APPLICATIONS AND EXAMPLES

Clearly, one of the complicated issues in beginning to approach the strategic planning process is to understand the different time-processing methods that exist in the organization. There are inherent conflicts in the needs of different types of processors.

Some companies become dominated in one direction or another. Many Asian competitors seemed to have taken a linear-procedural processing approach, committing themselves at whatever resource cost to build market share to profit down the road from the larger market share. In contrast, many organizations are dominated by *cyclical segmented* processing, focusing planning process around the reactions of the quarterly financial reports and the financial markets. Private firms and firms with sources of capital that are not too tightly tied to the world's capital markets tend to have more freedom to use other kinds of processing. Note that in the United States some of the most successful firms are those that are either private or in private control as they are not dominated by the *cyclical segmented* nature of the capital markets.

Finally, many companies have multiple timestyles, causing communications gaps. Large companies may be headed by management who speak in terms of procedural linear planning including scenario planning, traditional planning process, taking the time to accumulate information from the market side and analyze carefully before making a decision. This same management may keep its lower management so busy that they can only see what needs to be done in the immediate cycle and segment. The problem is that management must recognize that different operations require different time-processing approaches. What is missing is better translation from the linear procedural plan to linear segmented levels and to cyclical segments. Processing is needed consistent with its accomplishment and responsibility and assigned at the proper level to be triggered as objectives of the plan are met, such as the sales goals.

The Japanese style of processing may also vary with the task at hand. For instance, in negotiating a licensing agreement it may take three years for a decision, but once made, the Japanese may be ready to go into production within a few weeks and be highly critical of the delays made by US business (Harris and Moran, 1991). Thus, decision making and evaluation can follow a complex *linear procedural* process known as *ringi*, in which approval must pass numerous levels in the organization, and each level takes a somewhat procedural look at the decision, expanding the decision into vast amounts of time for those used to a linear segmented timestyle.

The flow of life, and hence business, in Saudi Arabia is related to the Islamic belief that their time is controlled to some degree by Allah. Thus planning some aspects of their time would seem pointless, since things will happen 'as Allah wills'. Such a fatalistic perspective imposes somewhat of an external procedural flow, in great contrast to Western *linear segmented* planning.

Harris and Moran (1991) report that African time is 'flexible, not rigid or segmented'. The inflexible time schedules typical of Western business time processing are likely to be viewed as inappropriate. Times for business are procedurally interwoven with times for socialization, in an informal style which evolves with the moment. Nigerians typically view time as unlimited. Since the typical traffic jams in business centers or 'go slows' are likely to restrict travel for hours, the limitations of infrastructure appear to be consistent with the ability to predict or plan time.

The processing matrix poses several challenges for management:

(1) Is everyone planning in the same way or is it necessary to recognize different timestyles? This extends vertically and

horizontally through the organization.

(2) How are the competitors planning and developing strategies? How will they approach the problem of shaping the future? How would your competitor array their functions on the Time Processing Matrix?

(3) Are there better opportunities if the planning process is considered in different ways? Looking at planning issues from the different perspectives covered by the matrix may help see different opportunities and threats.

(4) In the globalizing economy how do different types of time processing impact the competitive situation in terms of production, consumption, and planning?

CONCLUSION

Time is one of the most important resources of life for individuals, organizations and political units. In order to use that time most effectively it is important to eliminate as many of the time mismatches as possible. The Time Processing Matrix is a tool for helping to diagnose time-processing mismatches. The more there is time congruity or matching in the aspects of time such as time processing, the greater potential for maximizing the output of time resource.

Management, wondering why the strategic plan so carefully prepared by the top management team was not implemented, might use the TPM. An examination of the different functional areas as related to the options in the TPM might reveal some substantial differences. The top management may have placed themselves neatly in a *linear segmented* model but find that many of their personnel were as a function of those jobs, generally processing time in a *cyclical segmented* or *cyclical procedural* style.

In order to implement the plan some communication will have to take place to translate the plan into the type of processing time normally used by the staff. Conversely, top management may want to look at how personnel could be taught and encouraged to think about time in other ways. The goal should be the creation of time congruity in the processing area, reducing the time mismatches. This should lead to greater individual and corporate efficiency.

Similarly, in the era of regionalization and globalization increasing numbers of firms are operating in many different cultural environments. The Time Processing Matrix provides a tool to help analyze the many different national and corporate cultures that may be involved in one large corporation. This becomes very important in the management of production, in trying to understand the market's response, and in anticipating competitor response.

A corporation which is operating with a *linear segmented* processing style is likely to respond very differently to a competitive challenge from one that is operating in a *cyclical procedural* style. The procedural approach to the South Korean entry and eventual conquering of the microwave market is legendary. The South Korean team continued month after month and year after year to develop the process and then began the fight for shelf space. They attacked the market in the same way. Pressure on mid-management might lead to a firm processing time in a segmented fashion and might very well stop the project in any segment where proper progress was not being made.

The time-processing differences can also be seen in the way challenges are handled. In some environments employees given more work will attempt to work more efficiently to get the job done within the same time segment normally allowed. In others, those who need to work longer to accomplish the task do so. In others, whole groups of employees stay until the project is done, whether or not they are directly involved. In some countries legal requirements with respect to overtime work and union requirements for standardization of output severely restrict lower-level employee activity to standard repetitive units of work. These represent different processing styles and impact the way the organizations in the countries will compete. It also is a problem of mismatch for the multinational.

Using the Time Processing Matrix, there are many business functions that would seem to be oriented towards different processing styles. Planning tends to be linear while execution is cyclical. For example, the planning process tends to be *linear segmented*, marketing seems to be more of a procedural cyclical process, accounting tends to be more segmented, advertising needs to be broken down into at least two areas: the creative process would be procedural and scheduling would probably be *cyclical segmented*.

These differences could be important by themselves or in combination to the development and implementation of a strategic plan. A management that is sensitized by using the Time Processing Matrix can be proactive in dealing with these time issues, and in this way improve its competitive position and, potentially, its competitive advantage.

ACKNOWLEDGEMENTS

In this work we wish to recognize the very important contributions to the development of these ideas of Esther Page-Wood, our research associate at Western Michigan University, our co-author and reviewer in time Jay D. Lindquist, Ph.D., our graphics specialist Gary Goscenski, our editor/critic M. V. Lane, and the help of hundreds of people who have willingly taken their valuable clock time to help us understand the nature of time and in particular how it is processed.

REFERENCES

Copeland Griggs Productions, *Going International* Film Series, San Francisco, CA.

Gentry, J. W., Ko, G. and Stoltman, J. J. (1991) Measures of time orientation. In Chebat, J. C. and V. Venkateson, V. (eds), *Proceedings of the Time and Consumer Behavior Conference*. Val Morin, Quebec, University of Quebec at Montreal.

Graham, R. J. (1981) The role of perception of time in consumer research, *Journal of Consumer Research*, 7, March, 335–42.

Hall, E. T. (1959) *The Silent Language*, Garden City, New York, Doubleday.

Hall, E. T. (1983) *The Dance of Life: The Other Dimension of Time*, Garden City, New York, Anchor Press/Doubleday.

Harris, P. R. and Moran, R. T. (1991) *Managing Cultural Differences: High-performance Strategies for a New World of Business*, Houston, TX, Gulf Publishing Company.

Jones, J. M. (1988) Cultural differences in temporal perspectives: instrumental and expressive behaviors in time. In McGrath, J. (ed.), *The Social Psychology of Time*, Newbury Park, CA, Sage Publications, pp. 21–38.

Katzenstein, G. (1989) *Funny Business*, Englewood Cliffs, NJ, Prentice Hall.

Kaufman, C. F. and Lane, P. M. (1994) Time, potency, and exchange: making the most of the time resource. In Houston, F. (ed.), *Marketing Exchange Relationships, Transactions, and their Media*, New York, Quorum Books, pp. 77–98.

Kaufman, C. J., Lane, P. M. and Lindquist, J. D. (1991a) Exploring more than twenty-four hours a day: a preliminary investigation of polychronic time use, *Journal of Consumer Research*, **18**, December, 392–401.

Kaufman, C. J., Lane, P. M. and Lindquist, J. D. (1991b) Time congruity in the organization: a proposed quality of life framework, *Journal of Business and Psychology*. In Sirgy, M. J. (ed.), Special Issue on Quality-of-Life Studies in Marketing and Management, **6**, 1, Fall, 79–106.

Lane, P.M. (1986) Product market risk: a theoretical development of the concept of risk in the product market and its impact on management decisions in the capital and resource market. Unpublished dissertation, East Lansing, Michigan, Michigan State University.

Lane, P. M. and Kaufman, C. F. (1992a) The role of time in strategic marketing. In *Proceedings of the European Marketing Academy Conference*, pp.765–784.

Lane, P. M. and Kaufman, C. F. (1992b) Time in joint ventures, *Journal of Strategic Change*, 1, 259–272.

Lane, P. M. and Kaufman, C. F. (1993) Using time in strategic marketing. In *Perspectives on Marketing Management*, volume III. Chichester, John Wiley, pp.333–357.

Lane, P. M. and Kaufman, C. F. (1994) Retail processing time: Anthropology in the shopping center, *Proceedings of the American Marketing Association Winter Educators' Conference*, p. 281–287, 1994.

Levine, R. V. (1988) The pace of life across cultures. In J. McGrath (ed), *The Social Psychology of Time*. Newbury Park, CA, Sage Publications, pp. 39–62.

Morello, G. (1989) The time dimension in marketing, *Irish Marketing Review*, 4, 1.

Page-Wood, E. S., Kaufman, C. J. and Lane, P. M. (1990) The art of time. In B. J. Dunlap (ed), *Developments in Marketing Science*, volume XIII. Cullowhee, NC, pp.56–61.

The Colonel Comes to Japan, Film produced for Enterprise on Public Broadcasting Corporation, Deerfield, IL, The Learning Corporation of America.

OTHER SELECTED REFERENCES

Bluedorn, A. C., Kaufman, C. J. and Lane, P. M. (1992) How many things do you like to do at once? An introduction to monochronic and polychronic time, *The Academy of Management Executive*, 17–26.

Kaufman, C. F. and Lane, P. M. (1994) Time congruity: a tool for strategic change. Unpublished working paper.

Kaufman, C. J. and Lane, P. M. (1991) The language of time in the global marketplace. Enhancing knowledge development in marketing. In M. Gilly *et al.* (eds), *Proceedings of the 1991 AMA Summer Educators' Conference*, volume 2, pp.229–237.

Lane, P. M. and Kaufman, C. J. (1989) The standardization of time. Marketing: positioning for the 1990s. In R. L. King (ed) *Proceedings of the 1989 Southern Marketing Association*, pp.1–5.

*Numbering scheme indicates **volume**(number): page range. For example, **2**(1): 3–69 is Volume 2, Number 1, pages 3–69.

POSTAL ADDRESSES OF CONTRIBUTORS

Dott.essa Chiara Bentivogli *Banca D'Italia, Ufficio Studi, Via Nazionale, 186, Roma, Italia*

Professor T. K. Das *Associate Professor of Management, Baruch College, The City University of New York, 17 Lexington Avenue, New York, New York 10010, USA*

Mr J. Ellis *10812 Church Street, Dover, MA 02030-2501, USA*

Professor H. H. Hinterhuber *University of Innsbruck, Department of Management, A-6020 Innsbruck, Austria, Innrain 52*

Dr Sam Ho *Department of Corporate Strategy, De Montfort University, Leicester*

Professor Gert Hofstede *Den Bruyl 15, NL-6881 AN VELP, Holland*

Mr D. E. Hussey *Managing Director, Harbridge Consulting Group Ltd, 3 Hanover Square, London W1R 9RD*

Professor Carol F. Kaufman *Associate Professor of Marketing, School of Business, Rutgers University, Camden, NJ 08102, USA*

Professor Paul M. Lane *Associate Professor of Marketing Western Michigan University, Grand Rapids Regional Center, Grand Rapids, MI 49546-5936, USA*

Dr. M. G. Lynas *Centre for Management Studies, Aberdeen University, Edward Wright Building, Dunbar Street, Old Aberdeen, AB9 2TY*

Professor Briance Mascarenhas *Associate Professor Management and International Business, Rutgers University, Camden , NJ 08102, USA*

Mr Keith Ritchie *Halliburton, How Moss Avenue, Kirkhill Industrial Estate, Dyce, Aberdeen, AB2 OGP*

Professor Gen-Ichi Nakamura *SMI 21, I-27-7 Naka-cho, Meguro-Ku, Tokyo 153, Japan*

Professor Paul Strebel *Professor of Business Administration, International Institute for Management Development, Chemin de Bellerive 23, PO Box 915, CH-1001, Lausanne, Switzerland*

Dr Sandro Trento *Banca d'Italia, Ufficio Studi, Via Nazionale, Roma, Italia*

Ms Liisa Välikangas *International Institute for Management Development, Chemin de Bellerive 23, PO Box 915, Ch-1001, Lausanne, Switzerland*

Professor Wee Chow Hou *Dean, Faculty of Business Administration, National University of Singapore, 10 Kent Ridge Crescent, Singapore 0511*

INDEX TO THIS ISSUE

CUMULATIVE CONTENTS LIST
TO THE SERIES*

CUMULATIVE CONTENTS BY TOPIC

*Numbering scheme indicates **volume**(number): page range. For example, **2**(1): 3–69 is Volume 2, Number 1, pages 3–69.

National/Regional Aspects

Organizational Situations

Functional Aspects

Other

CUMULATIVE CONTENTS BY CONTRIBUTOR

CUMULATIVE INDEX (Volumes 1–5)